Praise for

Teaching Truly

"Penetrating, fearless and practical, this book offers educators (and anyone else with an interest in our future) a way to create a better world—before it is too late!"

—Thom Hartmann, award-winning syndicated progressive talk show host
and author of numerous books including *The Last Hours of Ancient Sunlight*

"This remarkable, nerve-touching book provides a missing link between the knowledge and ways of seeing and learning of indigenous peoples, that is 'part of the soul,' and the imperial education of the liberal West. In exposing and then pushing back a corporate screen behind which we all live and learn, Four Arrows hands us a new way to resist."

—John Pilger, Author, investigative journalist (International reporter of the Year
and recipient of a United Nations Peace Prize)
and academy award winning documentary film-maker

"This enlightening book reminds us that the grim prognosis for life on this planet is the consequence of a few centuries of forgetting what traditional societies knew, and the surviving ones still recognize. We must nurture and preserve our common possession, the traditional commons, for future generations, and this must be one of our highest values, or we are all doomed. To regain this sensibility from those who have preserved it we must pay careful attention to their understanding and practices, especially their educational practices as brought to us in these thoughtful chapters."

—Noam Chomsky, Professor Emeritus at MIT,
author of more than 120 books, recipient of the 2011 Sydney Peace Prize
and one of the top ten most-cited individuals in the world, living or dead

"*Teaching Truly* subtly raises the issue of the difference between education for the purpose of raising human consciousness and education for the purpose of creating workers for the global economy. Four Arrows makes it clear that our focus on the material and away from the spiritual aspect of our nature has created not only an imbalance in our mind/body/spirit that manifests in disease, dispirited communities and alienated children but also in the outward imbalance and disharmony on the planet that gives us life. In order to move forward, sometimes we need to connect with the best of our past. This book and its curriculum ideas are an opportunity and a gift to our children and the future. It is time to remember, to honor and to teach the great wisdom of our indigenous ancestors—this may be our last hope."

—Nancy Turner Banks, M.D., author of *AIDS, Opium, Diamonds and Empire*

"*Teaching Truly* is a singularly provocative book with the unsettling analysis that education is not about learning and economics is not about the well-being of society. As today's institutions crumble in their dysfunction, Four Arrows draws upon tens of thousands of years of empirical data within Indigenous societies, crucial intelligence on what works and how to unleash the kind of learning that will help us become human beings present and in balance with Mother Earth."

—Rebecca Adamson, president of First Nations Development Institute,
founder of First Peoples Worldwide
and inductee to The National Woman's History Hall of Fame

"This is a necessary book, a part of the revolution we so desperately need."

—Derrick Jensen, author of *A Language Older than Words*

"At a time when mainstream education is viewed as impoverished and lacking in meaning, this engaging book invites educators to start a self-reflective dialogue on educational innovation stimulated and inspired by the indigenous wisdom. With humility, sensitivity and force, *Teaching Truly* gives rise to the possibility of transforming education from inside out."

—Scherto Gill, Executive Secretary of the Guerrand-Hermès Foundation for Peace,
and author of *Learning Across Cultures and Exploring Selfhood*

"In this provocative new book, Four Arrows takes a principled stand on behalf of a significant educational perspective that has long been buried by corporate and political interests, that of the continent's Primary People. We would surely live more balanced, respectful and grounded lives if 21st-century educators were to read this book and learn from its lessons. If we hope to pass along to our grandchildren a healthy 22nd century, we need a richer education than the 'edupreneurs' have provided us thus far."

—Peter Smagorinsky, Distinguished Research Professor of English Education,
University of Georgia

"*Teaching Truly* is an important work. It outlines in great detail how we can bring Indigenous perspectives and practices into the K–16 curriculum. This book provides a powerful framework as well as many practical strategies that can inspire teachers. Rooted in the original vision of Indigenous peoples, Four Arrows has given us a way to educate the whole person including the soul. Educating the whole child is indeed our last hope."

—John (Jack) P. Miller, author of *The Holistic Curriculum*,
Ontario Institute for Studies in Education at the University of Toronto

"In my own work as an environmental activist, I've learned more from the indigenous environmental network than just about anyone else. If the Indigenous perspective can help even an old guy like me, then educators should be paying attention to what Four Arrows offers in this book. God knows we need some new ways of looking at things."

—Bill McKibben, founder of 350.org and author of *The End of Nature*,
The Age of Missing Information, and *The Global Warming Reader*

"Now more than ever, teachers overrun by the bankrupt Common Core hegemony need the wisdom and insights, the joyfulness and harmony offered in *Teaching Truly*."

—Susan Ohanian, author of *Caught in the Middle: Nonstandard Kids and a Killing Curriculum*

"This new book by Four Arrows bridges a gap, allowing for a renewed flow of wisdom from American Indian cultures. This perspective has always been crucial to us at AERO and we hope many will be able to use it before our mainstream culture goes over a cliff."

—Jerry Mintz, Founder and Director of Alternative Education Resource Organization

"This book needs to be taken seriously. It offers a perspective that has been missing in cultural storage and thinking promoted in public schools and universities and online learning systems. There are many reasons for learning from indigenous knowledge systems. It would be a mistake to read *Teaching Truly* as an appeal to going back in time, as the lessons to be learned from indigenous cultures are timeless."

—C.A. Bowers, author of the *Perspectives on the Ideas of Gregory Bateson*,
Ecological Intelligence and Educational Reforms, and *The Way Forward*

"Four Arrows has brought leading thinking about this vital necessity into this text. We have much to learn from our host First Nations about teaching, thinking, rhythm and curriculum that Four Arrows has concisely captured for all teachers. This book is vital to our collective learning for today and in the future."

—Tom Cooper, author of *A Time Before Deception* and *Fast Media/Media Fast*

"*Teaching Truly* is an incredible resource for staff in our schools who work with both Native and non-Native students. We will be using it."

—Elliot Washor, Ed.D., Co-director, Big Picture Learning

"In contrasting Western and Indigenous ways, Four Arrows is hard on the West, but that is because there is so much at stake. Under the circumstances, it is most expedient to take the merits of the Western way as a given and to focus on the imbalances it has created. He is sincere in his proposal that teachers look for ways to partner Western and Indigenous perspectives, and this book explains why and how to do it."

—Robert Lewis (Rafiq), author of *Gaj: The End of Religion*

"In *Teaching Truly* Four Arrows draws a frighteningly accurate map of the known world, and the spiritual and material collapse that's upon us: death and destruction at the heart of the liberal techno/imperial/capitalist juggernaut. Drawing on ancient and Indigenous ways of being and knowing Four Arrows offers a contemporary guide to what is to be done, and illuminates a path toward a future where schools might play a powerful role in truth-seeking, repair, and renewal for all children, youth, families, and teachers. After an encounter with Four Arrows, I reflected with renewed energy on the urgent questions that drive free people in pursuit of enlightenment and liberation: What are we? Why are we here? Where are we headed? How shall we live? What kind of world can we hope to inhabit? This handbook for teachers is a vibrant and essential text for anyone who wants to understand the broad dimensions of the mess we're in and pursue a wise and practical pathway forward."

—William Ayers, author of *Teaching Toward Freedom*; *Teaching the Taboo*; and *To Teach: The Journey in Comics*

"*Teaching Truly* is a masterful and liberatory book that not only moves between theory and practice but makes teaching a vocation of the highest order. Ever mindful of history and the context of teaching, this beautifully written book deals with the complexity of teaching in a language that is as accessible as it is insightful. This is a book that should be read by all educators and anyone interested in education."

— Henry Giroux, author of *Education and the Crisis of Public Values*

"Four Arrows is a combination of a visionary, a dreamer and a truth teller. While he is grounded in the realities of our global situations, and thus moves obstacles and creates better situational realities for the peoples he works with and for, he is motivated by a peaceful truth that radiates from the core of his being. If you are willing to listen and hear what might make you think and feel in an alternative capacity, Four Arrows is the gentle-hearted, educated soul to guide your path."

—Heidi Maston, Editorial Board, *International Journal of Science* and internationally known distance education consultant

"Four Arrows has cut to the core in *Teaching Truly*. Doing more than overcoming the omissions, misinterpretations, and outright fictionalization of our culture, traditions and spirituality that have been taught in American schools, he has put together generalizable teachings for specific subjects in ways that can point education toward achieving a more balanced world."

—Tim Giago, Nanwica Kciji (Stands Up for Them), author of *The Aboriginal Sin*, *Notes from Indian Country, Volumes I and II* and *Children Left Behind*

Teaching Truly

CRITICAL PRAXIS AND CURRICULUM GUIDES

Shirley R. Steinberg and Priya Parmar
Series Editors

Vol. 3

The Critical Praxis and Curriculum Guides series
is part of the Peter Lang Education list.
Every volume is peer reviewed and meets
the highest quality standards for content and production.

PETER LANG
New York • Washington, D.C./Baltimore • Bern
Frankfurt • Berlin • Brussels • Vienna • Oxford

Teaching Truly

A Curriculum to Indigenize Mainstream Education

FOUR ARROWS (DON TRENT JACOBS) WITH
KATHRYN ENGLAND-AYTES ■ GREG CAJETE ■ R. MICHAEL FISHER
BARBARA ALICE MANN ■ ED MCGAA ■ MARK SORENSEN

PETER LANG
New York • Washington, D.C./Baltimore • Bern
Frankfurt • Berlin • Brussels • Vienna • Oxford

Library of Congress Cataloging-in-Publication Data

Teaching truly: a curriculum to indigenize mainstream education
/ Four Arrows (Don Jacobs).
pages cm. — (Critical praxis and curriculum guides; vol. 3)
Includes bibliographical references.
1. Indians of North America—Education.
2. Indigenous peoples—Education—United States.
3. Native language and education—United States.
4. Curriculum change—United States.
I. Jacobs, Donald Trent.
E97.T43 370.89'97—dc23 2012050283
ISBN 978-1-4331-2249-1 (hardcover)
ISBN 978-1-4331-2248-4 (paperback)
ISBN 978-1-4539-1068-9 (e-book)
ISSN 2166-1367

Bibliographic information published by **Die Deutsche Nationalbibliothek.**
Die Deutsche Nationalbibliothek lists this publication in the "Deutsche
Nationalbibliografie"; detailed bibliographic data is available
on the Internet at http://dnb.d-nb.de/.

© 2013 Peter Lang Publishing, Inc., New York
29 Broadway, 18th floor, New York, NY 10006
www.peterlang.com

I dedicate this book to all who have worked, are working and will be working to promote traditional Indigenous perspectives from around the world that have in common a deep understanding of the sacred relatedness existing in all that Nature manifests on this planet.

Contents

THE SOUTH (The Color White) *Spiritual and Emotional Awareness*

Preface

Indigenous cultures are the only real source of resistance to the imperialism of market liberalism.

—CHET BOWERS, 2005, P. 118

I find it increasingly difficult to see in the recent history of the civilized world a greater respect for the quality of human existence than was manifested by our remote "primitive" ancestors.

—JAMES NEEL, 1970, P. 35

The Eskimos living absolutely isolated from civilisation of any kind are undoubtedly the happiest, healthiest, most honourable and most contented of peoples . . . my sincerest wishes for our Nechilli Eskimo friends is that civilisation may never reach them.

—ROALD AMUNDSEN, 1908, P. 93

I think we're on the brink of disaster on many fronts. I believe that that Native people can help us out of that, help push us back away from that brink.

—N. SCOTT MOMADAY, KIOWA, 1991, P. 439

Many say that public schooling is failing. The evidence offered depends upon the critic's viewpoint. Policymakers, politicians and the private education industry point to the inability of schools to meet federal mandates. Left-leaning reformers complain it is the take over of schools by corporations that defines school failure. Employers complain about job skills. Parents cry about dropout rates. Teachers refer to crumbling infrastructure and diminished finances. Students say the curricula is boring and irrelevant. On it goes. Schools *are* failing, but the evidence to substantiate the assertion is that life systems on Earth are at a tipping point. Schools are failing because the standards and curricula stifle even the best teachers, allowing for the harmful influences of corporatism and hegemony to continue the insanity dominating our world today. But growing numbers of teachers are ready to take control of what and how they teach in the classroom. They want practical guidelines for doing this in ways that have not been available until this book with its course specific guidelines offering both sufficient proof about educational hegemony and with clear guidelines for offering alternative and complementary lessons that can offset hegemonic influences.

It was not long ago when the U.S. government used education to harm our Indigenous neighbors to prevent the spiritual knowledge and values of Indigenous Peoples from threatening more materialistic goals. How federal education policies and common core standards today use education is not all that different, except now the same suppression of vital knowledge and values is hurting us all in ways soon revealed if not already known to the readers. As mainstream classroom teachers come to realize that standard curriculum and pedagogy have long been intended to suppress, not foster democratic ideals, they will embrace the solutions offered in this book without waiting for more school reform efforts to fail. *Teaching Truly* offers teachers the kind of authentic, truth-based teaching ideas most hoped they would be able to use when they first became teachers. "Partnering" mainstream curricula with Indigenous perspectives allows for such teaching. It can guide learning toward building rich, joyful relationships between diverse humans and between humans and non-human. It allows for a collaboration that can effectively counter the pitfalls of mainstream policies, politics and curriculum in ways that a more confrontational critical pedagogy alone has been unable to do.[1]

Bruce Lipton and Steve Bhaerman write, "True sanity must face and embrace the insanity of today's world and, in the process, offer to the temporarily insane a new awareness and a pathway to achieve harmony . . . sanity is about integrating opposites rather than taking refuge in one polarity or the other" (2009, p. 195). There is no question that the Indigenous perspectives offered here stand in stark contrast with the Western ones most readers have embraced. Yet this "partnership" between cultural assumptions about living and learning is essential in this era of crises. We are now forced to ask ourselves, "What must we do in this crucial moment as educators? Getting this book's message and practical lesson plans into classrooms is one answer. Using this handbook will significantly help education do better that which best serves joy, balance, health and justice for all.

—Wahinkpe Topa (Four Arrows), aka Don Trent Jacobs

Note

1. In his book *Theory and Resistance in Education,* Henry Giroux (2001) argues that resistance is essential for authentic school reform and that studying minority values and comparing them to dominant ones is the best form of resistance. He says that this reexamination of schools must begin with a study of hegemony in the curriculum. Critical pedagogy over the years has concerned itself largely with a hegemony that is mostly oppressive of subordinate groups. Today it is the "99 percent" of the population who are beginning to realize that the goals of hegemony serve a more concentrated elite.

Acknowledgments

We are friends; we must assist each other to bear our burdens

—OSAGE

I offer appreciation to: My wife, Beatrice, for belief in my work and her willingness to be a "writer's widow" again even after my saying that each of my last four books was my "last"; Rick Two Dogs and the brothers and sisters with whom I completed my Sun Dance vows on the Pine Ridge Reservation; my friends from the Seri, Tarahumara, Navajo and Oglala tribes; the many colleagues from around the world whose studying or living according to Indigenous perspectives offered me important material; Robert Lewis for his insights and his professional editing skills; my ELC colleagues at Fielding Graduate University for listening to my countercultural educational reform efforts for the past decade; my grandsons, Sage and Kaien, for the inspiration to continue this work; Jelle U. Hielkema for helping me with the many iterations of this book's title; to the contributing authors whose life work reflects the values reflected in this book; and finally, the late Joe Kincheloe, aka *Tiwa Sky*, and his life partner, Shirley Steinberg, for their published work that helped set the stage for a book such as this and helped give me the courage to write it.

Introduction

Up to now we have ignored the Younger Brother. We have not deigned even to give him a slap. But now we can no longer look after the world alone. The Younger Brother is doing too much damage. He must see, and understand, and assume responsibility. Now we will have to work together.
—ANONYMOUS KOGI INDIAN REPRESENTATIVE

The traditional Native Peoples hold the key to the reversal of the process in western civilization that holds the promise of unimaginable future suffering and destruction.
—FROM A POSITION PAPER OF THE SIX NATIONS PRESENTED TO THE UNITED NATIONS IN 1977

I believe it is time to think indigenous and act authentic even at the price of rejection. To disagree with mainstream expectations is to wake up, to understand what is happening, to be of service to a larger whole. You may even begin to work on behalf of our lands, water and air.
—MANU ALULI-MEYER

Curriculum development in the postmodern era must include attention to the wisdom embedded in Native American spirituality.
—PATRICK SLATTERY (1995, P. 45)

This book offers practical guidelines for creating a sort of partnership between mainstream[1] and generalizable Indigenous approaches to education, strange bedfellows that they are. Admittedly, these greatly differ and often oppose one another. Nonetheless, this book offers an opportunity for classroom professionals and their students to bring required standards and Indigenous perspectives into balance at long last. Whatever grade level,[2] background or cultural orientation, teachers and students who use this book to integrate Indigenous[3] perspectives into coursework will enjoy more meaningful, truthful and equitable educational experiences while being prepared to address the serious "real-life" problems facing the world today. As an alternative to radical resistance alone, teachers who embrace this book's message can more successfully counter hegemonic and corporatizing forces in education than critical pedagogy alone or strikes and other protestations have managed to do over the decades.

Although the Indigenous approaches[4] may seem strange at first to some teachers, they will likely resonate at some level. All of us have ancestors who once lived in one place long enough to understand how to exist in relative harmony with the rhythms of the natural world. This nature-based knowledge is in our DNA. Returning to or revisiting Indigenous knowledge will therefore not be completely foreign to non-Indian teachers and students. Realizing this does not mean we can master the knowledge merely by reading and implementing this book. We can, however, come to understand, respect and apply the ideas in ways that can make a serious difference in the classroom and in the world at large.[5]

I admit to having a sense of urgency in writing this book. Mainstream education is largely responsible for our era of crises. Its authoritarian assumptions of superiority over other creatures, races, cultures, spiritual beliefs and Nature, along with its continued dismissal of Indigenous, nature-based values, have brought humanity to the brink of near extinction and has helped cause many other species to already become extinct. Every major life system on our planet is at a tipping point. Forest and ocean vegetation is losing the ability to absorb sufficient carbon dioxide. Fresh water sources are precarious. Coral reefs may die out within a decade. Ocean fisheries are at risk of depletion in the near future. The loss of biodiversity proceeds at unprecedented rates. In 2009 a team of twenty-eight distinguished scientists identified nine planetary life-support systems vital for survival that are close to irreversible destruction (Roberts, 2009), explaining that:

- Ocean acidification is now significantly higher than pre-industrial levels.
- Climate change impacts are worse than imagined.

- Over one-fourth of the world's river systems no longer reach the ocean.
- Extinction rates are up to 1,000 times higher than at any time in recorded history, with 100 extinctions per million species per year causing 30 percent of all mammal, bird and amphibian species to be threatened with extinction in the twenty-first century.
- There is too much nitrogen and phosphorous production destroying soil fertility and causing increasing numbers of dead zones in our oceans.
- There is overwhelming and continuing loss of rainforests.
- Chemical pollution is widespread, with nearly 100,000 human-made chemical compounds in use.

In June 2012, the prestigious journal *Nature* emphasized the same problems with even more urgency in a report authored by twenty-two of the world's most respected scientists (Barnosky et al., 2012).). As will be seen, there is ample evidence that Indigenous perspectives, including those related to science and psychology, can help bring us back into balance.

I emphasize these facts not to frighten but to motivate action out of love for life and for future generations. Courage and fearlessness, not fear, is the ultimate mandate in most Indigenous cosmologies, with great generosity being the highest expression of courage. They use courage and fearlessness for truth-seeking in ways that require engagement with and reflection on the laws of Nature. Thus, consider this text a handbook that can help instill the courage to:

1. Revitalize Nature-based systems thinking;
2. Encourage an appreciation for diversity and multiple interpretations of reality;
3. Develop character and emotional intelligence across the curriculum;
4. Stimulate meaningful self-reflection;
5. Question the problem of anthropocentrism;
6. Move away from authoritative status quo paradigms and into experiential-becoming ones;
7. Embrace the mysterious and recognize the spirit in all;
8. Encourage respect for and survival of all life on this planet;
9. Learn enough about academic subjects to contribute significantly to the public good.
10. Expose educational hegemony

Courage often relates to transformation and many scholars and philosophers have referred to the potential of using Indigenous wisdom to transform learning.[6] For example, Chomsky writes that "The American Indian perspectives have been far too little understood in our culture" (2001). Parker Palmer, author of *The Courage to Teach,* calls for education to embrace "one of the most neglected and abused resources of our continent: the deep knowing of the American Indian people" (2001). On the back cover of John Perkin's book *Shape Shifting* (1997), Dr. Edgar Mitchell, Sc.D., an Apollo astronaut and the founder of the Institute of Noetic Sciences, writes, "Only a handful of visionaries have recognized that Indigenous wisdom can aid the transition to a sustainable world." Noted curriculum studies scholar Patrick Slattery says in his classic 1988 text (as well as in the second edition in 2006), "Curriculum development in the postmodern era must include attention to the wisdom embedded in Native American spirituality" (p. 79). Kincheloe and Steinberg, citing others, write:

> Some indigenous educators and philosophers put it succinctly: We want to use indigenous knowledge to counter Western science's destruction of the Earth. Indigenous knowledge can facilitate this ambitious 21st-century project because of its tendency to focus on relationships of human beings to both one another and to their ecosystems. Such an emphasis on relationships has been notoriously absent in the knowledge produced in Western culture over the past four centuries. (2008, p. 137)

In addition to these non-Indian educators, a group of First Nations educators from the National Indian Education Association has endorsed the "Interdisciplinary Manual for American Indian Inclusion," which also proposes to indigenize the Western curriculum. This manual states in its preface that:

> The type of inclusion we address in this manual goes beyond merely including Indian students in public schools, or including Indian-related content in a math lesson. In our view, American Indian inclusion is something that should permeate an entire educational system. (Reinhardt & Maday, 2005, p. vi)

The noted Indigenous scholar Marie Battiste also speaks of how Indigenous knowledge can significantly complement mainstream curricula:

> Indigenous scholars discovered that Indigenous knowledge is far more than the binary opposite of western knowledge. As a concept, Indigenous knowledge benchmarks the limitations of Eurocentric theory—its methodology, evidence, and conclusions—reconceptualizes the resilience and self-reliance of Indigenous peoples, and underscores the importance of their own philosophies, heritages, and educational processes. Indigenous knowledge fills the ethical and knowledge gaps in Eurocentric education, research, and scholarship. (Battiste, 2005)

In "Indigenous Knowledges in Education: Complexities, Dangers, and Profound Benefits," Kincheloe and Steinberg explore the value of Indigenous knowledge and its "compelling insights into all domains of human endeavor" but warn that it can be a challenging "twenty-first century project" (2008, p. 135). Many reasons for this are addressed in the following pages that relate to the unique phenomenon of "anti-Indianism"(Cook-Lynn, 2007; Four Arrows, 2006). We must also consider challenges relating to borrowing sacred values from another culture. The Indigenous perspective contrasts significantly with mainstream values, so much so that even the great American awakening being referred to as the Occupy Wall Street movement tends to ignore the Indigenous perspective in its quest for a fair share of the "American Dream." Yet, as we shall see, in many ways it is this dream itself that the Indigenous perspective questions.

Chapter Overview

Honoring the Four Directions, this text is organized into four sections of a Medicine Wheel or "Sacred Hoop" as it is often referred to in English.[7] We start in the West with Mystery and Introspection represented by the color Black. The two chapters in this section intend to help the reader reflect on the mysterious phenomenon of anti-Indianism and its effects. Chapter One, "Anti-Indianism in Education and in the Academe," offers an overview of how intentional misinformation has largely been responsible for our continued tendency to ignore past and potential Indian contributions to Western society. This chapter also reveals that our ecological crises, numerous wars, rampant authoritarianism and large-scale personal unhappiness stand in contrast to the experience of the majority of traditional Indigenous societies. It explains how and why American Indians, Alaskan Natives, Canadian Aboriginals and other Indigenous Peoples from around the world remain a unique "cultural contrary" among minority groups and why anti-Indian hegemony is so widespread in American, Canadian and Australian cultures especially. Understanding anti-Indianism and its impact on the thinking of non-Indian teachers is a prerequisite for non-Indigenous teachers' success in partnering with Indigenous perspectives in the classroom.

The second chapter in this section, "Historical Trauma and Its Prevention in the Classroom," explains the phenomenon of historical trauma, the impact of centuries of continuing "anti-Indianism" schooling on today's First Nations, and the specific role education continues to play in suppressing Indigenous wisdom. Guest author Kathryn England Aytes (Delaware/Cherokee descendant) presents this chapter in a way that can help educators who have Indian children in their classroom be more aware of how education can continue the trauma if they are not careful. The phenomenon of historical trauma is also relevant to the lives of non-Indian children, and understanding this history can help us learn how to prevent similar problems from happening to future generations.

We move from the West to receive Wisdom and Nurturing from the North and the color Red. This part also has two chapters. Chapter Three, "The STAR (Service To All Relations) School Experience," written by guest author Mark Sorenson in concert with members of the school board that oversees his school for Navajo children, reveals how nurturing it can be for children and communities when educators passionately weave Indigenous perspectives into mainstream state standards. In describing the profound benefits of their efforts to indigenize the school, this chapter also reveals challenges that will likely be magnified in mainstream schools.

Chapter Four, "Indigenous Teaching and Learning Pathways," presents more nurturing ideas, requirements, strategies, skills and recommendations that will help assure that non-Indian teachers can optimally weave the Indigenous perspectives and values into their standard curriculum and instructional approaches. Included in this chapter is a presentation on Indigenous approaches to discipline and conflict resolution that work well for most children. It also describes sensitive issues surrounding the appropriation of Indigenous knowledge, spirituality and traditions. "Indian country" itself is divided on who can teach what. However, the suggestions in this chapter have been accepted as appropriate by a number of respected elders, and I believe that most First Nations educators will endorse these guidelines and requirements, allowing teachers to successfully modify daily lesson plans that partner Indigenous approaches with mainstream ones.

The third direction, the East, represented by the color Yellow, is about New Beginnings and Illumination on Truth. This section consists of eight chapters, each representing lesson plan options for an important mainstream subject area and offering supplementary guidelines that allow students to question mainstream curriculum[8] and enhance it in light of Indigenous perspectives. Teachers in K-6 grades who combine multiple subjects will likely want to use all the relevant chapters. Teachers of higher grades who specialize in only one of these courses will want to look at additional subject areas owing to the Indigenous understanding that all of these subjects interrelate in some important ways. The fragmented nature of separate subjects stands in contrast to the more holistic Indigenous learning. The format of each chapter makes such interdisciplinary connections relatively easy.

Whether teachers adapt these lesson plans for kindergarten or graduate students, there are also at least three ways that they can use the lesson plan guidelines and exercises with their students. The first option is to devote the initial quarter or third of the time scheduled for a particular subject. Such a "preface" to the usual approach will make an exciting difference in desired outcomes by offering a different perspective up front that can be returned to as you and/or the students choose. A second option is to incorporate various parts of the five-step lesson plan throughout the course where it seems most relevant to the text or standards being used. The third option is to use these lesson plans for the entire course, inserting specific objectives and requirements along the way for context. Again, keep in mind that grade levels where one teacher teaches all or most of the subjects have the advantage of being able to use all the lesson plans. In higher grades and in university settings, teachers and students will benefit from looking at Indigenous perspectives for subjects other than the one they are studying but will likely focus primarily on only one of the chapters in the West listed below.

Ch. 5:   Health
Ch. 6:   Music
Ch. 7:   English Language Arts
Ch. 8:   United States History, with guest author Barbara Alice Mann
Ch. 9:   Mathematics
Ch. 10:   Economics
Ch. 11:   Science, with guest author Greg Cajete
Ch. 12:   Geography

Each chapter is organized according to four subsections, described below:

1. Corporate and Hegemonic Influences on Education
2. Real-World Outcomes
3. Indigenous Perspectives
4. Questions for Research, Dialogue, Choices and Praxis

1. Corporate and Hegemonic Influences on Education

Each chapter begins by exploring corporate and hegemonic influences relating to the chapter's specific subject area. Today there may be little distinction between the two, although there exist neoliberal and neoconservative ideologies that are more or less separate from the profit motivation per se. Awareness of educational hegemony enhances motivation and balanced use of the Indigenous learning paths but many teachers are unfamiliar with the term. It refers to the insidious ability of those "in power"[9] to use schooling to convince everyone that the values implied in the curriculum they have managed to insert are working for the greater good when they are not. It is a way that this "ruling elite" preserves their interests by getting people to voluntarily act in opposition to that which may have better served their own well-being and that of the greater good.

Closely aligned with corporatism and nationalism, hegemony stems from the belief that decision-making can effectively be made only by the "intelligent minority," whose wealth "proves" their stake in maintaining best policies. This minority believes that too much democracy in the hands of the working-class citizenry is dangerous and that education can keep it in check rather than support it. They worry that the masses might rise up in protest and take their wealth away.[10]

Thus, in addition to offering Indigenous perspectives for the teaching of specific subject areas and exercises for learning them, lesson plan guidelines presented for eight mainstream courses presented Part Three introduces one or two examples of hegemonic influences aligned with on of the subject areas targeted. This work is in alignment with Indigenous truth-seeking priorities and can open minds; stimulate critical reasoning and truth-seeking dialogue; and open the door for legitimate consideration of Indigenous alternative ideas that follow. By so doing, students can address the source of the problems we have in the world and consider an equally deeply rooted solution. Such reflection is part of the Indigenous teaching and learning that is vitally missing in mainstream education. An education that does explicitly identify "features of the Western tradition or worldview that produce many of the problems we are immersed in today" is falling short (Wildcat, 2001, p.10).[11]

Educational hegemony is sometimes referred to as a "hidden curriculum" that can socialize a population so that it will come to believe that the interests of those in power support the public good even when they in fact do the opposite. Through schooling, media and the manipulated creation of common cultural assumptions, beliefs continue benefitting only a few in spite of damage to the public welfare (Bullock & Trombley, 1999, pp. 387–388). Hegemonic education neutralizes opposition without needing force to do so (Williams, 1977). "Crucial to the hegemonic relationship is the belief of the masses that the lifestyle and values of the hegemonic group are inherently, naturally, and objectively superior" (Zurayk, 2010). Awareness at the teacher level may be the only way we can overcome the subtle power of hegemony to influence educational policy, curricula and textbooks.[12]

A classic example of educational hegemony relates to what most teachers teach about Helen Keller. Very few know she was a socialist who was outspoken about the pitfalls of capitalism, a labor unionist who was a member of the International Workers of the World and who participated in a strike against her own biographical film for unfair wages, and an anti-war activist whose beliefs caused her to be attacked by her critics. All of these attributes make her a much greater hero than merely a woman who overcame her disabilities to write books. Yet in the bestselling children's biography of Helen Keller, Gare Thompson's *Who Was Helen Keller?* (2003), none of this is mentioned. Instead, on the back cover, the author presents a multiple-choice question about her identity (honoring today's continuing emphasis on standardized assessments) and offers the following answers:[13]

[ ] A woman who could not see or hear
[ ] A best-selling author
[ ] A famous world traveler
[√] All of the above!

Indigenous knowledge has been and will continue to be dismissed if hegemony is allowed to work unsuspected. This book offers a way for teachers to try a different approach in their own classrooms by simply teaching specific examples of course-related hegemony and addressing or reversing the problems with Indigenous alternatives. Awareness of corporate and hegemonic influence on schooling is thus an important benefit of the partnership with Indigenous education. Indigenous paradigms oppose deception of any kind and gently allow for their exposure. Above all, "truth-seeking" opportunities emerge naturally via Indigenous approaches to teaching and learning.[14]

2. Real-World Outcomes

This section of each chapter offers some evidence of how the mainstream approach to teaching the particular chapter's subject has played out in society with real-world impacts. Test scores and grades mean little if the ultimate goals for learning the subject are not met. For each subject covered in these chapters, real-world outcomes show that in the absence of Indigenous values and perspectives, mainstream approaches have failed to achieve the generally assumed outcomes, giving evidence perhaps to the truer hegemonic goals. Real-world outcomes demonstrate that a change must occur if the highest purpose for education is not met, such as that asserted by the National Council for Social Studies:

> The primary purpose of social studies is to help young people make informed and reasoned decisions for the public good as citizens of a culturally diverse, democratic society in an interdependent world. (National Council for Social Studies, 1994, p.1)

The truth is that citizens, whether in the United States, Canada, Australia or most other countries whose curriculum is without Indigenous perspectives, are not making such informed and reasoned decisions. Bowers recognized this problem long ago in his text *Education, Cultural Myths and the Ecological Crises: Toward Deep Changes*: "We have only to observe how few public school and university teachers would be able to recognize the many ways in which an anthropocentric world view is represented in the curricula to recognize how complex the problem is" (1993, p. 186). In an interview with Amy Goodman, David Suzuki also spoke about our ecological crises, warning that until we realize and then educate others to realize that we are part of the fragile biosphere, we are doomed. He added that the leadership in this awakening waits within the knowledge of our Indigenous Peoples (Democracy Now at democracynow.org, June 26, 2012).

3. Indigenous Curricular Alternatives

This part of each of the chapters presents ideas that allow for Indigenous knowledge, wisdom, values, and traditional goals and objectives to be applied specifically to the content area targeted for the chapter. These ideas have been condensed from hundreds of books, chapters and articles over many years and from personal experience among traditional Indigenous Peoples from a number of First Nations in Canada, the United States and Mexico. They are intended to foster a new partnership between traditional Indigenous and Eurocentric/American wisdom. As Rebecca Adamson says, "Both Western and Indigenous cultures can mutually benefit from accessing and sharing beliefs, customs and technology" (n.d.). Such interaction between cultures creates a new dynamic—one that fosters the creativity and prosperity of creation.

Because true Indigenous education would not be as fragmented as the subject areas we address here, it would be most optimally effective if teachers were able to tie the various subjects together with course work. However, the goals are for teachers to act immediately in classrooms across North America and beyond to use what they are obligated to use but to do so in a way that will make it possible to "teach truly."

4. Questions for Research, Dialogue, Choices and Praxis

Each chapter ends with questions and specific activities intended both to enhance learning the Indigenous ways and to facilitate actually practicing them. These simple lists of questions and activities can help promote authentic and enthusiastic research and dialogue that will lead to making choices about what aspects of mainstream education and Indigenous perspectives to either keep or throw away. These questions and activities also help students turn their choices into real-world actions. Teachers can modify the questions for any age group and for any aspect of the standard curriculum. They can use the questions to guide and encourage students to carefully reflect on the material with the goal of deciding what mainstream ideas are best replaced with Indigenous ones.

The fourth direction, the South, emphasizes spiritual and emotional awareness that helps guide us back to the introspection and reflections of the West. This section has but one chapter, Chapter Thirteen, entitled, "From Fear to Fearlessness." Originally intended to address two additional subjects-religion and psychology-instead it combines spirituality and psychology as inseparable paths to "always thinking the highest thought" (Cajete, 2000, pp. 276–279). Early on, I refer to the work of three respected Indigenous colleagues who have conflicting ideas about who is qualified to teach Indigenous spirituality. It also brings to the surface important questions that are vital for any serious study of psychology, religion and spirituality. Is Indigenous spirituality compatible with Christianity? If not, can it be made to be so and how? If it cannot be made to be compatible, what impact might this have on indigenizing mainstream education systems that are largely founded upon Christian perceptions? What role does fear and fearlessness play in resolving these questions as they relate to learning spiritual and psychological principles for a healthy, balanced world?

This chapter has two guest authors. Ed McGaa, also known as Eagle Man, shares his ideas about Lakota spirituality and the fearlessness it embraces and requires. R. Michael Fisher shares ideas from his research on cultures of fear and education. Both of these presentations lead into my presenting a "fear hypothesis" along with a tool for using fear as a catalyst for living a virtuous life that can be used in the classroom. From an Indigenous perspective, courage and fearlessness are essential components for "thinking the highest thoughts" and acting accordingly.

The Prophesy

The idea of an eventual partnership between white and red cultures was prophesized long ago. Ancient Kogi and Hopi myths tell about the selfishly inventive and deceptively articulate Younger (White) Brother, who strays from the spiritual path known to his Elder (Red) Brother. Using any means to get what he wants, White Brother wreaks havoc on our planet's life systems. If nothing changes, Mother Earth's purifying upheavals eventually lead to renewal, but the process is devastating for humanity. Since First Nation's prophesies do not announce facts but rather offer intuited visions of living currents of probabilities, another outcome is possible. In this one, White Brother realizes his errors and commits to relearning how to honor the spirits and walk in balance again. As a result, Nature's purification process is less catastrophic for human beings.[15]

Some related stories foresee collaboration between White Brother's creative genius and Red Brother's deep wisdom as a way to accomplish the scenario that restores the health of our life systems before it is too late. According to Hopi spiritual leader Dan Evehema, one prediction describes the awakened White Brother as "large in population and belonging to no religion but their very own" (n.d.). I interpret this phrase as describing non-Indian educators around the world commencing to indigenize mainstream schooling. "Belonging to no religion but their very own" means the teachers will be spiritually guided by their understanding that "everything is related."

Ultimately, the opportunity to partially indigenize mainstream schooling is about remembering our relationship to and our love for place. It is about letting go of our sense of superiority over and our fear of the natural world so that we can return to a life that deeply respects Mother Earth. We can wait no longer for educators to challenge the hegemony that cuts children off from their natural roots and keeps them away from the sights, sounds, aromas, colors, sensations and the sacred sense of space that ultimately give us the multidimensional capability for harmonious relationships. D.H. Lawrence expresses this idea poetically:

> Oh, what a catastrophe, what a maiming of love when it was made personal, merely personal feeling. This is what is the matter with us: we are bleeding at the roots because we are cut off from the earth and sun and stars. Love has become a grinning mockery because, poor blossom, we plucked it from its stem on the Tree of Life and expected it to keep on blooming in our civilized vase on the table. (n.d.)

Teaching Truly offers a way to reclaim the joy and beauty of this magic planet. "In the end, a Red pedagogy is about engaging the development of a community-based power in the interest of a responsible political, economic and spiritual society. That is, the power to live out active presences and ability to survive rather than an illusionary democracy (Grand, 2008, p. 250).[16] We seem to have reached a time in human evolution for entering into a new age of enlightenment based on the experiences of the past, including our past detour from the unified path of relationships.[17] This collaboration between current mainstream education and Indigenous knowledge paths may be the most realistic possibility for transforming future education. With it, each plant, person and animal offers a perspective to help understand something of importance. When we realize this synthesis of relationships, we come to a higher level of thinking that, according to many American Indians, is a requirement for living a good life. Greg Cajete, a Tewa Indian, writes in *Native Science*, "Thinking the highest thought means thinking of one's self, one's community, and one's environment 'richly'—essentially, it is a spiritual mind-set in which one thinks in the highest, most respectful, and most compassionate way, thus systematically influencing the actions of both individuals and the community" (2000, p. 276).

Ultimately mainstream education has failed to achieve "a life in balance" as did Indigenous education prior to conquest. In 1744 the Virginia Commissions offered to pay for a number of young Indian men to attend Williamsburg College to learn the white man's way. After a day of reflection and discussion, a representative of the Six Nations of the Confederation of the Iroquois conveyed the following reply:

> We know that you highly esteem the kind of learning taught in those colleges, and that the maintenance of our young men while with you would be very expensive to you. We are convinced, therefore, that you mean to do us good by your proposal, and we thank you heartily. But you who are wise must know that different nations have different conceptions of things, and you will therefore not take it amiss if our ideas of this kind of education happen not to be the same with yours. We have had some experience of it. Several of our young people were formerly brought up at the colleges of the northern provinces, they were instructed in all your sciences, but when they came back to us they were bad runners, ignorant of every means of living in the woods, unable to bear either cold or hunger, knew neither how to build a cabin, take a deer, or kill an enemy, or speak our language. They were, therefore, neither fit for hunters, warriors, or counselors; they were totally good for nothing. We are not, however, the less obliged by your kind offer, though we decline accepting it, and to show our grateful sense of it, if the gentlemen of Virginia send us a dozen of their sons we will take great care of their education, instruct them in all we know, and *make men of them*. (Hopkins, 1898, p. 240)

Whether this book can or will sufficiently produce the kind of education the future demands or whether a more radical replacement of Western education entirely will be necessary remains to be seen. At least what we propose herein is a reasonable starting place in accordance with Indigenous prophesies that indicate this is one of many possible solutions to our current crises during what many see as a crucial time of transition into a more beautiful, balanced way of living in the world. Here is where real-life knowing is invigorating and where interpretations matter. Indigenous perspectives "bring something unique to the table. We bring dreams, food, elders, courage and the clarity of speech and purpose. After all, there is no time to waste" (Aluli-Meyer, 2006, p. 230).

Notes

1. I use the term "mainstream" instead of "Western," or "dominant" or "Eurocentric," but these terms are relatively interchangeable. By "mainstream," I mean primarily American-dominated influences on teaching, learning and curriculum, whether in the United States or in other countries such as Canada, Mexico and Australia. Mainstream education is based on values that stand in stark contrast to Indigenous ones.

2. Although the K-12 curriculum is specifically addressed and the primary emphasis is on K-12 students, the creative university teacher can easily adapt the material for university-level work.

3. "Indian," "American Indian," "Alaskan Native," "Aboriginal," "Indigenous," or specific tribal names are used to describe Indigenous peoples in different contexts and generally refer to any people who have in some significant way maintained cultural values stemming from their having lived in one place long enough to understand deep connections to nature and its laws, including those who continue these values in spite of continual efforts to suppress them.

4. Reference to "Indigenous knowledge" or "Indigenous perspectives" throughout this text generally refers to those common themes that are unique to many tribal cultures and that differ significantly from most non-Indigenous ones. There is no universal Indigenous perspective per se. Diversity is the hallmark of Indigenous knowledge, and only through deep reflection, experience and commitment can anyone, Indian or non-Indian alike, easily grasp the way that respect for diversity collaborates with respect for interconnectedness.

5. It is also important to do what we can to stop the "culturecide" of Indigenous Peoples. It would be most unfortunate to think we can borrow from traditional cultural wisdom and at the same time allow its disappearance, along with the disappearance of those who for thousands of years have maintained it.

6. The phrase "transformational learning" is used here with caution. The idea of transformation is often connected to the antithesis of Indigenous knowledge paths and has been a cause of our ecological ignorance. Transformation often embodies individualism, progress, change, technology and the sense that we are always on a trajectory toward something better. This ignores traditional wisdom. Red Cloud says that when we move, we simply need to remember what to leave behind and what to take with us. Thus my use of this phrase refers to making fundamental changes where needed while remembering those ideas that should not change.

7. Medicine Wheels have been found as stone structures dating back nearly 5,000 years. Many contemporary uses by Indigenous peoples as well as New Age–oriented individuals use the structure as an organizing paradigm for human learning and adapting to nature and natural movements or stages in life. I have adapted the Lakota version with my own symbolic representations for this book in hopes to bring balance into the four sections.

8. When referring to curriculum standards throughout the book, I refer to either current California standards revised in 2011 or to the "Common Core State Standards" which California and all but four states have adopted at the time of this writing. These are pro-

moted by the Bill & Melinda Gates Foundation and the Obama Administration as well as the National Council for Teacher Education as "state of the art" guidelines for core subjects in spite of a number of concerns of progressive educators listed in Chapter Four.

9. We can refer to the ruling class, the elite population, those with the money and influence to control politics, media and culture as being those "in power." Four hundred individuals in the U.S. now have the wealth equal to the lower 185 million citizens. They and the most powerful corporations have ideological and financial incentives for constantly maintaining a society that serves their continued success.

10. This philosophy has a long and remarkable history that will never be taught in classrooms. This book only gives course by course examples of hegemony, but a quick way for the reader to better understand its history in America is to watch the one-hour presentation, "Education for Whom and for What?" on YouTube by Noam Chomsky at the University of Arizona in February 2012. Chomsky describes the universal application of education as a tool to control, not enlighten, the population. See Chomsky, "Education for Whom and for What?" at http://www.youtube.com/watch?v=e_EgdSh01K8.

11. Wildcat was referring to the problems in Indian country and addressing Native educators and students, but the same call now applies to all of us and the "features" are largely to be found hidden in educational and cultural hegemony. I see the exposure of educational hegemony as getting to the source of educational reform. I also believe that although this book does not address Indian education reform for our Indigenous Peoples beyond the guest chapter three, that indigenizing mainstream education will indirectly enhance the dignity of Indigenous Peoples and an eventual change in anti-Indianism that continues cultural genocide.

12. In essence, today curriculum is largely determined by textbooks, and which textbooks are used is largely determined by the Florida, Texas and California School Boards. Whether the adoption of the national "common core standards" will change this is debatable, but these standards will most likely increase dependency on textbooks.

13. More about the Helen Keller example appears in the chapter on U.S. history hegemony. See also the article "The Truth about Helen Keller," by Ruth Shagoury, in "Rethinking Schools" at http://zinnedproject.org/posts/175.

14. Two excellent resources for understanding the Indigenous paradigm of honesty include Thomas Cooper's *A Time before Deception* (1998) and *Critical Neurophilosophy and Indigenous Wisdom* (Four Arrows, Cajete, & Lee, 2010).

15. Two of the most credible sources on the Hopi and the Kogi prophesies are Thomas Banyacya's speech to the U.N. (http://www.welcomehome.org/rainbow/prophecy/hopi.html) and Alan Ereira's BBC documentary "From the Heart of the World: Elder Brother's Warning" (http://www.linktv.org/globalspirit/Kogi).

16. The idea of "survivances" comes from Vizenor's 1993 article in the *American Indian Quarterly*, entitled "The Ruins of Representation," and from his notion that we must move beyond survival to thriving.

17. Charles Eisenstein offers an interesting perspective on the evolution of consciousness that expands on this idea. He says that after a great "separation," we are now at a crucial time

when the wisdom of the ages from all cultures, the great stories and the surviving Indigenous Peoples themselves are the keys to our rebalancing. Eisenstein's book *The Ascent of Humanity* is available for free reading at http://www.ascentofhumanity.com/text.php.

THE WEST

The Color Black

Introspection

Anti-Indianism[1] in Education and in the Academe

I think we're on the brink of disaster on many fronts. I believe that that Native people can help us out of that, help push us back away from that brink.
—N. Scott Momaday, in Nabakov,1992, p. 436

The repression of American Native Peoples during the last century is one of the least known genocidal stories of our time.
—Cook-Lynn, 2008, p. 188

I don't go so far as to think that the only good Indian is the dead Indian, but I believe nine out of every ten are, and I shouldn't like to inquire too closely into the case of the tenth.
—Teddy Roosevelt, in Hagedorn 1921, pp. 354–356

The sense of loss, alienation and indignity is pervasive throughout Indian country. It is evident that there have still not been adequate measures of reconciliation to overcome the persistent legacies of the history of oppression, and that there is still much healing that needs to be done.
—James Anaya, in his May 2012 official report to the United Nations Human Rights Council

Understanding anti-Indianism is a prerequisite for respectfully and authentically indigenizing mainstream curriculum and instruction. It is deeply ingrained in our culture and is likely influencing the thinking of most readers, teachers, administrators, parents and students right now. In spite of a growing intuitive desire to embrace the sacred understandings that are a legacy for us all, most non-Indian teachers will harbor anti-Indian assumptions at least unconsciously. Grant and Gillespie acknowledge this:

> Teachers, who have themselves been educated to believe that Native Americans lacked a culture of their own and needed to be civilized by the Europeans, are not in a good position—without additional learning—to teach their Native students respectfully or with an appreciation for Native heritages. Teachers with Eurocentric attitudes trying to teach Native students could be compared to the agriculturally untrained trying to raise a crop. At best, such teachers offer condescending sympathy—a response to Native students that can be as stultifying to growth as overt disrespect. (1993, p. 4)

Although other minority groups suffer prejudice and structural inequalities, there is a unique reason for anti-Indianism that sets it apart from other forms of racism and prejudice.[2] Axtel puts it succinctly when he argues that American Indians have provided the European invaders with a continual enemy against whom to defend their contrasting values in ways that assure the status quo:

> Without Indian targets and foils, even the New England colonists might not have retained their Chosen People conceit so long or so obdurately. The Indians were so crucial to the formation of the Anglo-American character because of the strong contrasts between their cultures and that of the intruders, which the English interpreted largely as native deficiencies....For example, while English society was divided into "divinely sanctioned" strata of wealth, power and prestige, Indian society fostered an "unnatural" contrast of democratic individualism in the people. (1987, p. 983)

Thus European ethnocentrism, in contrast with the holistic, tolerant, and non-materialistic views of Indians, helped make Indians a sort of cultural contrary that rationalized campaigns of genocide and cultural genocide. This is why the U.S. still honors Christopher Columbus with a national holiday. It is why U.S. schools continue to ignore or deny evidence that the American form of democracy was largely inspired by the Iroquois Confederacy (Johansen, 2006, pp. 45–66). In effect, educational hegemony designed to maintain status quo benefits for a ruling elite is by definition a form of anti-Indianism. This is why each chapter in Part Two begins with exercises to expose subject-related hegemony before engaging Indigenous alternatives and supplements. Chris Hedges refers to the continuing hegemonic war against Indigenous cultures in one of his recent essays:

And as we race toward the collapse of the planet's ecosystem we must restore this older vision of life if we are to survive. The war on the Native Americans, like the wars waged by colonialists around the globe, was waged to eradicate not only a people but a competing ethic. The older form of human community was antithetical and hostile to capitalism, the primacy of the technological state and the demands of empire. (Hedges, 2012, p. 1)

Seeing First Nations People as a "cultural contrary" is pervasive in mainstream education. Cultural gatekeepers, who are largely responsible for contemporary educational policy and social studies curriculum, maintain the phenomenon, whether conservative textbook publishers and influential historical societies (Crocco and Thornton 1999) or right-wing legislators and "well-intended" Christian groups. Anti-Indianism is also sustained via teacher education programs and the general inability of K-12 schooling to cultivate open-minded considerations about white privilege. Most people are so completely socialized with Eurocentric values and ruling-class hegemony that they are unaware of the extent to which they use these values as normative. Abram refers to this problem in his book *Becoming Animal*:

There are many intellectuals today who feel that any respectful reference to indigenous beliefs smacks of romanticism and a kind of backward-looking nostalgia. Oddly, these same persons often have no problem "looking backward" toward ancient Rome or ancient Greece for philosophical insight and guidance in the present day. What upsets these self-styled "defenders of civilization" is the implication that civilization might have something to learn from cultures that operate according to an entirely different set of assumptions, cultures that stand outside of historical time and the thrust of progress. (2010, p. 267)

Anti-Indianism is ultimately promoted by disinformation. This is why education plays such a crucial role in countering or maintaining its pervasiveness. Metaphorically, disinformation can be a weapon of mass destruction every bit as horrible as an atomic bomb, and it has been used against Indigenous People for hundreds of years. Water and land theft, corporate contamination of reservation land, continual attacks on sovereignty, loss of language and cultural rights, rates of disease as bad or worse than in third world countries, and extreme poverty are just some of the consequences of contemporary anti-Indianism for Native Peoples. Ultimately, it "displaces and excludes; thus its purposes have been to socially isolate, to expunge or expel, to fear and menace, to defame and to repulse Indigenous Peoples" (Cook-Lynn, 2001, p. 4).

Many readers are likely aware of the role Hollywood has played in promoting anti-Indianism in the world. For scholarly reading on this topic, the University of California's Media Resource Center lists more than forty publications that have explored the negative stereotyping in film.[3] A blatant example of such stereotyping is Walt Disney's story of Peter Pan. The children in the story go to Never-Never Land, where they find mermaids, pirates, and Indians. The Indians fulfill every stereotype ever invented about them in terms of appearance, actions, and customs, replete with a vocabulary that consists of "Ugh" and "How," whereas the pirates and mermaids have a good command of the English language. "To further insult Native people, Western values are attributed to them. They are 'red' because they are embarrassed about kissing, they devalue women, and so on. These ingratiating stereotypes, which so misrepresent Natives, last a lifetime" (Grant and Gillespie, 1993, p. 2). Even films wanting to show that Native Peoples have substance, like *Dances with Wolves* (1990), still make the white hero the most important figure while continuing to present romantic images that see "good Indians" as a remnant of the past:

> The movie *Dances with Wolves* (1990) might have improved on the "Whites Suffered, Too" theme by showing army depredations against the Lakotas, but even *Wolves* ended before the end, by allowing the two settler adoptees to peel off into the sunset. Left unexplored by the movie was the fact that, simply by removing their buckskins, changing their hair styles, and putting on cotton fabrics, they could easily move back into the safety of the settler world, something that none of the Lakota friends they left behind could have done. (Mann, 2012)

Hollywood's negative stereotypes of Native Peoples are made possible by the stories read to children that set the stage for accepting them. Anti-Indianism in children's literature begins a lifetime of anti-Indian consciousness in non-Indigenous children and a lifetime of pain for Indigenous children. According to Aziyatawin Angela Cavender Wilson, a professor of American Indian history at Arizona State University, "anti-Indian educational and ideological hegemony is so firmly established, most Americans cannot recognize it even when it appears before their eyes" (2006, p. 67). She points out in her chapter in *Unlearning the Language of Conquest* that an example of anti-Indian literature is Laura Ingalls Wilder's classic *Little House on the Prairie*. Debby Reese, an Indigenous scholar who has devoted much of her career to this topic, has an excellent website that provides critical perspectives on how Indians are and have been depicted in children's literature. For instance, on her website we learn about the findings of a major study of forty-five children's books about the Nahua/Mexica/Aztec People:

> Colonized Nahua/Mexica/Aztec children's books…consist of incorrect information, reinforced stereotypes, and racist characterizations such as the Nahuas being extinct or violent "savages," having practiced human sacrifices, and the application of Western concepts such as "God," "King," and "Lord," to describe the Nahua culture. (Reese, 2011)

Yet it is neither children's literature nor Hollywood movies that are mostly responsible for anti-Indianism. The most significant way anti-Indian disinformation makes its way into our world is through academic publications that sanction the more popular flow of anti-Indian attitudes. A number of professors have published works that dismiss anything positive about Indigenous ways, present or past. F.R. McKenna, a professor of Native studies and a consultant to numerous Indian tribes and federal agencies, categorized this policy of dismissal in an article for the *Journal of American Indian Education* in 1981. His words apply still.

> Academics generally have little interest in Indians. Scholars can be divided into three categories: (a) Those who are overtly racists. An example is John Greenway, a folklorist at the University of Colorado. Greenway posed the question, "Did the United States destroy the American Indian?" and answered, "No, but it should have." (b) Those who exclude Indians from academic life. To Illustrate, witness the rejection of the application of the American Indian Historical Society for participation in the International Congress of Historical Sciences; and (c) those who neglect to include the Indian in scholarly presentations. For example, the revisionist historian, Colin Greer, in an otherwise excellent collection of works of ethnicity in America, makes no mention of American Indians. (pp. 22–23)

A number of university professors seem to dedicate their careers to work that sets the "good" dominant cultures against the "bad" Indigenous ones. Such popular texts by academics establish the tone for education curricula (Four Arrows, 2006). For example, James Clifton, an anthropologist, argues in his book *The Invented Indian* (1990) that "acknowledging anything positive in the native past is an entirely wrongheaded proposition because no genuine Indian accomplishments have ever really be substantiated" (p. 36).[4] Robert Whelan, director of a pro-free-market think tank and author of *Wild in the Woods: The Myth of the Peaceful Eco-Savage* (1999), also dismisses any positive contributions of Indigenous Peoples from around the world: "Indigenous peoples of the earth have nothing to teach us about caring for the environment" (p. 23). UCLA anthropologist Robert Edgerton, in *Sick Societies: Challenging the Myth of Primitive Harmony* (1992), writes that the problems in "primitive societies" prove the superiority of Western culture. Most recently, Steven Pinker's newest text, *The Better Angels of our Nature: Why Violence Has Declined* (2011), continues the anti-Indian propaganda that essentially supports current wars and anti-terrorism policies by offering poor scholarship about the "warlike Yanomamo" and using stories about Indigenous violence against European colonists to make the case (once again) that we are far better off now than in pre-state societies. The following quotation reveals another typical example of how "scientific" interpretations of Indigenous history result in false conclusions. On a website specializing in science and metaphysics, we can read about the Kogi People and how warlike the authors claim they are:

> The figurines depict human subjects—thought to be noblemen or chiefs—in ornate dresses and with a large animal mask over the face. Many elements of their body posture (e.g., hands on their hips) and dress signal an aggressive stance and hence are interpreted as evidence for the power of the wearer and the bellicose nature of Tairona society. (http://www.crystalinks.com/kogi.html)

Without ample supporting evidence, the existence of one figurine that seems to depict "an aggressive stance" is insufficient to conclude that an entire culture is warlike or bellicose.

Such arguments can and must be challenged appropriately and effectively in mainstream curricula. One way to help students question anti-Indian claims in scholarly publications is to compare them with authentic narratives of Aboriginal Peoples. For instance, to help decide whether it is likely that Smohalla Indians of the Columbia Basin tribes trashed their environment, one might consider a Smohalla representative's complaint about European attitudes in the 1880s:

> You ask me to plow the ground! Shall I take a knife and tear my mother's breast? Then when I die she will not take me to her bosom to rest. You ask me to dig for stone! Shall I dig under her skin for her bones? Then when I die I cannot enter her body to be born again. You ask me to cut grass and make hay and sell it, and be rich like white men! But how dare I cut off my mother's hair. (Quoted in Mooney, 1991, p. 46)

When a collection of firsthand statements such as these is contrasted with a Western anthropologist's deductions after studying a few ancient artifacts, one quickly realizes that the anthropologist, no matter how well intended, often interprets through the anti-Indian lens. In Four Arrows, Greg Cajete and John Lee's text *Critical Neurophilosophy and Indigenous Wisdom* (2011), this problem is explored as relates to neuroscience. The authors conclude that interpretations of human nature as relates to brain research and concepts like generosity and honesty are largely swayed by Western assumptions. As for the arguments touting significant pre-contact warfare among Indigenous Peoples, we suggest that teachers and students also study the assertions carefully and compare them with more substantial research that is easily accessible. For example, one can Google the research presented in Yale University's Human Resource Area Files, an internationally recognized database in the field of cultural anthropology founded in 1949 to facilitate worldwide comparative studies of human behavior. We also recommend visiting the website peacefulsocieties.org for similar research. In these places and in others, people will learn that most human societies prior to the rise of monarchies and monotheism were relatively peaceful. For example, Leavitt's (1977) research found war absent or rare in 73% of hunting and gathering societies and in nearly half of those employing some form of agriculture.

Referring to claims that Indigenous Peoples were more warlike than contemporary people, Johan M.G. van der Dennen's doctoral dissertation and subsequent 900-page book, *The Origin of War: The Evolution of a Male-Coalitional Reproductive Strategy* (1995), support Axtel's "cultural contrary" theory:

> Peaceable preindustrial (preliterate, primitive, etc.) societies constitute a nuisance to most theories of warfare and they are, with few exceptions, either denied or "explained away." In this contribution I shall argue that the claim of universal human belligerence is grossly exaggerated; and that those students who have been developing theories of war, proceeding from the premise that peace is the "normal" situation, have not been starry-eyed utopians. (p. 2)

Unfortunately, mainstream education continues to support ideas about war as a necessary part of life and an unfortunate aspect of human nature, except of course when it is in behalf of freedom and democracy, which it is falsely claimed to be with regards to the U.S. Some educational material claims that modern societies are much more peaceful than pre-contact Indigenous ones. This idea about the violence of Indigenous people has even spilled into policies to ban ethnic studies that legislators claim incites anti-American violence. Such sentiments were used to pass a recent Arizona law that essentially bans ethnic education (Amster, 2010). In implementing this law, the superintendent of the Tucson Unified School District ordered teachers to stop using Bill Bigelow's book *Rethinking Columbus: The Next 500 Years*, one of the few scholarly texts that has been used for over twenty years to teach the truth about Columbus and his legacy. The district also banned Arturo Rosales's *Chicano! The History of the Mexican Civil Rights Movement*, Paulo Freire's *Pedagogy of the Oppressed* and a number of others. This is not surprising given Arizona's law allowing for the profiling of suspected illegal immigrants crossing the border. What social studies students and educators do not likely know, however, is that most of the illegal immigrants are Mexico's Indigenous farmers forced to find work outside of their own country due to the consequences of free trade laws.

In effect, the increase in discrimination against "illegal immigrants" and the prohibitions against legal Mexican students learning about their histories of oppression are tied to a policy of anti-Indianism that actually started in Mexico long ago. A process of "de-Indianization" in Mexico has essentially managed to get the people to renounce their own cultural Indigenous identity. Buillermo Bonfil Batalla writes, "The Spanish colonizers were able to convince the colonized of their own inferiority" (1996, p. 59) until the population stopped considering itself Indian. Dr. Mario Garza, board chair of the Indigenous Cultures Institute, says, "This de-Indianization continues today as an increasing number of Mexican Americans prefer to identify as 'Latino' or 'Hispanic,' Eurocentric labels that totally ignore our indigenous heritage" (n.d.). (It is not likely that 7,000 Spanish conquerors inseminated a large enough number of Indigenous women to have created a population where the Indigenous Peoples are so diluted as not to claim their heritage.)

Unfortunately, Canadian social studies education and policy have not done much better in attending to Indigenous perspectives. In 2003 a study of 520 first-year university students from throughout Canada showed that two-thirds of them could not recall discussing current Native issues in elementary or high school. Eighty percent said they didn't learn enough about Aboriginal Peoples to equip them as responsible citizens. Only 17% could offer an example of how Native culture contributed to Canada, and fewer than 10% could name one fact about the federal Indian Act, which governs life on Canada's Aboriginal reserves. The report also revealed that 80% of the Canadian students expressed dissatisfaction with the education they obtained regarding Aboriginal Peoples in their elementary and secondary schooling.[5] These students called directly for an improved pedagogy based on honesty and respect. Unfortunately, in 2012 a national report revealed not only that there is insufficient education about Aboriginal Peoples for non-Indian students but also that there is no organized federal plan for educating Aboriginal children in either reserve or Canadian schools. In a news article entitled "First Nations education gets poor grade from federal panel" (2012), the panel's chair says that in spite of the desires of many people, there is no system of support for Indian education: "There isn't, in fact, a First Nations education system in Canada" (Canadian Press, Feb. 2012).

McDiarmid and Pratt (1971) wrote a pioneering book that exposed how anti-Indian bias manifests in schools via how teachers and teaching materials address Indians. Their work was adapted by the Manitoba Indian Brotherhood (MIB) to examine Grade 6 social studies textbooks. *The Shocking Truth about Indians in Textbooks* (Manitoba Indian Brotherhood, n.d.) details the methods used by the brotherhood and clearly demonstrates that children in Manitoba, Canada, were being taught biased information that glorified the accomplishments of settlers while denigrating Native inhabitants. The MIB researchers identified ten kinds of biases commonly found in school materials. The following categories are taken from *The Shocking Truth about Indians in Textbooks* (pp. ia, iia), as is the definition of each category. Grant and Gillespie (1993) list these biases along with examples from their own experience:

1. Bias by omission—selecting information that reflects credit on only one group, frequently the writer's or speaker's group. **Example:** the omission of Native people from both historic and contemporary material. North American history is taught as beginning with European colonizers; contemporary Native people and their contributions are not part of mainstream consciousness.

2. Bias by defamation—calling attention to the Native person's faults rather than virtues and misrepresenting the nature of Native people. **Example:** the teacher who says, "Indian children are shy" without considering the role the teacher is playing in maintaining the children in their "shy" role.

3. Bias by disparagement—denying or belittling the contribution of Native people to mainstream culture. **Example:** the teacher who does not involve Native parents in school activities but then alleges that Native parents do not value an education for their children.

4. Bias by cumulative implication—constantly creating the impression that only one group is responsible for positive development. **Example:** The United States prides itself in being a "nation of immigrants." Native people, by definition, are not a part of the proud heritage.

5. Bias by (lack of) validity—failing to ensure that information about issues is accurate and unambiguous. **Example:** A study of Native civilizations before the coming of Europeans is not included in school curricula. An excellent reference article, "Indian Contributions to the World" by D. B. Sealey, is found in the text edited by Sealey and Kirkness entitled, *Indians without Tipis* (1973).

6. Bias by inertia—perpetuation of legends and half-truths by failure to keep abreast of historical scholarship. **Example:** Teacher training institutions have long ignored the need to take culture and race into account when training teachers.

7. Bias by obliteration—ignoring significant aspects of Native history. **Example:** American victory over Japan in WWII is touted without acknowledging the fact that many Native people suffered from nuclear testing as the bomb was being developed in the southwestern United States and on several Pacific Islands.

8. Bias by disembodiment—referring in a casual and depersonalized way to a group of people. **Example:** educators who do not bother to learn names of community members.

9. Bias by lack of concreteness—dealing with a race or group in general-

izations that apply shortcomings, or positive characteristics, of one individual to the group. To be concrete, the material must be factual, objective, and realistic. **Example:** generalizations like "Native people abuse the welfare system" or "Native people live in harmony with nature."

10. Bias by (lack of) comprehensiveness and balance—failure to mention all relevant facts that may help form the opinion of the students. **Example:** Though many Indian people practice traditional spirituality, they are also represented in other major religions in the country.

Beyond teaching and educational materials and policy, the law of the land itself is anti-Indian. For example, in upholding a treaty provision in 1883, Justice Mathews of the Supreme Court wrote:

> The law tries superiors of a different race, according to the law of a social state of which they have an imperfect conception, and which is opposed to the traditions of their history, to the habits of their lives, to the strongest prejudices of their savage nature; one which measures the red man's revenge by the maxims of the white man's morality. (*Ex parte Crow Dog*, 1883, p. 556)

In his chapter for *Unlearning the Language of Conquest*, entitled "Conquest Masquerading as Law," the late Vine Deloria Jr. describes how anti-Indian attitudes and disinformation have continued to be engrained in both U.S. and international laws:

> Law is often a means of expressing and enforcing the prejudicies of the majority. In the Indian case, law quite often does not deal with facts but with beliefs accepted as facts. The belief that God appointed the Pope to rule over planet earth until the Second Coming of Jesus produced for many of the world's people a kind of legal limbo where justice could not be served, nor was it ever intended to be served. (p. 107)

The endemic nature of anti-Indianism as a legal construct is exemplified in how four major countries have responded to the United Nations Declaration on the Rights of Indigenous Peoples (UNDRIP). In December 2011, President Barack Obama finally signed this document which had been adopted by 143 countries in 2007 after nearly thirty years of hard-fought negotiations and activism. Australia, Canada, New Zealand and the United States were the only four countries that voted against the declaration in 2007. They worried that its language would contradict current law and treaty interpretations, especially those still supported legally via the Christian Doctrine of Discovery, which stems from a 1452 papal bull. However, activism advocating these countries' support of the declaration continued, and in

2009 Australia changed its position, followed by New Zealand in April 2010 and Canada in November 2010. On December 16, 2010, President Obama announced his decision to sign at the Second Annual White House Tribal Nations Conference (which was not at the White House but at the Department of the Interior nearby). His words, as usual, were on target and hopeful, offering great respect for the cultures of Native Peoples. However, shortly after his speech, the U.S. did what the other three countries did shortly after they signed the Declaration. They passed legislation that makes the declaration non-binding. In fact, many current policies and practices of the U.S. government under President Obama's administration violate the letter and the spirit of UNDRIP at home and around the world.

All of this is to reveal to the reader how strongly entrenched is the phenomenon of anti-Indianism. Clifton (1990) and others like him may feel it is "wrongheaded" to expect that any contributions might be made by Indigenous cultures to our contemporary world. They may believe that the proper role of education is to continue celebrating the genocidal legacy of Christopher Columbus until the contemporary First Nations Peoples whom they have made "invisible" ultimately vanish from the Earth. However, as Weatherford (1991) notes in his text about positive Indigenous contributions, the dominant culture's neglect of Indigenous truths implicates it in Columbus's folly, for it does not know where it truly is in the world or how to get to where it wants to go. You, the educator about to study a way to indigenize your curriculum, have a map to discover where we are, where we must go, and how we can get there!

Notes

1. I borrow this phrase from Elizabeth Cook-Lynn, who uses it in her excellent text *Anti-Indianism in Modern America* (Urbana: University of Illinois Press, 2001). I also used the phrase as a subtitle for my edited book *Unlearning the Language of Conquest: Scholars Expose Anti-Indianism in America* (Austin: University of Texas Press, 2006).
2. Unlike other suppressed and oppressed minority groups who wish to assimilate into the dominant culture with more equality, a culture where wealth redistribution is terribly out of balance, Indigenous Peoples wish to live according to their own very contrasting cultural values. A number of talented American Indians who have graduated from top universities and obtained high-paying jobs have quit the "rat race" to return to their impoverished reservations and help save their languages and cultures while waiting for Western culture to run its fatal course.
3. See the list at http://www.lib.berkeley.edu/MRC/IndigenousBib.html.
4. In response to Clifton's work, Vine Deloria Jr. writes, "Clifton's argument is that the modern Indian point of view is wrong because Indians do not have the right to have a point of view when scholars know reality to be different. Here, then, we have the crux of the prob-

lem. Clifton et al. are simply fighting for the right to continue defining Indians in whatever manner they see fit" (quoted in Mihesuah, 1998, p. 71). As for Indian accomplishments, besides coffee, rubber, corn, beans, popcorn, chewing gum, quinine, cotton, lacrosse, toboggans, sleeping bags, and hundreds of other products, many further contributions to our world can be listed, such as psychological insights, communication skills, and scientific skills. In Part Two of this book, many of these will be revealed.

5. Read about this report at http://www.turning-point.ca/?q=node/176.

Historical Trauma and Its Prevention in the Classroom

By guest author Kathryn England-Aytes*
(Delaware/Cherokee descendant)

Whoever controls the education of our children controls our future.
—WILMA MANKILLER, PRINCIPAL CHIEF,
CHEROKEE NATION, 1985–1995

How different would be the sensation of a philosophic mind to reflect that instead of exterminating a part of the human race by our modes of population that we had persevered through all difficulties and at last had imparted our Knowledge of cultivating and the arts, to the Aboriginals of the Country by which the source of future life and happiness had been preserved and extended. But it has been conceived to be impracticable to civilize the Indians of North America—This opinion is probably more convenient than just.
—HENRY KNOX TO GEORGE WASHINGTON, 1790s

Inclination to remove from this land has no abiding place in our hearts, and when we move we shall move by the course of nature to sleep under this ground which the Great Spirit gave to our ancestors and which now covers them in their undisturbed peace.
—CHEROKEE LEGISLATIVE COUNCIL,
NEW ECHOTA, JULY 1830

> *After the devastation of tribal economies and the deliberate creation of tribal dependence on the services provided by this agency, this agency set out to destroy all things Indian....These wrongs must be acknowledged if the healing is to begin....I extend this formal apology to Indian people for the historical conduct of this agency....Never again will this agency stand silent when hate and violence are committed against Indians. Never again will we allow policy to proceed from the assumption that Indians possess less human genius than the other races. Never again will we seize your children, nor teach them to be ashamed of who they are....Together, we must wipe the tears of seven generations.*
>
> —BIA ASSISTANT SECRETARY KEVIN GOVER (PAWNEE) ON THE 175TH ANNIVERSARY OF THE ESTABLISHMENT OF THE BUREAU OF INDIAN AFFAIRS IN SEPTEMBER 2000

Although this is a book about teaching all children, it is important that educators understand how historical trauma, unresolved grief and cultural decimation over an individual's lifespan and across generations has affected Native students, families and communities. If a teacher has only one Indian student, this understanding could be vital for that child. For non-Indian students, this awareness is of significance not only for cultivating a more empathetic concern with the continuing plight of their nation's hosts but also because non-Indian students themselves may be suffering their own forms of trauma resulting from the structural inequalities their families have experienced. Moreover, in the difficult times facing all people today, the discussions provided here might stimulate changes in the educational process that will reduce the legacy of trauma in future generations.

Nearly three centuries after the arrival of the European colonists, the impact of their policies aimed at civilization and assimilation through education can still be felt within Native communities. It is difficult to view these results as anything less than disastrous. As a result, sometimes directly and sometimes more insidiously, mainstream education may still challenge tribal identification and traditional values and thus remain a source of cultural conflict and negation of the individual (Marr, 2012; Jacobs, Cajete & Jongmin, 2010; Grande, 2004; Deloria and Wildcat, 2001). This chapter intends to help educators become more aware of how mainstream (Eurocentric) education has historically affected Native students. It concludes with some recommendations for honoring the source of Indigenous wisdom and knowledge paths in educational settings.

Over the past two decades, a substantial body of research has emerged on cumulative and historical trauma involving American Indian and Alaskan Native populations. Dr. Maria Yellow Horse Brave Heart's landmark work defines historical trauma as cumulative emotional and psychological wounding, over the lifespan and across generations, emanating from massive group trauma experiences (Brave Heart-Jordan, 1995, Brave Heart-Jordan & DeBruyn, 1998; Brave Heart, 1998). In other work with Native child populations, Dolores Subia-Bigfoot examines three primary types of trauma in Indian Country: *cultural trauma*, which is caused by an attack on the fabric of a society that affects the essence of the community and its members; *historical trauma*, which is caused by cumulative exposure to traumatic events that affect an individual and continue to affect subsequent generations; and *intergenerational trauma*, which refers to trauma that is not resolved but internalized and passed from one generation to the next (Subia-Bigfoot, 2007).

In the context of this chapter, historical trauma refers to the individual, community, and intergenerational effects of the cataclysmic events of European colonization, including genocide, warfare, ethnic cleansing, forced assimilation and relocation. Using educational settings to address the ongoing cumulative impact of historically traumatic events on Native peoples requires some understanding of colonization, cultural identity, tribal citizenship, sovereignty and federal policies directed at Native people.

Early Educational Policies on American Indians: Missionaries, Treaties and Becoming Wards of the State

Education for American Indians began as missionary efforts by European colonizers as early as the 1630s. Jesuit missionaries traveled to America to convert Native Americans to Christianity, and although some were successful, others were not able to displace Native religious practices, as revealed by the following Huron Native comment to Jesuit missionary Jean de Brébeuf in 1635:

> You tell us fine stories, and there is nothing in what you say that may not be true; but that is good for you who come across the seas. Do you not see that, as we inhabit a world so different from yours, there must be another heaven for us, and another road to reach it? (Smithsonian Institute, 2007, p. 6)

Colonizers regarded education as a necessary bridge to Christianize and successfully assimilate Native Americans. Curricula and teaching were implemented with Eurocentric views and without consideration for the values of Native peoples themselves, setting the stage for generations of miseducation (Boyer, 1997) and cumulative trauma. Ultimately, American Indian educational policy became inextricably intertwined with federal policies directed toward the elimination or assimilation of Native populations.

During the American Revolution, as European colonists evolved into "Americans," Native nations fought on both sides of the conflict. Even those who wished to remain neutral were forced to fight on one side or the other to protect their homelands. The 1783 peace treaty between Great Britain and the newly created United States of America was not extended to Native Americans who had fought as allies of the British. Instead, they were treated as a conquered people who had forfeited their land as a spoil of war. Although it is true that the newly formed U.S. government, eager to expand, did so by purchasing Native land, in many instances land was taken by means of dishonored treaties and acts of warfare (Zinn, 2003).

Throughout the nineteenth century, the U.S. federal government initiated hundreds of treaties with sovereign Native American nations that exchanged Native lands for the provision of education, healthcare and protection from continued expansion. In spite of government promises to leave Native territories unmolested "as long as grass grows or water runs," conflicts continued over land ownership, religion and culture. Westward expansion continued, and accelerated, fueled by the fur trade, an ever-growing push for land for white settlement, gold discoveries and the higher calling of Manifest Destiny. U.S. federal policies were implemented through federal and state laws to appropriate Native lands, to exterminate or remove Natives to reservations, to disrupt sacred relationships to the land, to use education and religion as forces of indoctrination and assimilation and to exploit economic necessity as justification for forced relocations. Finally, although the tragic effects of differential immunity to diseases between populations are well documented as an unintended consequence of peoples coming into contact with one another for the first time, Europeans interacting with Native Americans also deliberately used diseases and their transmission as a biological weapon of choice with which to decimate the Indigenous peoples of the North American continent, resulting in countless deaths (Brave Heart, 1995; Deboe, 1940, 1983; Duran and Duran, 1995; Jacobs, Cajete and Jongmin, 2010; Ross, 1998; Strickland, 1980).

Even those charged with enforcing the federal government's early policy on American Indians struggled with the morality of it. In his observations of conditions in the Indian Territory in the early 1840s, Major Ethan Allen Hitchcock heatedly described his views of conflict between the U.S. government and the five "civilized" tribes:

> The government is in the wrong, and this is the chief cause of the persevering opposition of the Indians, who have nobly defended their country against our attempt to enforce a fraudulent treaty. The natives used every means to avoid a war, but were forced into it by the tyranny of our government. (Hitchcock, 1930, p. 120)

Federal policy on the "civilization" of Indians clearly focused on acquiring possession of Indian land, as indicated by Secretary of the Interior Caleb B. Smith in 1862 in a description of land grants for higher education in agricultural and mechanical arts:

> The rapid progress of civilization upon this continent will not permit the lands which are required for cultivation to be surrendered to savage tribes for hunting...although the consent of the Indians has been obtained in the form of treaties, it is well known that they have yielded to a necessity to which they could not resist....Instead of being treated as independent nations [as in the past] they should be regarded as wards of the Government. (Bureau of Indian Affairs [1956] as cited in Phillips, 2003, p. 23)

Removal and Resilience: Walking to Indian Country

Initially, the federal government created Indian territories in Oklahoma and the western portion of South Dakota for Indians to be out of the way of westward expansion. The effort also contributed to successfully casting Indians as perpetual villains in American fiction and films, as an obvious contrast to American heroes who looked even more heroic when killing bloodthirsty savages (Andrews, 2010). In 1830, U.S. President Andrew Jackson convinced Congress to pass the Indian Removal Act, which appropriated funds for relocation—by force if necessary—of all Native Americans. Federal officials were sent to negotiate removal treaties with southern tribes, many of whom reluctantly signed, exchanging one form of genocide for another (University of Nebraska, *The Reservation System: Native American Lands Sold Under the Dawes Act*, 2010).

Arguably, although all tribes removed to the Indian Territory shared similar experiences of hardship and suffering, the Cherokee removal, known as the Trail of Tears, continues to be one of the most recognized accounts of Indian removal in American history. The Cherokee had sought to retain rights to their remaining lands in Georgia by bringing a lawsuit against the state, eventually prevailing in a companion suit decided in favor of Cherokee boundaries by the U.S. Supreme Court (*Worcester v. Georgia*, 1832). Ignoring the Supreme Court's ruling, President Jackson initiated policies to terminate title to Indian land in a number of states (including Georgia shortly after gold was discovered on Cherokee land) and to relocate all Indian populations to the Indian Territory, which eventually became the state of Oklahoma (Cherokee Nation History Course, 2000, pp. 3–5).

The final removal of the Cherokee nation's last remnants from its members southeastern homes came in the winter of 1838–39 after U.S. president Martin Van

Buren ordered immediate implementation of the 1830 Indian Removal Act. United States Army troops rounded up an estimated 16,000 Cherokee men, women and children and interned them in forts built in North Carolina, Georgia, Alabama and Tennessee, where hundreds died from illness and harsh conditions before they could be removed to the Indian Territory (Foreman, 1934). The Cherokee removal was so ruthlessly accomplished that it shocked even army personnel assigned to supervise the process. There is no official government record of the number of Cherokee who died as a result of the removal, but it is estimated that some 4,000 died en route or shortly after arrival. Once there, the survivors found themselves "destitute of every convenience and comfort" (Foreman, 1934, p. 282) previously enjoyed in former homes from which many had been driven by bayonet:

> These unhappy people were delivered here upon the raw virgin soil, destitute, possessed of little besides the primitive instinct to live and protect the lives of their helpless children. They were compelled to start life anew, many of them fortunate to possess an axe with which to construct wherewith to shelter them against the storm and sun. (Foreman, 1934, p. 282)

For the Cherokee, removal meant that their vast original landholdings, which had included all or part of what would become eight southern states from Virginia to Georgia, were drastically reduced, leaving them with less than one-third of 1 percent of their original land simply in acreage alone, not taking into account the significant qualitative differences between the lands in terms of their ability to maintain and sustain traditional life and culture (Cherokee Nation History Course, 2000; Sultzman, 2002).

In spite of the multilayered decimation of the Cherokee people, it was just two years after their removal, in 1841, that the Cherokee established a school system that taught Cherokee children, including female students, to read and write in English and Cherokee, a system that exceeded the academic standards of the education provided to the surrounding white populations in Oklahoma, Texas and Arkansas (Allen, 1999).

During a brief period between the last removals and the outbreak of the Civil War, Native communities in Oklahoma lived in what historians have called the "Golden Years" (Gibson [1985] as cited in Cherokee Nation History Course, 2000, p. 2). Many tribes re-established tribal councils and reclaimed some autonomy in the relative obscurity of the Indian Territory. Following the Civil War, which found Indians fighting on both sides of the conflict, the federal government abolished all Native educational systems, stating its own education philosophy for American Indians as an effort to educate the Indian in the ways of civilized life in order to preserve him from extinction, not as an Indian, but as a human being…he cannot exist encysted, as it were, in the body of this great nation.…To educate the Indian is to prepare him for the abolishment of tribal relations to take his land in severalty, and in the sweat of his brow and the toil of his hands to carry out, as his white brother has done, a home for himself and family. (Cited in Clarke, 1993, p. 15)

The Boarding School Experiment: Killing the Savage—Saving the Man

In 1871 Native "wards of the state" were offered minimal education on reservations by the Appropriation Act for Indian Education. Indian resistance led to the Compulsory Indian Education Act of 1887, which promoted a system of boarding schools that historians have compared to penal systems. Indian children were taken from families and housed in overcrowded, inadequate facilities, forbidden to use their Native language, and punished for noncompliance with ankle chains and solitary confinement. Refusing to send one's children to boarding school could result in parents' arrest and a reduction or elimination of food rations (Clarke, 1993, p. 5). Henry Pratt, a decorated officer in the Civil War who had supervised POW camps for the Union, was the architect of residential school policies, which he justified with the argument that "It is a great mistake to think that the Indian is born an inevitable savage. He is born a blank, like all the rest of us. Left in the surroundings of savagery, he grows to possess a savage language, superstition, and life. Transfer the savage-born infant to the surroundings of civilization, and he will grow to possess a civilized language and habit" (Capt. Richard H. Pratt, Carlisle School Founder, 1892).

The Bureau of Indian Affairs established twenty-five residential boarding schools to which hundreds of thousands of children were sent or forcibly removed between 1880 and 1960 (Kellogg Foundation, 2002). Designed as quasi-military institutions that employed harsh indoctrination and systematic suppression of Native culture, the schools banned Native spiritual practices and Native languages. Children learned English, Christianity and agricultural and domestic skills, and they were away from their families for months or years at a time. Conditions at many schools included long-term physical and sexual abuse of students, malnutrition, and medical neglect (Adams, 1995; Andrews, 2002; American Indian Heritage Support Center, 2012; Grande, 2004; University of Oklahoma, American Indian Institute, 2012).

The legacy of residential schools continues to be experienced in subsequent generations as unresolved historical trauma and grief (Riche, 2007; Bigfoot, 2007;

Duran and Duran, 2006; Duran, 2005). In addition, because the level of education at most residential boarding schools prepared students only for menial vocations, many Native students today do not have several generations of family who have completed higher education. Often, they are first or second-generation college students—not due to intellectual inferiority or academic indifference but due to the lack of an equitable educational system. Many of the psycho-social ills that persist in American Indian communities today have roots in the boarding school era and the systematic enforcement of child maltreatment (University of Minnesota, 2012).

The dismal failure of educational policies, including residential schools, was the subject of a 1928 report to Congress known as the Merriam Report. This report highlighted the failed operation of boarding schools and day schools and argued for an individualistic, decentralized education focusing on the Indian child's relationship with family and community. The report also recommended access to postsecondary education for Native Americans (Langford & Riley, 1986). As a result of the Merriam Report, reform efforts included the 1934 Indian Reorganization Act (known as the Indian Bill of Rights) and the Johnson-O'Malley Act, which promised Indian self-government, eligibility for positions with the Bureau of Indian Affairs, authorization of student loans and state reimbursement for public school education (Clarke, 1993). Funding was provided for bilingual education, adult basic education, and training of Indian teachers, but unfortunately, the Second World War intervened before significant reforms were implemented, and an opportunity for change was lost (U.S. Senate, 1969, as cited in Lankford & Riley, 1986).

Culturally Responsive and Respectful Teaching

Gay defines culturally responsive teaching as using "cultural knowledge, prior experiences, and performance styles of diverse students to make learning more appropriate and effective for them" (2000, p. 29). This pedagogy embraces the effectiveness of teaching to and through the strengths of Native students and can be reasonably implemented in K-12 education in the U.S. It requires an awareness and acknowledgment of the legitimacy of the cultures of Native students and an effort to connect academic abstractions with socio-cultural realities. According to Smith (1991), culturally responsive pedagogy benefits all students but requires a degree of cultural literacy often absent in mainstream classrooms. Regrettably, the vast majority of American Indian students are taught by non-Native teachers, and no attempt to assist Native students can occur apart from an acknowledgment that mainstream educational policy has failed Native students and damaged tribal efforts to preserve cultural identity.

In their insightful book *Critical Neurophilosophy and Indigenous Wisdom*, Jacobs, Cajete and Lee suggest that awareness of one's own place in the world is critical to meaningful relationships with other people. As defined in their book, Indigenous wisdom "holds that technology, including that which supports the neurosciences, is an important aspect of humanity, but that without a deeper understanding of the sacred, natural world, its consequences will continue to disrupt the balance of life on Earth" (2010, p. 11). This view honors the Native understanding that education is a comprehensive process of life and learning, undertaken within a cultural experience. According to Gay (2000), this perspective can produce high-quality educational experiences that cannot be produced if minority ethnic groups and their contributions to society are ignored or demeaned.

By the late 1960s, with the hard-won prominence of the self-determination movement, tribal leaders were able to promote educational systems that provided education based on cultural traditions. The Dine Community College, established in 1968, became the first of thirty-three tribally controlled higher education institutions to offer accredited programs in a variety of fields ranging from business management to environmental sciences.

Tribally controlled colleges provide access to quality higher education for Native students, combining preservation of tribal history, culture and traditions with academics, vocational training and basic adult education (Brown, 2003; Pavel, 2004). Most are institutions that offer two-year programs, but nine offer bachelor's degrees and two offer master's degrees; in addition, most have transfer agreements in place with other institutions that offer four-year programs (AIHEC, 2007).

In 1994, under the Elementary and Secondary Education Reauthorization Act, tribal colleges were authorized as land-grant institutions by the U.S. Congress, allowing them to apply for public funds as agricultural and technical educational institutions. In part, this act validated the need for education that addresses the unique environment of Native students. Many Native students with high school diplomas or GEDs have not acquired the academic skills to succeed in higher education (American Indian Higher Education Consortium, 2012). The small but steady increase in attendance at tribal colleges attests to their success for Native communities, and although continually underfunded, these institutions have proved effective in providing the basic education skills necessary for degree completion, job placement assistance and advocacy for Native students. By 2010 more than 30,000 Native American students were enrolled in tribal colleges, and nearly half of those completing studies there went on to universities or colleges that offer four-year programs (Kellogg Foundation, 2010).

Todd Fuller, co-founder and former president of the Pawnee Nation College in Pawnee, Oklahoma, poignantly captures the range of historical losses suffered by Native people in *To the Disappearance*:

To the Disappearance

Call me the great
Colonizer, the one
Who conquers with
Abandon and *Bible*
Armed with sword
& ideology. Watch
Me on the feather of
An angel's wing. I
Have seen ancient
Tongues disappear
With a woman's last
Breath. I have seen
Ways of classifying
The world dissolve
With a man's final
Heartbeat. I have
Calculated salvation
One heathen and acre
At a time. Watch me
Divide the land into
Perfect squares, cut
The continent in half
With silver railroad
Lines. With this, I
Have cut the skins of
Buffalo off their hides
And watched the red
Man whither on his
Weak horse. His drum
Nearly quiet, his flute
Nearly broken. I am
The bullet and flame
That destroys silence.
I am the holy massacre
That pierces a child's
Eyes. I am the wool
Blanket that incubates
Infection. I am *all* of
This in the name of pro-
Gress. I am your forced
Removal and forced
Assimilation. I am your

Negotiated treaty with
An "X." I am your
Bottle of spirits known
As manipulation. I am
Your headmaster at all
The boarding schools,
Poised to strike with
The ruler and unfazed
By your rehearsed tears.
I am the recorder of
Black and white photos
And wax cylinders.
I have divvied up the
Land in allotments &
Called it yours. I have
Been certain of your
Farming future. I follow
You on your powwow
Highway and see your
Bald tires. I follow your
Children to school and
Nurture moments of self-
doubt. I am the creator
Of political turmoil &
Kakistocracies* all across
Indian Country. I weave
Perpetual stereotypes
Of the buckskin and tipi.
I listen to your 49 songs—
Recognize the yearning
In your voice. I hear
The *Hey-ya* yearning
In your voice. I know
You sing with your eyes
Closed. You sing in
Languages that have
Started slipping into
Mist. One breath at a
Time, you sing until
Your heart bursts into
Memory.

*Government by the least qualified or most unprincipled citizens

Historical Trauma: A Disease of Time

Historical trauma has been called a "disease of time," with the accumulation of disease and social distress reaching into succeeding generations (Aboriginal Healing Foundation, 2004, p. 6). One of the challenges in understanding this concept is that it entails the ability to conceptualize how events that took place in the distant past affect the present. Brave Heart's and Bigfoot's models propose that historical trauma originates with a dominant group's subjugation of a population by at least four means: (1) overwhelming physical and psychological violence, (2) segregation and/or displacement, (3) economic deprivation, and (4) cultural dispossession (Brave Heart-Jordan, 1995; Brave Heart-Jordan & DeBruyn, 1998; Bigfoot, 2007; Sotero, 2006).

In a consideration of historical trauma for clinical practitioners, Ringell and Brandell propose a similar model in which historical trauma begins with "Initial cultural conflict where a dominant culture/society has a clear technological or military advantage and the establishment and exercise of hegemonic power through policies and institutions" (2008, p. 207). A combination of social and economic inequities, mass traumatic events, and cultural subjugation and persecution disrupt key cultural protective systems, practices and healing processes. As the initial generation transmits this intergenerational legacy to subsequent generations—ecologically, individually, socially and culturally—the resulting cultural loss, social and economic disadvantage and maladaptive responses are propagated in contemporary generations' physical and emotional health disparities (ibid., p. 208). Generations that did not experience the originating trauma are transgenerationally affected by subsequent trauma that becomes embedded as a feature of the new environment of their families and communities. Thus, according to Ringell and Brandell,

> The cumulative intergenerational experiences of trauma and cultural loss act to perpetuate legacies of social systems, policies and institutions that disrupt the natural protective and adaptive features of a culture. Over time, critical cultural protective factors are displaced by the shared experience of the cumulative trauma. In this way, historical trauma becomes a self-perpetuating phenomenon, woven into the tattered tapestry of cultural identify. (p. 207)

Those contemporary links to historical trauma include the mental, physical, spiritual and emotional health disparities of Native people, as well as the contemporary emergence of dysfunctional coping mechanisms that have formed in response, including alcohol and substance abuse (Duran and Duran, 1995; Brave Heart and DeBruyn, 1998; Bigfoot, 2007). Although resiliency and protective factors may mitigate the cumulative effects of historical trauma, certain social and physical ills remain strongly correlated with population-specific health disparities.

Today, the Native American population has the poorest health status of any racial/ethnic population in the United States. According to the U.S. Department of Health and Human Services, Native Americans experience death rates 1.2 times higher than all other races in the U.S. in general and have much higher death rates from certain diseases (8.5 times for tuberculosis, 4.2 times for chronic liver disease and cirrhosis, and 2.9 times for diabetes), from substance abuse (6 times for alcohol and 1.5 times for drugs), and from unintentional injuries (2.5 times). They experience violent crimes in general and rape/sexual assault in particular at more than twice the rate of the general population and are more likely than all other victims to report the offender as being from a different race.

The homicide rate for Native Americans is twice the rate for all other races in the U.S. They experience elevated rates of maltreatment, including physical abuse, sexual abuse and neglect: 14.2 per 1,000 Native children versus 9.1 per 1,000 white children (U.S. Department of Health and Human Services, 2009). For some Native populations in the U.S., life expectancy is lower than that for every country in the western hemisphere, with the exception of Haiti (U.S. Health and Human Services, 2010).

There is considerable research linking a trauma response to psychological and emotional disorders in primary generations of Native Americans. This link is seen in elevated levels of conditions such as post-traumatic stress disorder (PTSD), depression, self-destructive behaviors, severe anxiety, guilt, hostility, and chronic bereavement (Brave Heart & DeBruyn, 1998; Evans-Campbell, 2008; Sotero, 2006; Subia-Bigfoot, 2007; Whitbeck, Adams, Hoyt and Chen, 2004). Given the link between PTSD and illness, it is certainly possible that such disorders may translate into an elevated incidence of physical disease as well. Epigenetics, the study of gene expression, suggests that the epigenome (the cellular material atop our genetic code) activates or silences genes through the mobilization of molecules, called methyl groups, that are triggered by the environment. Research suggests that environmental toxins, pollutants, diet deficiencies, and exposure to stressors may alter the way genes are expressed and, furthermore, that such changes in gene expression may be passed down to our offspring (Brave Heart, 1999; Bigfoot, 2007; Sotero, 2006; Hopkins, 2011).

The Pedagogy of Remembering: Responding to the Soul Wound of Historical Trauma

According to Ringell and Brandell (2010), on an ongoing basis, Native Americans experience contemporary events that have the potential to be traumatic at individual and cultural levels at much higher rates than do other racial groups. Research on the interaction between the response of Native Americans to historical trauma and their contemporary experiences of trauma, mistreatment, injustice and discrimination has resulted in the suggestion that the interplay between direct trauma experiences and transgenerational trauma is best understood against the backdrop of "distal patterns of collective harm" (Whitbeck, Adams, Hoyt and Chen, 2006; Evans-Campbell, 2008). First-hand experiences of discrimination, injustice, poverty, and social inequality may reinforce ancestral knowledge of historical trauma (Brave Heart, 1999; Williams, Neighbors and Jackson, 2003).

Drawing from the literature on intergenerational transmission of trauma among Holocaust survivors' descendants, Native researchers have suggested that contemporary responses must be understood in terms of cumulative trauma in Native cultures, including the impact at the individual, family and community levels. Ancestral pain can result in secondary generations experiencing feelings of unresolved grief, persecution and distrust, in addition to the original losses of culture, tradition, language, sacred ritual and homelands (Brave Heart, 2003; Brave Heart and DeBruyn, 1998; Evans-Campbell, 2008).

As a teacher on the Holocaust and a second-generation survivor, Baum asks students to see themselves "as guardians of memory" even as she contemplates the difficult task of immersing them in historical, and traumatic, narratives:

> Second generation texts reveal the tension between the redemptive claims of memory, that memory can honor the dead, and teach the living, and the experience of an unredeemed memory, which perpetuates the horror of the past. Although it may be clear that the memory of survivors lies as an open wound, there is a common belief that such tainted memory can be cleansed in the next generation, particularly through education. Remember! students are told, as if remembering were only a question of moral choice. Yet narratives of the second generation reveal the limitations of such a view. (2000, p. 94)

The vicarious traumatization of secondary and subsequent generations may occur through collective memory, storytelling and oral tradition as traumatic events become embedded in collective social memories and viewed as compatible within a broader view of historical abuses.

According to Brave Heart's seminal work in this area, resolving the historical grief that has left individuals "impaired, delayed, fixated, and/or disenfranchised" requires four acts of intervention: (1) confronting historical trauma, (2) understanding the trauma, (3) releasing the pain, and (4) transcending the trauma (Yellow Horse Brave Heart, 2003).

Gone discusses a number of educational programs that include

> an unfolding process of self-transformation—characterized by an acknowledgment of past personal pain, dealing with one's problems through disclosure and catharsis, looking

at oneself through consistent introspection, working on oneself toward improved self-understanding, and finding one's purpose as an Aboriginal person—that reorients and motivates vulnerable and wounded selves toward renewed and meaningful engagement in the world. This expansive vision of healing is what sustained…program participation, comprehensively bridging past and present, self and community, psyche and spirit. (2009, p. 758).

Cherokee educators and writers Robert Thomas and Tom Holm explored concepts of Native identity, suggesting that it eventually transcends "notions of statehood, nationalism, gender, ethnicity, and sectarian membership" (in Holm, Pearson and Chavis, 2003, p. 16). This theoretical model, called the Peoplehood Matrix, identifies four interdependent, interpenetrating components of Indian people: language, sacred history, place or territory, and ceremonial cycles. The model was shaped from Spicer's definition of cultural enclaves, or "enduring peoples," which he views as resulting from colonialism and which he states are "most often identified as having distinct languages, religions, and territories that the colonizers sought to destroy or, in the case of territory, claim for themselves" (Spicer, 1980, p. 11).

Peoplehood Matrix

Source: Holm, Pearson and Chavis (2003)

To Spicer's three factors of enduring peoples, Thomas and Holm added sacred history in defining peoplehood, and as shown in overlapping spheres, the four factors are interwoven and dependent on one another. The matrix itself appears to be nearly universally applicable to Native tribes and nations and possibly to all Indigenous groups. The idea that groups of human beings constitute various peoples has always been understood, but this model explains how these four essential characteristics are linked together. No single factor is more important than the others; all support one another and contribute to a particular group's larger sense of identity. The Peoplehood Matrix demonstrates the essence of Native American knowledge as the understanding of how all things are interrelated, and are continuously interacting (Holm, Pearson and Chavis, 2003, p. 14). As a complete system of cultural, social, political, economic and environmental behaviors, the matrix defines codes of conduct and relationships between and among individuals and the environment. According to Holm, describing societies as "uncivilized" and "primitive" has generally been a way to justify theft, cultural destruction and genocide (Holm, personal communication, June 2010). Applying this peoplehood perspective to an understanding of Indian people's historical trauma and unresolved grief can increase awareness of how sacred history and ceremony inform kinship structures and maintain group cohesion. This holistic concept gives an accurate picture of the ways traditional people may connect with the ordinary as well as the supernatural worlds (Holm, Pearson and Chavis, 2003). The authors observe that Western science has finally embraced the "mind, body, soul" connection, but remains reluctant to see any connection between the loss of environment or place and Native experiences of harm. Holm suggests that current thought rejects as "superstition" any effort to bring healing to a place as part of healing a people (Holm, personal communication, June 2010), but the power of place is well defined by Deloria and Wildcat (2001) in their extraordinary review of Indian education in America. The Peoplehood model acknowledges the Native view that one's very existence is inextricably tied to the existence and welfare of other living beings and places on the planet. Traditional and cultural practices in Native communities engage the sacred by their experiences in those places.

While there is no single *correct* way for educators to address the complexities of historical trauma and unresolved grief among Native students and their communities, this chapter offers the following for consideration:

1. Acquire at least a basic understanding of the experience of Indigenous people in the United States. If one is interacting with a specific tribe or tribes, become familiar with specific tribal history and events. With over 560 federally recognized tribes in the United States, there is no generic "Native American." Indian identity exists on a continuum ranging from traditional to highly assimilated. Native beliefs and spirituality exist in modern day life as tribal cultures, traditions and languages, and they are incorporated into the ways that American Indians and tribes govern and manage their affairs.

2. *Go beyond simply acquiring knowledge.* Culture is a complex concept with a variety of features that can be difficult to define. Explore the internal representations of Indigenous culture—such as the values,

beliefs and attitudes—with tribal members, particularly elders, and learn how those internal experiences are expressed and shared externally, namely through artifacts, rituals and social structures. Be respectful of differences and preferences.

3. *Introduce community-level connections and collaborations with Native institutions.* Educators know that students learn best when they are actively engaged in the material. Ongoing relationships and collaborations with Native institutions can provide opportunities throughout the year to engage in applied, hands-on learning about Native culture and traditional communities.

4. *Do not limit student learning about "Indian Country" to a historical context.* There are currently more than 4 million people in the U.S. who identify as American Indian or Alaska Native (National Urban Indian Family Coalition, 2008). Nearly 70 percent live outside of specific tribal areas, and many live in urban areas. Regularly engage students with contemporary Native experiences; use local Indigenous experts and sites. Do not teach Native history as a separate category of U.S. history: American history *is* American Indian history.

5. *Pay attention to behaviors that could indicate experience of traumatic events, including psychological stress.* Knowing the historical, social, economic and cultural contexts in which students live can help educators respond appropriately to behaviors indicating primary or secondary trauma. Make the connection between current behaviors and historical distress.

6. Recognize and acknowledge current experiences of discrimination and social injustice of Native people and the failure of most institutions to acknowledge responsibility in past wrongs. In 2004 a joint resolution before the 108th Congress called for the U.S. government to "acknowledge a long history of official depredations and ill-conceived policies by the United States Government regarding Indian tribes and offer an apology to all Native Peoples on behalf of the United States" (United States, 2004). Thus far, no apology has been offered.

It is a privilege to share in the discourse of educators who seek to preserve and honor Indigenous knowledge in ways that encourage respect for all life, embrace diversity of thought and restore balance for Native people. My own work honors the memory of Minerva Brock England, a Cherokee educator who began teaching in 1907 in the Ozark hills. Her seventh child was my father. As a Native woman born a year after the Dawes Act and educated at the height of misguided attempts to "civilize" Indian people, she carried her own soul wounds in silence. As an educator, she weathered the challenges of teaching in a culture that devalued everything Indian. She was tough, sharp-witted and resolute. Her extraordinary story survives in private letters and surprisingly intimate poetry, as well as in hand-painted images of the people and places she loved for well over ninety-five years. From the wisdom of age, she shared her perspective of our human struggle to discover the truths of life:

> The truth shall make us free from all the frustrations and extra baggage or rubbish that we try to carry. What a joy if all we carried was pure truth! The actual truths of life, boiled down, would be no heavier than a small piece of pure gold. Life's road was made simple. We now walk through the clutter left by civilization. (Brock-England, 1964, p. 22)

Some Native traditions speak of reaching into the future for seven generations. I think often about Minerva's small piece of pure gold—she was right about a lighter load, although she had no way of knowing the privilege it would be to carry on her behalf.

Note

* Kathryn England is an Oklahoma Native and teaches at California State University, Monterey Bay. She was the first visiting scholar at Northeastern State University in Tahlequah, Oklahoma, for the Cherokee Studies Program in 2010. She has served as a curriculum consultant for the Cherokee Nation, is a board member of the Native American Children's Alliance, and is a curriculum consultant for Kinship Center Education Institute in Salinas, California. Kathryn is a doctoral candidate at Fielding Graduate University, Santa Barbara, California, where she is completing a doctorate in educational change and leadership.

THE NORTH

The Color Red

Wisdom

3

The STAR (Service To All Relations) Navajo School Model

By guest author Mark Sorensen*

The Navajo Nation Council is greatly concerned that knowledge of these fundamental laws is fading, especially among the young people; the Council is also concerned that this lack of knowledge may be a primary reason why the Diné are experiencing the many negative forms of behavior and natural events that would not have occurred had we all observed and lived by these laws.

Earth and universe embody thinking, Water and the sacred mountains embody planning, Air and variegated vegetation embody life, Fire, light, and offering sites of variegated sacred stones embody wisdom.

It is the right and freedom of the people that there always be holistic education of the values and principles underlying the purpose of living in balance with all creation, walking in beauty and making a living;

Mother Earth and Father Sky is part of us as the Diné and the Diné is part of Mother Earth and Father Sky; The Diné must treat this sacred bond with love and respect without exerting dominance for we do not own our mother or father.

From "Transcript of the Fundamental Laws of the Diné"
http://www.nativeweb.org/pages/legal/navajo_law.html

As an early Star School board member who helped us to refine and focus our vision, Four Arrows asked me to write this chapter about the STAR School's efforts to indigenize the curriculum for its mostly Navajo students. He felt there would be some useful parallels for readers who intend to do the same for their non-Indian students. Of course, I had the significant advantage of starting the school with a vision to sustain Indigenous values and learning paths. Administrators, teachers, students, parents and community members supported this vision. The learning styles and dispositions of our students also make them more receptive to Indigenous ideas. Still, as a non-Native educator who has indigenized a mainstream state curriculum, I agree that our story can be of help to all who see the value of incorporating Indigenous perspectives into coursework.

I have been the director of the STAR School since it began in 2001 as a one-room, solar-powered school serving 24 Navajo students in grades 1 through 5. It has since grown in many ways and now educates 135 mostly Native American students from preschool through grade 8, with the original building fulfilling the role of Community Resource Center. The STAR School from the very beginning has been a vision-driven school that honors traditional Navajo principles. The most important one is that relationships are important and that we need to broaden our ideas about who and what we are related to. Inspired by the Diné (Navajo) concept called "K'e," we see relations as encompassing all life on this planet, including the rivers, trees, and animals. We also consider our relatedness to the larger universe, seeing the sun and stars as relatives as well.

When my wife, Kate, our friend Thomas Walker Jr., a Navajo tribal member, and I started the STAR School as a public charter school on the edge of the Navajo nation, it was the first off-grid solar- and wind-powered school in the country. (Although sustainability was also a value for the school, this was also a necessity. There were no utility lines within ten miles of the area.) We each had much experience with Navajo education and tribal schools, which had been forced to use Arizona state's curriculum and policies. We felt the need to provide an education that was more empowering for the Navajo children and more culturally relevant. In this chapter, relying also on our other two current board members, Rick St. Germaine (Ojibwe) and Evelyn McCabe (Navajo), I share here a brief overview about the real-world effort to indigenize a school while still having to meet mainstream state and federal requirements in order for the school to survive.

There are five core values that we adhere to at the STAR School, and we try to ensure that they are reflected in all of our decisions. The first of these is embedded in our name: STAR is an acronym for "Service to All Relations." We chose the name to remind us of the importance that the Navajo and other Indigenous peoples place on service to others and on the idea that we are all related to all things in Nature: plants, animals, rocks, rives, mountains, the sun and the wind. As one elder puts it, "I know who I am through my relations, and my relations are my medicine." Navajo elders, as well as elders of many other Indigenous peoples, have frequently taught us that we are interconnected to all of Nature and that we ignore this relationship at our peril.

Since such ideas are not included in any of the standards that Arizona state or the federal government monitors to determine the success of our school, it is up to us to determine what actions are examples of such values, how to operationalize them and whether we are being successful. Every Monday morning, for example, the entire school gathers in our circular amphitheater outside, and one by one each student and staff member shakes the hand of every other person at the school and greets that person either by clan or with another friendly greeting. This practice takes a while, and of course the state might say that this time would be more effectively spent providing students with direct instruction in reading and math. Nonetheless, we believe it is vital to our character as a school, and it sets the tone for the entire week.

As of 2012 our governing board developed a service graduation requirement for all STAR School students specifying that before graduating from grade 8, each student must complete a project either individually or as part of a group of students that (1) is of service to the environment around the school or in the community, (2) addresses a need in the school and/or the surrounding community, and (3) demonstrates at least one core standard of STEM (science, technology, engineering, and math). Implicit in this graduation requirement is the board's expectation that each class at all grade levels will meet state standards. The three parts of this graduation requirement show that we have successfully combined mainstream subjects with our Indigenous goals.

Another way we weave Indigenous ideas into the curriculum is exemplified in our reading program. Using a literature-based program called Voices, which we have further enriched with texts by Native American authors, we focus on six themes: identity awareness, conflict resolution, freedom and democracy, friendship and love, perspective taking, and social awareness. Teachers are encouraged to include in the readings biographical information on inspiring leaders of change like Mohandas Ghandi, Martin Luther King Jr., and Ceasar Chavez so that students can begin to sense how Native peoples can develop a certain kind of sovereignty through service to others. Our hope is that students will see that when they are of service to their community or the larger world, they develop the right and the courage to speak to the powerful about the needs of their community. Our goal is to have all of our students develop a sense of how they can increase their "sovereignty through service" and make their contributions to the community matter.

Although we feel we have been very successful in helping to develop future citizens with this approach, we have not yet found a way to have the majority of our students perform well on the state standardized tests. There are, of course, some students who do well in both areas, and we have had years when the majority of our students met or exceeded the state standards, but generally slightly less than 50 percent of our students meet or exceed the state standards in reading and math. Although in this respect the STAR School has a better record than most of the Indian schools nearby, as a school that is subject to charter renewal, it enjoys no guarantee that the state will decide to renew its charter after 2014. Unfortunately, the state has not shown much interest in the school's Indigenous values and their influence on building character. The No Child Left Behind Act of 2001 sets rigid guidelines for how a school must use its supplemental federal monies if its students' standardized test scores do not meet the state standards required by the act. The consequence of not meeting these standards is either a reduction in the school's federal funds, a reduced amount of freedom for the school to determine its own approach to teaching, or both.

Living with the desire to sustain Indigenous values that we feel are vital for both the students' well-being and the survival of their culture, as well as for their contribution to restoring balance in this "era of crises" we all are experiencing, requires a difficult balancing act. Admittedly, in these times it is difficult to get all of our students to truly understand and live according to our STAR vision and to the Navajo learning paths and values. For example, service to community is still not where we want it to be, and there is enough litter on the playground to show that not everyone understands our environmental priorities. We have seen situations in which our students demonstrate no clear knowledge of how to properly recycle, and students don't always know how to respect the living things on our campus. We have more work to do in order to get all students to really take these principles and their application in daily life to heart. Still, in spite of having to compete with current social problems as well as the negative influence of television and other media, we have been truly inspired over the years by the actions of many students. We know that even in a society that puts forth values different from ours, we can instill healthy attitudes via our program.

The second of our core values is actually a cluster of four values that emerge out of traditional Navajo peacemaking: respect, relationship, responsibility, and reasoning. We refer to these values throughout our school—in the classrooms, on the playground, on the buses and in school assemblies—as the "4 R's." We have developed a rubric that allows everyone in the school to assess their own behavior in light of these 4 R's on a daily basis. We also have incorporated the 4 R's into our grading system. Each quarter the 4 R's are part of the students' progress reports. We have defined each of these 4 R's as concepts, and we have defined them with sample behaviors as well so that students can see how these values work in everyday life. The 4 R's grew out of values as articulated by Navajo elders and were expanded by the co-founders of the school and its board to show students how this applies operationally at the school.

Respect is demonstrated by active listening, by allowing each person the expression of emotion without ridicule or non-acceptance, by honoring the ability of all to make up their own mind about something, and by acting to make sure that personal space and possessions are treated with dignity. Respect allows us to recognize that each person has something to offer; each person has value even if we don't see right away what his or her value is. At its highest level, respect may be thought of as the ability to see and acknowledge the sacredness of each person and each living thing.

Relationship is demonstrated by exercising K'e (a Navajo tradition of acknowledging to one another how we are related by clan and that "my relations are my medicine"), by doing one's best to communicate clearly and empathetically with others, and by helping the group you are working with to progress toward a worthwhile goal. The value of relationship, we believe, is similar to Jesus' teaching to "love your neighbor as yourself." At its highest level of application in one's life, relationship involves recognizing that other persons or beings are not separate from, but are interconnected with, oneself as part of the same whole.

Responsibility is demonstrated by honouring one's word, by continually working to improve one's performance, and by willingly taking on a job or duty that one believes is going to help another. Responsibility is also demonstrated by showing that one is "able to respond" to the needs of others, by going the "extra mile" when someone needs help, and by looking for ways that one can make a situation better and then acting on it without being told. According to Navajo traditional values, we show responsibility by *protecting* those who are weaker or in danger and by *nurturing* those who need to know they are cared for. To be truly responsible, we need to be able and willing to protect and nurture ourselves and others.

Reasoning is demonstrated by thinking things through before one acts and by talking things through in conflict situations instead of resorting to violence. Reasoning is also demonstrated by problem solving in which one works to clarify what the facts are and then looks for the best choices to solve the problem. Reasoning is important in helping us to improve our choices when we are presented with facts or other viewpoints that raise our level of understanding. It is obviously an important value for students in school as well as in life outside of school. Such reasoning as relates to educational hegemony and the corporatizing of the standardized curriculum is also important.

There are many signs to indicate that we are being successful in implementing the core values of the 4 R's into the school's culture. The 4 R's have become integrated into the daily language of the students at the STAR School through the application of the 4 R's rubric and through consistent reminders from the staff about what kinds of student behavior conform to the 4 R's. Virtually every student in the school is able to tell you what the 4 R's are, and all of the students from grade 1 on up can give you an example of what kinds of behaviors can show the 4 R's. One of our staff members wrote "The 4 R's Song," which all staff and students sing together and which contains both descriptions and American Sign Language representations of the 4 R's. Perhaps more important, the proactive teaching and modeling of the 4 R's by the staff set a standard of behavior that makes the whole school feel safer and more respectful. For example, in the 2011–12 school year, there was only one physical fight among the students throughout the whole year, and it was fairly minor. Students report that they feel very safe while they are at school. Another indicator of integration of the 4 R's values into the school culture is that all students in the school learn how to introduce themselves in Navajo by their four clans. Even non-Navajos, including staff members, are expected to learn how to introduce themselves by their parents' and grandparents' cultural roots. Finally, we hear reports from parents that when our students are in their home community and playing basketball or some other sport with students from other schools, they will still remind all the players to "practice their 4 R's" and then briefly explain to the other students the expectations inherent to this practice.

Although the state has never expressed its formal support for teaching the 4 R's values, state monitors and accreditation agencies at least recognize that "school climate" is an important factor in a successful school. Since the daily practice of these values results in a respectful, safe and friendly atmosphere at the school, which in turn results in more time for teachers to teach the intended curriculum to the students rather than dealing with behavior problems, the state has not put in place any obstacles to practicing these values. Nevertheless, these values have their roots in Navajo culture and do not coincide in many ways with more mainstream "character education" programs. In truth, when older students enroll in our school and have not yet learned our values, many of them come in with disrespectful and irresponsible behaviors. We have found that in order for these values to remain part of the fabric of the school, we must do continual training to keep the focus on practicing these values among all the adults as well as the students. Success is a matter of constantly recognizing that we are responsible for creating an atmosphere full of the 4 R's and that we can't expect these values to abide in our school without our continuous efforts.

Our third core value is "expecting excellence in the preparation of our students for life." As a school, one of our main purposes is to prepare our students academically for further success in meeting their learning needs so that they can perform at or above their grade level in all major subjects. We also strive to keep challenging our staff and students so that we can help students to discover what they are passionate about learning and can help them to become truly excited about learning. This is important in a school that truly emphasizes preparing people for lifelong learning. We keep striving to improve our teaching techniques, teaching materials, and classroom management so that we can see steady improvement in students' academic skills and knowledge. We pay attention to data, and we do our best to respond to the data with meaningful ways to enhance student performance within the context or our school values. One of the recent outcomes of looking at our data has been the extension into grades K through 3 of our highly successful preschool math instruction program, which uses Montessori materials. We are convinced that high-quality early childhood education is vitally important to the future academic success of our students.

Our approach to this third value is based upon the belief that schools play a critical role in transmitting knowledge from one generation to the next. In a world as out of balance as ours is, this means we must not forget that academic excellence includes the values of mutual respect, motivation, creativity, teamwork, and sharing.

It is clear from the research and from our own experience that success in school is a combination of developing academic as well as social-emotional skills. As a school that is rooted in Indigenous (Navajo) values, academic excellence must consider the development of the physical, emotional, and spiritual aspects of all children, in addition to their mental development. Although as a school it is not our job to instruct students in any particular set of spiritual teachings, we recognize that students who have this guidance at home or in the community tend to do better in school, so we welcome opportunities for students to express themselves spiritually in whatever way they choose. The physical aspects we must consider include the food students eat at school, the amount and quality of exercise we involve them in, the amount of time students are active and outside, the safety of the environment, and the healthy habits we help students to develop. The emotional aspects we must consider include the ability of students to work cooperatively with one another, the ability of students to resolve conflicts peaceably with one another, and the emotional safety students feel at school (free from excessive teasing and taunting). All of these spiritual, social-emotional and physical factors contribute to students' readiness to learn. To create a school-wide atmosphere that supports this readiness, all staff members at the school must seek to create this same atmosphere in how they treat one another. One of the attributes of the STAR School that may make it unusual among schools is that we firmly believe that we adults must treat one another in a way that reflects not only how we would like to be treated but also how we expect the children to treat one another. In the words of Mohandas Ghandi, "we must BE the change we wish to see in the world."

How are we doing on excellence in preparation of our students for life? Several of our former students have told us that the study skills and methods they learned at our school they still use in high school to great advantage. They have also told us the same thing when they have decided to major in an environmental area. We have had one former student major in environmental engineering and another major in environmental communications, and both said their interest in these goals was sparked when they attended the STAR School. We also have tracked our former students to determine what percentage have graduated from high school within four years. The state and national graduation average for Native American students is around 50 percent. Our rate is over 80 percent even though our graduates attend several different high schools in the area. Two of our graduates (out of a total of sixty-eight over the past seven years) have received Gates Millenium Scholarships to complete their doctorates, and one of our graduates has earned the Arizona Board of Regents Scholarship for undergraduate work. Several others have received other scholarships and awards, including fellowships to the 2012 Student Climate Conservation Convention outside of Washington, DC.

On the other hand, according to Arizona state's rating system, our school received a letter grade of D for 2012 based on the average performance of our students on the state-approved standardized tests. Not surprisingly, most of the public schools of the Navajo nation have also received a D or C, and the schools funded by the Bureau of Indian Education are not even given a letter grade. We are told that if we want to bring up our test scores, we should eliminate our Monday morning gatherings of the entire school, our interschool sports competitions, and the time we spend on Navajo language and service projects around the campus and in the community. This we are not willing to do because we see these activities as essential to the development of our school culture and the social-emotional learning we want the students to achieve to help them in life. The risk that we take by not focusing more on our students' performance on these standardized tests is that when our charter comes up for renewal in 2014, the State Charter Board may point to our average test scores and threaten not to renew the charter unless we accept some other educational program or priorities. Our only choice at that point would be to seek private support to keep our school going. We are working hard on finding ways to increase our effectiveness in teaching the students how to do well on the standardized tests without compromising our values, and we have had great success in a couple of classes. Nevertheless, since mainstream society has accepted that the results on standardized tests are the measure by which we must assess the success of our schools, the challenge remains that many schools—especially those serving Indigenous populations whose members traditionally have never done particularly well as a whole on these kinds of tests—will abandon richer, more thought-provoking curricula in favor of curricula that are focused specifically on what these standardized tests measure and the idea that there is only one right answer to each question. We all know that in life there are often situations in which there is more than one possible solution to a given situation. For example, when traveling from one location to another, one must choose which route to take based on a variety of considerations, and it can rarely be said that there is only one correct way to go; it all depends on which variables we decide to include in our appraisal of possible routes. Especially for Indigenous youth who come from very rural upbringings, it is more important to learn how to problem solve in the complex situations in which they may find themselves than to learn how to pick the correct answer when presented with four possible answers in a multiple-choice test.

Our fourth core value is "honoring our place and place-based education." The STAR School is a small rural charter school on the edge of the Navajo nation that serves a population of almost entirely Navajo families. Since the late 1800s, this area has been the scene of much interaction and some conflict among Navajos, Anglos, and Hopis. It is on the interface between cultures. The area where the school is built is surrounded by volcanic cones, some as high as 1,300 feet, and is on the edge of a juniper forest as it turns into rich desert about twenty miles northeast of Flagstaff and the San Francisco Peaks, which are known as Dook'o'oosliid in Navajo, the sacred mountain of the west. The whole area is part of the Colorado Plateau, which extends across the Navajo nation not only to the north and east but also to the west, which includes the Grand Canyon. It is an area of incredible cultural, botanical, and geographic diversity and awesome beauty. This is our place. The STAR School's location in this place is purposeful, so it is part of our core values to honor this place, its people, the plants and animals who live here and have lived here, as well as the cultures that have grown out of this land.

Even though our area is quite arid and does not have land that would normally be considered good or even fair farmland, Indigenous people have lived in this area for many centuries and have successfully supported their families and communities without needing to have food shipped in from anywhere else. Thus one of the goals at STAR is to weave into our curriculum lessons in the uses of the area's native plants and local knowledge about how to successfully farm and garden as well as about how people from the area provided nutritious food for their families for so many generations. As modern technologies develop that can help the communities to be more self-sustaining, however, it is entirely appropriate to apply the more modern techniques and technologies. For example, before starting the school, the co-founders lived for twenty years on a ranch near the school, where they used only solar and wind power and gathered water off the roof. This knowledge and experience has been utilized and expanded at the STAR School in the form of robust solar arrays and wind turbines. The three most recent wind turbines installed at the school, in fact, were first designed by and developed by an inventor when he lived only a few miles from where the school now stands. Thus the school has the expectation not only that the STAR teachers and students will utilize knowledge developed locally but also that students will help to advance this knowledge and share it with the community.

One particularly dramatic example of how we have honored our place was demonstrated a few years ago when we involved the whole school in researching an event that had happened over 100 years ago in the same area where the school now stands. In 1901 there was an encounter between a group of Anglo ranch hands and a group of Navajo hunters that resulted in gunshots being fired and people being killed on both sides. The two groups returned to their separate communities to prepare for what seemed like an inevitable range war. However, there was an Anglo missionary living in the area who had learned Navajo and who had become the trusted friend of a Navajo headman. The Navajo headman reached out to this missionary to see what could be done to restore harmony. The two men trusted each other. A trial was set, and given the hostilities between the two groups of people, the Navajo families were afraid that their hunters would be found guilty and hanged. But the missionary was able to bring in skilled attorneys, and the all-white jury found the Navajo hunters innocent based on their claim of self-defense. After the ruling, there was great celebration in the Navajo community. These facts were researched by students by interviewing elders in the community, some of whom were even the students' own grandparents. Then students prepared and wrote a play, and using clay masks to depict the characters, they put on the play for the community. One student was so moved by the play that he began to write poetry to describe his perspective and feelings. It is our premise that researching and documenting our place using filmmaking as a medium is also a way to honor our place. These student-made films can be seen on the school's website: www.starschool.org.

Two of our student-made films that depict aspects of our place (*Nitsidigooii* and *STAR Energy*) won First Place and Best in Show respectively in two consecutive years of the Arizona Student Film Festival.

The fifth core value of the STAR School is to "be in harmony with our environment." In 2012 the STAR School was awarded the U.S. Department of Education's Green Ribbon Schools Award for being an outstanding example of the three pillars of being "green": (1) a healthy and safe environment at the school; (2) reducing costs, reducing water and energy requirements and reducing waste through various environmentally friendly design elements and programs at the school; and (3) integrating environmentally aware approaches and information into the school curriculum. These three pillars represent well the values of the school in terms of operationalizing what it means to be an Indigenous school that is "green" in a remote rural area. The following indicates what the school is doing that meets these criteria:

1. To ensure a safe and healthy school environment, the STAR School is committed to utilizing recyclable products whenever possible, utilizing environmentally friendly materials for cleaning whenever possible, and checking for good air quality and low noise levels in all of our buildings. As part of a safe and healthy environment, the school provides ample structured exercise and involvement of students in outside activities during free time. Also deeply connected to our honoring of place, the STAR School provides fresh vegetables to the school breakfast and lunch program, which come as much as possible from local Navajo farms and gardens. The First Nations Development Corporation just funded a program for STAR in which a local Navajo farmer is growing ten acres of vegetables for use in the community and in the STAR School's breakfast and lunch program. To ensure that students actually want to eat these vegetables, the school also has a Home Economics Program that involves students in the preparation of food so that they will try eating various preparations of locally grown vegetables and traditionally raised sheep.

2. The water and energy requirements of the STAR School had to be severely reduced in the early days of the school's existence because the school was built ten miles from the nearest utility lines. These utility lines are no closer to the school now, so the school has to be supported by its own off-grid solar and wind system, and for many years water has been hauled in and stored in tanks. In order to make the school function with these limitations, everyone has had to pay close atten-

tion to how these precious resources are being used. Initially, the consequence of not being very cautious about our power and water use was that we would run out of power or water on a given day and would have to send the students home. The school eventually drilled its own well and developed an adequate solar power supply, but it is clear that in order to be more self-sufficient, we must be aware of and practice ways we can reduce our need for more power and water resources than we have. The school uses water runoff to irrigate planting areas. With every building built on the campus, we plan for ways that the building can be designed to minimize power usage. Our school makes extensive use of natural lighting through skylights and south-facing windows. Nearly two-thirds of the square footage on the campus is heated by radiant water coils in the floors. Not only is this kind of heating system more efficient when heated by fossil fuel, but it is also adaptable to being fully supplemented by solar heating panels.

3. At the STAR School, it is expected that each class will develop year-long projects that show students how they can help the environment and that give them opportunities to actively do things that are helpful to the school and the community environment. It is expected that in each grade the lessons associated with these projects will be integrated into the academic learning and into the efforts to meet core standards. Every department in the school is also expected to demonstrate in its own way how it is caring for the environment. For example, buses will not sit with their motors idling when waiting for children to come out of classes to board the buses at the end of the school day. Also, the kitchen staff works actively with students to promote the composting of vegetable waste from breakfasts and lunches.

Admittedly, mainstream standards and state policies have done little to help us live in harmony with the environment. This is why indigenizing the mainstream curriculum independently in the classroom is so important for all of us. State officials have even looked with suspicion and mistrust at our dedication to being off the grid and to remaining one of the first off-grid solar- and wind-powered schools in the U.S. They have been unwilling for the most part to allow us any deviations from a set of plans designed for a school building with an unlimited power supply from the grid. Although local building officials may have good intentions respecting the safety of students, their unwillingness to open up the regulations to accommodate innovation has been frustrating.

Such frustrations are to be expected in any effort to indigenize mainstream education. I encourage the reader to take heart, however, by the many successes I have tried to share. You are embarking upon a great and important adventure, and if you do not do it, no one else will. The project envisioned by this book is a big one. It is clearly a challenge, and it is not for the faint of heart or for those who are easily discouraged. However, our future generations depend on your courage as you endeavour to integrate Indigenous perspectives and values into the mainstream curriculum. Keep noticing each step you are taking forward, and celebrate the little victories as you work toward your goal. We need to recognize those times when we are not truly challenging the hegemony of the state, but doing so is not enough to succeed. We cannot lead by simply being against the way things have always been. Rather, we must have a vision of what we want to see, and we must pursue it with enthusiasm. If we get too caught up in criticizing the system or our own efforts, we will not have enough energy to realize our visions. Encourage one another! Love one another! Cherish what you are creating! *Hozho Nahasdlii! May you walk in beauty!*

Note

* Dr. Sorensen has been an administrator of schools (as principal or superintendent) that serve students living on the Navajo Reservation for the past thirty-six years. He is the founding executive director of the Native American Grant Schools Association, which comprises thirty community-controlled schools, both tribal and charter, that serve Native American communities throughout the Southwest. In 1993 Dr. Sorensen was selected as Principal of the Year by the Bureau of Indian Education. He was awarded a fellowship from the Open Society Institute to develop a guide to implement traditional Navajo peacemaking in Navajo schools, a project undertaken in collaboration with board member Thomas Walker Jr. He was the co-founder with Rick St. Germaine of Four Winds Academy, a graduate-level leadership training program for principals that serves Native American grant and Native Hawaiian charter schools throughout the nation. He is currently the co-founder and director of the STAR School, the first off-grid, totally solar-powered charter school in the U.S.

4

Indigenous Teaching
and Learning Pathways

The accumulated knowledge of the remaining indigenous groups around the world represents a body of ancient thoughts, experiences and actions that must be honored and preserved as a vital storehouse of environmental wisdom. Modern societies must recapture the ecologically sustainable orientation that has long been absent from its psychological, social and spiritual consciousness.

—Greg Cajete 1994, p. 78

It is the theory that decides what can be observed.

—Albert Einstein

Words only point to truth, genuine knowledge must be experienced directly.

—Francesca Fremantle

Subjectivity is your starting point to reality.

—Leroy Little Bear

Indigenous Learning Theory

The above quotations are intended to set the tone for understanding that Indigenous teaching and learning paths are ultimately about cultivating cognition and consciousness via spiritual awareness and reflection on lived experience. They direct us toward realizing that human awareness is a part of life's web. They connect us to smaller and larger elements in the universe. They allow us to see the "whole" as a sacred mystery that we cannot fully know but that we can nonetheless change with our thinking and actions. They are about relationships, with the ultimate one being our relationship with our planet. This chapter offers some generalized guidelines for the kind of teaching and learning typical of Indigenous traditions. In Part Three, more specific guidelines relating to particular subject areas represent are offered but still generally reflect the perspectives offered here.

How can such a theory of learning be adopted and adapted by mainstream education? One way is to not look at the curriculum as something to cover but rather as a catalyst for discovery. A more self-directed approach to education is thus preferred when possible to teacher-directed learning. Whatever combination of the two approaches a teacher wishes to employ, the goal is to express "community-based power in the interest of a responsible political, economic and spiritual society" (Grande 2008, p. 256). An indigenized approach weaves the empirical and the symbolic, nature and culture, self and community, power and love into a unified and unique vision of the world. It sees rituals, ceremonies, rights of passage, places and family histories and connections as integral and vital to the learning experience.

Aluli-Meyer has attempted to organize these ideas so as to help non-Indian educators integrate Indigenous knowledge "into a context of world awakening" (2008, p. 233). Her simple overview provides non-Indian teachers with a new "theoretical" construct for heeding Einstein's words above:

1. Finding knowledge that endures is a spiritual act that animates and educates.
2. We ARE earth, and our awareness of how to exist with it extends from this idea.
3. Our senses are culturally shaped, offering us distinct pathways to reality.
4. Knowing something is bound to how we develop a relationship with it.
5. Function is vital with regard to knowing something.
6. Intention shapes our language and creates our reality.
7. Knowing is embodied and in union with cognition.

Cognition and consciousness exist in an inseparable body-mind-spirit-nature unity that normal mainstream education breaks apart. The body offers us a microcosm for understanding community, earth and the cosmos. The mind, starting with subjective interpretations of reality, helps move us into higher levels of thinking about and understanding reality. Spirit gives significance to all and allows the mind to let go so as to open the psyche to direct and intuitive experience. Nature offers continual opportunities for learning and sustenance. Together, this interconnectedness moves us away from the binary thinking and oppositional dualities common in mainstream thinking. In terms of "instruction," all of this means that learning is a natural phenomenon and that extrinsic "unnatural" influences are barriers to it.[1]

In *Solar Light, Lunar Light* (2012), Howard Teich implements a similar approach to non-binary thinking by using expressions of solar and lunar awareness to help people achieve what he refers to as a "flowing balance" between solar and lunar energies. This idea of balance plays a huge role in Indigenous knowledge paths. This is why male and female roles in traditional cultures are egalitarian. Teich does not see male energy as solar and female energy as lunar but rather views males and females as having both solar and lunar potentials. Respect for sexual orientation and multiple gender interpretations is also common in Indigenous thinking, as reflected in Teich's model, for such orientations merely indicate a variety of balances between solar and lunar dynamics, whether spiritual or biological. Teich uses Navajo stories and ancient pictographs about solar-lunar understanding in his work as well. In his interactive "quick-fix" exercises on his website, solarlunar.com, he charts the symbolic dispositions that relate to solar and lunar balancing. Below is a table from this site that helps identify behaviors and dispositions related to solar and lunar energies. Those with challenges in the solar columns can rebalance by working on these characteristics in the lunar column. Since most student learning problems relate in one way or another to imbalances in these characteristics, students can use this website as a tool for addressing the problems of binary thinking in ways not all that dissimilar from how traditional Indigenous medicine wheels are used.

In *Reclaiming Youth at Risk: Our Hope for the Future* (1990), Brendtro, Brokenleg and Van Bockern offer another chart that complements Teich's solar-lunar one. These authors emphasize the power of caring in Native cultures and introduce the "circle of courage," which can also serve as a guide for wellness psychology and classroom discipline for youth:

> Native American philosophies of child management represent what is perhaps the most effective system of positive discipline ever developed. These approaches emerged from cultures where the central purpose of life was the education and empowerment of children. Modern child development research is only now reaching the point where this holistic approach can be understood, validated and replicated. (p. 35)

Being out of Balance		Achieving Balance	
If solar without lunar	*If lunar without solar*	*Solar*	*Lunar*
Over-concerned with self-image/pride	Self-effacing, self-doubting	Confident (courage to enact ideas)	Willingness to admit limitations and mistakes
Dominating, disconnected or isolated	Appeasing others, weak	Assertive	Cooperative
Aggressive	Lenient, lax	Responsible	Empathetic
Compulsive	Lacking focus	Precise	Connecting the dots
Perfectionist	Lack of will	Desire to achieve	Willingness to fail
Closed to different perspectives	Living in a fantasy world	Goal oriented	Visionary
Authoritarian	Follow the herd	Powerful	Compassionate
Rigid	Aimless	Structured	Flexible
Arrogant	Helpmate	Self-conviction	Receptivity

H. Teich, "Chart of Flowing Balance," http://solarlunar.com/articles/quick-fix/chart-of-flowing-balance.

The Circle of Courage Chart represents Indigenous educational goals that reflect balance between the spirit of belonging, the spirit of mastery, the spirit of independence and the spirit of generosity. Belonging is perceived as relatedness to family, to community and to all of the natural world. Mastery is about developing cognitive, physical, social and spiritual competence, beginning with self-control, which aims especially at survival for self and community. Independence is a sense of individual uniqueness balanced with humility and a sense of being part of the whole; it is nurtured by encouraging children to be intrinsically motivated. Generosity is considered to be the highest expression of courage; it is fundamental to Indigenous cultures and reflects a natural democracy focused on the welfare of all. The chart below shows various ways that these four concepts can be in or out of alignment. Employing this chart also mimics traditional medicine wheel use (pp. 44–46).

Belonging	Distorted	Absent	Mastery	Distorted	Absent	Independence	Distorted	Absent	Generosity	Distorted	Absent
Attached	Gangs	Unattached	Achiever	Overachieve	Failing	Autonomous	Dictatorial	Submissive	Altruistic	Overinvolved	Selfish
Loving	Craving	Guarded	Success	Arrogant	Avoids risk	Confident	Reckless	Unconfident	Caring	Plays martyr	Affectionless
Friendly	Promiscuous	Rejected	Creative	Risk seeker	Fearful	Assertive	Bullying	Inferiority	Sharing	Codependency	Narcissistic
Intimate	Clinging	Lonely	Motivated	Cheater	Unmotivated	Responsible	Manipulative	Irresponsible	Loyal	Servitude	Disloyal
Gregarious	Cults	Aloof	Persistent	Workaholic	Gives up	Inner control	Rebellious	Helpless	Empathetic	Bondage	Hardened
	Dependent	Isolated	Competent	Delinquent	Inadequate	Leadership		Easily led	Pro-social		Anti-social
		Distrustful							Supportive		Exploitive

Bringing such thinking and philosophy into the classroom calls for preparedness and open-mindedness. In their monograph for the Ontario Association of Dean's Education, entitled "Incorporating Indigenous Philosophies and Practices" (2011), Beckford and Nahdee encourage teachers and students to:

- Recognize traditional and indigenous ways of knowing as valid and useful.
- Understand the benefits of including Aboriginal and other indigenous ecological perspectives in lessons.
- Understand the potential of these perspectives to precipitate interrogation of current mainstream human and environmental interactions, broaden and deepen students' sources of information and engender social transformation.
- Avoid Sentimentalism and Romanticism. Aboriginal ecological knowledge should not be romanticized. Aboriginal societies do not possess a single view or type of relationship with nature. Also, there are often gaps between philosophy and practice. Note that today many Aboriginal cultures are quite mainstreamized and have become estranged from the traditional knowledge and practices once associated with their relationship with the land. Thus, despite the many great lessons to be learned, a realistic and balanced approach is prudent.
- Use factual accounts of the lived experiences of Aboriginal peoples to teach concepts like climate change. Stories of indigenous groups in the Canadian and American Arctic provide a rich source of cultural evidence of climate change, as manifested in impacts on economic livelihoods. Examples include negative impacts of changing ice conditions on hunting, trapping, fishing and ecosystems; wildlife exhibiting atypical consumption behaviors, which are linked to a diminishing supply of their traditional food sources; alterations in the migration pattern of birds and other animals, which adversely affect food security for local peoples; changes in animals' behavior, fur condition, and meat color and flavor, as a result of their feeding in polluted areas.
- Use Aboriginal ecological philosophy to teach positive environmental values and attitudes, stewardship, and sustainable consumption and lifestyles. For example, the principle of only harvesting the resources you need and minimizing waste could be used to introduce critical lessons to students in mainstream schools; it could be tied into lessons on cultural differences, consumption patterns, poverty, global hunger

and resource conservation. This could be introduced across the curriculum through stories, mathematical games, case studies, poster competitions and poem writing.

- Invite Aboriginal persons—including elders or senators (the custodians of traditional indigenous knowledge), local community members, parents, and business and community leaders—into classrooms as resource persons and guest teachers. Plan and prepare for field trips to ensure cultural sensitivity and respect. Teachers and their students should work with Aboriginal community members to understand traditions and cultural values, including the roles of gift giving and knowledge sharing. Aboriginal community members can help you to make contact and act as guides and facilitators.

- Use examples of Aboriginal groups and indigenous peoples who have lived harmoniously with the natural world for thousands of years. To be authentic, it is important that Aboriginal perspectives be seamlessly integrated into classroom practice. Activities like those listed below should, therefore, become part of the teacher's repertoire.

- Employ traditional Aboriginal activities like talking circles and explore their origins and importance to Aboriginal peoples. Introduce medicine wheels as graphic organizers. Add Aboriginal traditions, cultures and perspectives to the curriculum and co-curricula program.

- Be aware of Aboriginal students in class and draw on their knowledge and expertise of their culture.

- Build a bank of Aboriginal books, resources and classroom activities for students to use.

These directives relate to "Indigenous learning styles," but I have long contended that such styles are not cultural per se but are natural for all children. Although it is true that Indigenous students raised in families that still honor these ways come into a classroom with a unique perspective on how they best learn, I submit that the approach to teaching and learning practiced by Indigenous cultures for thousands of years is natural and thus best for most children. With this in mind, I offer further guidelines below for ways classroom teachers can modify mainstream education for all students to bring forth more natural learning in the classroom.

1. Allow for ample observation and imitation rather than verbal instruction. Also allow students to take their time before attempting a task so that the chances for success are higher even on the first effort.

2. Make the group more important than the individual as often as possible in terms of both the learning process and learning goals.
3. Emphasize cooperation versus competition whenever possible.
4. Make learning holistic rather than sequential and analytic. Spend more time in dialogue talking about the big picture associations before looking at details.
5. Use imagery as often as possible. Einstein wrote that "imagination is more powerful than knowledge," and Indigenous education takes advantage of this fact.
6. Make learning connect to meaningful contexts and real life.
7. Be willing to allow spontaneous learning opportunities to change pre-planned lessons.
8. De-emphasize letter grading and standardized evaluations and use authentic narrative assessments that emphasize what is actually working best and what needs more work.

By following all of the above guidelines as often as possible, not only will teachers create a new, nature-based ethic in the minds of children, but they will also find that the discipline problems common in most schools at all grade levels will quickly start to diminish. Classroom management problems are listed by teachers as being the most frustrating and time-consuming issues in the classroom. I believe discipline issues are really curriculum issues. Using the charts above and the guidelines in this chapter can help develop the kinds of dispositions and behaviors that prevent disrespectfulness. When problems do arise, however, specific Indigenous approaches to conflict resolution work like magic as well. Here are some basic precepts that teachers can consider to help mitigate disciplinary problems:

1. Make bringing everyone back into community the main objective.
2. Widen the circle of blame and involvement to include all possible individuals who may have some influence on the problem or the solution.
3. Use ample and appropriate humor throughout the process.
4. Appeal to a universal sense of love and power that connects all participants.
5. Discuss cognitive dissonance in ways that show it is human to react to it.
6. Avoid punishments and instead seek honorable reciprocity.
7. Refer when possible to the non-human kingdoms for metaphors.

These concepts, since they emphasize regaining balance, work remarkably well for children who have not experienced them. I used them when I directed a large facility for troubled youth, and my faculty could not believe the difference. In one year, we reduced physical take-downs in which a staff had to bring a child to the floor to prevent injury to someone from 122 per quarter to only 11! (Admittedly, there were other measures I implemented besides these conflict resolution techniques. We took out the Coca-Cola machines, took children off Ritalin, engaged them in exercise, used Larry Brentro's Circle of Courage and assigned animals to each student for care.) Note that all of these things ultimately are about respecting relationships with oneself and others. Prior to conquest by Europeans, traditional Indigenous education in the Americas emphasized oral histories, teaching stories, ceremonies, apprenticeships, learning games, formal instruction and informal tutoring. Dreams and visions as well as teachings from non-human entities such as animals or clouds were also valued as sources of knowledge. The goal of all these forms of education is to maintain and sustain relationships among the human, natural and spiritual worlds.

As in the Solar-Lunar and Circle of Courage charts above, balance in these relationships as well as within oneself is paramount. Furthermore, in all these approaches to learning, there is a cautious awareness of the power of the unconscious mind and its susceptibility to being influenced by fear, words, and external authoritarianism. More on this is presented in the chapter on psychology, but for now it is enough to say that instructional methodologies embracing Indigenous wisdom must work toward employing courage and fearlessness as catalysts for practicing a virtue; toward making a student's authentic reflection on experience the primary locus of authority; on seeing words as sacred vibrations that require truthfulness; and on recognizing that Nature is in us and around us as the ultimate teacher (Jacobs 1998).

Another set of guidelines to help non-Indian educators indigenize coursework comes from Eber Hampton. He interviewed a number of American Indian students at Harvard University to come up with a definition of "Indian education." He wanted to create a theory of Indian education that could not only serve contemporary schooling for Natives but also overcome the limitations of mainstream schooling. Hampton felt that non-Indian educators must realize that mainstream education is hostile in its structure, curriculum, context and personnel. While at Harvard he wrote that contemporary American schools are politically motivated, transmitting values and behaviors to prevent authentic diversity for the sake of Anglo values, especially those of the ruling powers. He referred to the call for higher standards in education as being only a call for the standards of the Anglo, not a call "for more adequate presentation of the knowledge of devalued minorities, creative thinking about pressing social problems, higher standards of equity and respect, or recognition of institutional racism" (1995, p. 301). Upon completion of his research project at Harvard, he came up with the following precepts for Indian education:

1. Spiritual concerns are an important part of Indian education.
2. There are distinctive Indian styles of thought and communication.
3. Education has the dual purpose of promoting Indian cultures as well as providing skills and information relevant to non-Indian society.
4. Indian education cannot be understood apart from historical analysis.
5. Indigenizing the curricula takes place in a cultural atmosphere that is permeated with both strong group bonds and great individual freedom.
6. Indian education is service oriented.

He distilled the following concepts from his many interviews with Native students (ibid.):

1. Identity
2. Spirituality
3. Service
4. Culture
5. Vitality
6. Affiliation
7. Freedom
8. Tradition
9. Respect[2]
10. Diversity
11. Education, history and relentlessness
12. Place

While serving as president of Saskatchewan Indian Federated College, Hampton created "12 Standards of Education for Aboriginal Students" from the results of this research. Although they were intended only for Indian students, all of them have relevance for indigenizing the mainstream curriculum.

1. *spirituality*—At the center of spirituality is respect for the spiritual relationships that exist between all things.
2. *service to the community*—The individual does not form an identity in opposition to the group but recognizes the group as relatives

(included in his or her own identity). The second standard is service. Education is to serve the people. Its purpose is not individual advancement or status.

3. *respect for diversity*—The respect for diversity embodied in the third standard requires self-knowledge and self-respect without which respect for others is impossible.

4. *culture*—Indian cultures have ways of thought, learning, teaching, and communicating that are different than but of equal validity to those of White cultures. These thought-ways stand at the beginning of Indian time and are the foundations of our children's lives. Their full flower is in what it means to be one of the people.

5. *contemporary tradition*—Indian education maintains a continuity with tradition. Our traditions define and preserve us. It is important to understand that this continuity with tradition is neither a rejection of the artifacts of other cultures nor an attempt to "turn back the clock." It is the continuity of a living culture that is important to Indian education, not the preservation of a frozen museum specimen.

6. *personal respect*—The individual Indian's sense of personal power and autonomy is a strength that lies behind the apparent weakness of disunity. Indian education demands relationships of personal respect.

7. *sense of history*—Indian education has a sense of history and does not avoid the hard facts of the conquest of America.

8. *relentlessness in championing students*—Indian education is relentless in its battle for Indian children. We take pride in our warriors and our teachers are warriors for the life of our children.

9. *vitality*—Indian education recognizes and nourishes the powerful pattern of life that lies hidden within personal and tribal suffering and oppression. Suffering begets strength. We have not vanished.

10. *conflict between cultures*—Indian education recognizes the conflict, tensions, and struggle between itself and White education.

11. *sense of place*—Indian education recognizes the importance of an Indian sense of place, land, and territory.

12. *transformation*—The graduates of our schools must not only be able to survive in a White-dominated society, they must contribute to the change of that society. Indian education recognizes the need for transformation in the relation between Indian and White as well as in the individual and society. (http://www.usask.ca/education/ccstu/guiding_documents/12_standards_of_ed.html)

All of the lists and conceptual frameworks presented above comprise a theory of Indigenous education that makes more practical sense when specifically applied to the various core subjects, as seen in Part Two of the book. As I mentioned in the Introduction, however, it is important to remember that the fragmentation of various subjects is itself a violation of Indigenous educational theory. Authentic Indian education would not separate mathematics, economics, history, or health education from other subjects such as language arts, music, ecology, or science. Nonetheless, remembering the basic values in this chapter and doing your best to incorporate other subjects into the one you are teaching in an interdisciplinary way will adequately facilitate the partnership.

Non-Indian Teacher "Requirements" for Indigenizing Mainstream Education

Aboriginal nations rightfully have concerns about non-Indian intellectuals writing about or non-Indian teachers teaching Indigenous perspectives, knowledge and values. What knowledge is to be presented? Will it just be more personal, invented or white-washed anthropology? Will it appropriate Indigenous rights, as continues to happen worldwide? Remembering that Indigenous knowledge is always spiritual knowledge, what right does a non-Indian have to teach the spiritual traditions of Indigenous Peoples when he or she does not speak the language and has no true stake in Indian politics and suffering? These are important questions. Even well-intentioned teachers might wind up marginalizing and silencing the very people whose appropriated ideas they attempt to share.

There are no easy answers to these concerns. Indian Country itself is divided on who can share what with non-Indians. In an era when anti-Indianism and structural inequalities are becoming more and more oppressive, this chapter's ideas may indeed be potentially dangerous to the sanctity of Indigenous knowledge. Respected Indigenous scholars such as Elizabeth Cook-Lynn and Marie Battiste are concerned that Indigenous knowledge will be "contaminated by colonialism and racism" (Battiste 2008, p. 422). They insist on the Native voice and on ethical protection and rights relating to who can offer tribal knowledge.[3] Most of us, including myself, would prefer that all mainstream teachers had a traditionally raised Native person as a co-teacher in the classroom. Such a goal is worth discussion, but we cannot afford to wait for such a policy to happen before we share knowledge that might turn us back from the brink. Most public and private school teachers, including those who teach Native studies, are non-Indian. The majority of teachers in schools on reservations and reserves are non-Indian. Our world is in too precarious a condition to wait until this situation changes before starting the process of indigenizing education. It must begin now.

For those of my Indigenous brothers and sisters who worry about sharing Indigenous spirituality with others, I remind them of the Lakota prayer "Mitakuye Oyasin," which asserts that "we are all related" and in the same sinking boat. The goal here is not to equip corporations or entrepreneurs to utilize Indigenous knowledge but to encourage school teachers to follow the guidelines contained in this text as best they can. It is time for courage and ultimately fearlessness to take hold in all of us for the sake of all future generations. I ask you to join me in helping teachers to use this book's ideas in the most respectful and accurate way possible. Encourage them to teach their students how to regain balance in our world by adhering to Indigenous knowledge paths. There is no time to waste in implementing precepts that I believe are our only means to turn things around.

That said, the following lists offer powerful reminders of how you can begin to indigenize your coursework right away!

1. Be willing to be attacked for teaching about Aboriginal Peoples and cultures no matter how well you do it.
2. Use good, triangulated scholarship and critical thinking to counter anti-Indian academics and white-washed textbooks.
3. Work to counter, correct or inform "New Age" appropriation of Indigenous ceremonies, especially in those instances where money is charged for such experiences as Sun Dances, purification ceremonies, vision quests, and the like.
4. Understand and accept that you teach in a school that is a product of colonialism, realizing that what and how you teach is essentially a political position no matter what.
5. Realize that you can never really know everything important about Indigenous wisdom.
6. Appreciate that a sense of the sacred is inseparable from Indigenous knowledge paths and that this is likely compromised when teaching "outside the circle," especially if you have no social or emotional commitment to the knowledge and values. So work on developing this commitment.
7. Remember that Native spirituality infuses all knowledge and is not a religion per se.

In addition to this list, Ronald Grimes (1995) offers one that comes from a discussion he initiated in several forums involving a number of Indigenous and non-Indian students and faculty at Harvard University about who should be able to teach Native American "religions." This list details what is desirable and/or permissible if non-Natives teach about Indigenous cultural understandings:

- The sanctity, privacy, feelings and rights of those studied must be respected.
- The topic is taught critically and contextually and in dialogue with those involved.
- Teachers should work outside of class as change agents to help rectify imbalances.
- There should be multiple interacting voices including all impacted by the topic.
- Native speakers and authors must be prioritized in learning.
- Constant attention to the limits of one voice is important.
- Native views are allowed to challenge the dominant worldview and values.
- Any research of Indigenous Peoples should be shared with them.
- Presentations in class should be comparative and cross-cultural.
- European-American teachers should admit their mistakes publicly.
- Extra care must be exercised when studying sacred rites in current use.
- Knowledge is for the sake of decision and action.
- Teachers are always respectful of students.
- The teacher does not try "to be Indian."

The California Critical Thinking Disposition Inventory, developed in 1987, is often used in psychological research, and the conclusions reveal consistently low scores for a variety of people from a variety of occupations. They include truth seeking, open-mindedness, analytic skills, perseverance, confidence in ones critical thinking, inquisitiveness, and the ability to see complexity in problems. I dare say that few people gain such skills from typical schooling (Facione, Facione and Giancarlo, 2001)

Because one never knows which precept will be of most value to the reader, I offer more of them below for consideration. Scanning the various lists in this chapter before class time may be of great help when working to indigenize a curriculum. This list is my own collection of ways to help ensure that you are on the right path:

1. Vitality: The idea of "vitality" is foundational to Indigenous knowledge paths (Hampton 1995). Vitality, when integrated into any subject area, can make whatever material you are teaching more relevant and meaningful. Ideas associated with this concept that can be used to indigenize various social studies subjects include health and wellness; responsibility for personal and community health; input from elders; and the degree to which fear or fearlessness impacts the subject area.

2. Nature, Place and Cycles: Here teachers and students address two questions: (1) How can we better use the natural world, including non-human "teachers," as resources for better understanding this topic? (2) In what ways does this topic impact life systems on Earth? In Nature we also learn about how virtues must be a primary factor in life. Social studies teachers using Indigenous values will constantly look at topics in light of fortitude, courage, patience, honesty, humility and generosity.

3. Natural Democracy: Whether a teacher is addressing law, anthropology, economics, government, civics or history, keeping the Indigenous understanding of "natural democracy" in mind and how it contrasts with current forms of "illusionary democracy" ("the best democracy money can buy") can lead to authentic democracies. Various aspects of this theme include discussions about gift economies; social/ecological justice; diversity; service; critical inquiry; consensus; applying the above listed virtues; and considering empathy, equality and participation.

4. Technology and Science: Concepts relating to community wellness and ecological harmony are prioritized here. These include initiation; ceremony; stories; experience and context; body-heart-mind-spirit learning; subjectivity; readiness to learn; visions and dreams; and an orientation to place.

5. Conflict Resolution: The main idea here is to bring individuals back into community. Indigenous approaches emphasize humor; respect; language; community reinstatement; interconnectedness; respect for cognitive dissonance; and reciprocity.

6. Critical Thinking and Place: Although courage will be required to implement the kind of critical observations common in Indigenous learning, including criticism of one's own uninvestigated assumptions, doing so is an educational necessity. Red Cloud said going forward is easy: "You just decide what to take and what to leave behind." (In his new book, *The Way Forward: Educational Reforms that Focus*

on the Cultural Commons and the Linguistic Roots of the Ecological/
Cultural Crises* (2012), Chet Bower writes about the need for curricular reforms that stem from the kind of evaluation of the contrasts
between Indigenous and mainstream perspectives that my proposal
involves.)

7. Transformational Learning: Many education books use the rhetoric of
   transformation, yet Indigenous knowledge strategies are designed to
   engage in transformation differently. For example, in *Primal Awareness*
   (Jacobs 1998), I show how Indigenous versus mainstream beliefs related
   to fear, authority, words and Nature impact natural and induced trance
   states and thus determine whether positive or negative transformational learning occurs. Also the term "transformative" is loaded with
   assumptions that Indigenous perspectives oppose, assumptions related
   to a constant pursuit of individualism and progress, for example.

Finally, in addition to these categories of ideas for enhancing curricula by integrating Indigenous values into the classroom, I offer a "pedagogy and procedures
checklist" that can help teachers employ dialogic and Indigenous approaches to
teaching and learning. For a detailed description of each of these "requirements,"
along with examples of their importance to the teaching of Indigenous virtues in elementary grade coursework that follows typical state standards, see *Teaching Virtues:
Building Character across the Curriculum* (Jacobs and Jacobs-Spencer 2001, pp.
41–43). The more of these "requirements" a teacher meets, the more automatically
will Indigenous ways of learning emerge to counter the mainstream curriculum's stifling standards, which, without this partnership, are dangerous for our world.

1. Field experience
2. Cooperative learning
3. Intrinsic motivation
4. Student ownership of subject matter
5. Critical reflection
6. Intuitive work
7. Visualizations and dream work
8. Honoring student pace
9. Using song and music
10. Honoring place
11. Using natural world as teacher
12. Involving community

13. Doing activism and serving others
14. Remembering that everything is connected/related
15. Using humor whenever possible
16. Employing wellness/fitness considerations
17. Using peer teaching
18. Allowing for observation rather than participation
19. Using storytelling prolifically and interactively that is related to the students' world
20. Being aware of sustainability issues in the class, school and home environment

Before concluding this consideration of the theory, philosophy and tools for rebalancing cognition and spirit and moving on to specific coursework, it may be useful to end this chapter with a hint at how each of chapters in the next section begin- with a critical look at possible hegemony built into the state standards. Since as of this writing all but five states (Alaska, Texas, Virginia, Nebraska and Minnesota) have adopted the "Common Core State Standards," I offer this list of ways a number of educators already believe these standards reflect such hegemony. I quote this list from the noted educator, author and activist, Marion Brady, published in her op-ed piece in the *Washington Post* on August 13, 2012 entitled, "Eight Problems with the Common Core State Standards."

One: Standards shouldn't be attached to school subjects, but to the qualities of mind it's hoped the study of school subjects promotes. Subjects are mere tools, just as scalpels, acetylene torches, and transits are tools. Surgeons, welders, surveyors—and teachers—should be held accountable for the quality of what they produce, not how they produce it.

Two: The world changes. The future is indiscernible. Clinging to a static strategy in a dynamic world may be comfortable, even comforting, but it's a Titanic-deck-chair exercise.

Three: The Common Core Standards assume that what kids need to know is covered by one or another of the traditional core subjects. In fact, the unexplored intellectual terrain lying between and beyond those familiar fields of study is vast, expands by the hour, and will go in directions no one can predict.

Four: So much orchestrated attention is being showered on the Common Core Standards, the main reason for poor student performance is being ignored—a level of childhood poverty the consequences of which no amount of schooling can effectively counter.

Five: The Common Core kills innovation. When it's the only game in town, it's the only game in town.

Six: The Common Core Standards are a set-up for national standardized tests, tests that can't evaluate complex thought, can't avoid cultural bias, can't measure non-verbal learning, can't predict anything of consequence (and waste boatloads of money).

Seven: The word "standards" gets an approving nod from the public (and from most educators) because it means "performance that meets a standard." However, the word also means "like everybody else," and standardizing minds is what the Standards try to do. Common Core Standards fans sell the first meaning; the Standards deliver the second meaning. Standardized minds are about as far out of sync with deep-seated American values as it's possible to get.

Eight: The Common Core Standards' stated aim—"success in college and careers" —is at best pedestrian, at worst an affront. The young should be exploring the potentials of humanness.

As we move to the next direction we now actually engage curricular supplementation for specific subjects and for state adopted examples from the Common Core Standards. Keep this list of problems in mind as you study the hegemonic and corporate influences on the standardized curricula; the real-world outcomes prior to supplementation with Indigenous perspectives; the Indigenous perspectives themselves and the lists of exercises, questions and dialogue topics. Also note, as stated in the Preface, a truly Indigenous approach would not focus as we do here on individuals subjects without connecting them to the others. Wanting to make these guidelines as teacher friendly as possible, I have kept the focus for each subject as per mainstream structures but nonetheless recommend that the reader look at subjects other than those taught to see how these interconnections can serve the teachers highest goals.

Notes

1. For proof of this assertion, see J. Scott Armstrong, "Natural Learning in Higher Education," in the *Encyclopedia of the Sciences of Learning* (Heidelberg: Springer, 2012).
2. Although I have not been able to relocate it, I recall a study on ethics that compared responses of Indian and non-Indian law students. The word "respect" was used repeatedly by the Indians but not at all by any of the non-Indians.
3. These scholars and other Indigenous academics are also critical of Indian people, especially mixed-blood, urban-raised ones like myself, who teach or profit somehow by sharing Indigenous knowledge. This is a sensitive, controversial and important topic that I address in Chapter 13.

THE EAST

The Color Yellow

Energy and Action

5

Health

The conquistadors had a general lack of confidence in their own medical skills and frequently sought out Aztec practitioners for health complaints in preference to their fellow countrymen.

—Verano & Ubulaker, 1993, p. 82

Diabetes, hypertension, obesity and atherosclerosis is unknown among the modern Kenyan Kikuuy, Broaya pastoralists and other pre-industrial cultures in Africa, Australia and South America.

—Eaton & Konner, 1985, p. 34

They are very well formed, with handsome bodies and good faces. All alike have very straight legs and no belly.

—From Christopher Columbus's Diary dated October 12, 1492 in Dunn & Kelley, 1989, p. 113

The medical-pharmaceutical-industrial complex was taken over long ago....The aim was to create profit, not to conquer disease.

—Nancy Turner Banks, 2010, p. 62

K-16 Teacher Instructions:

Adapt and use this chapter's information according to your students' cognitive levels. Use as an introduction to your standard course content, or weave values, ideas or critical reflections into it throughout the course. Encourage students to carefully reflect on this information with the goal of deciding what mainstream ideas are best replaced with Indigenous ones, which ones are best as they are, and how the two might be partnered in terms of practical benefits for the students and their community (local and global). Use the questions at the end of the chapter to help with this process and to stimulate primary source research and enthusiastic, critical dialogue. Since in Indigenous ways of thinking the ideas relating to this subject have relevance to all the other subjects, you may want to incorporate some of this chapter's material into the study of another subject area. As with all chapters in this section, this chapter is organized as follows:

1. Corporate and Hegemonic Influences
2. Real-World Outcomes
3. Indigenous Curricular Alternatives
4. Questions for Research, Dialogue, Choices and Praxis

Corporate and Hegemonic Influences

The opening quotations suggest that traditional Indigenous cultures place a higher priority on health, fitness and healing skills than do European civilizations. Of course, in the Americas Indigenous Peoples have largely lost their abilities to live according to the old ways. The evidence is clear, however, that before their societies were forcefully destroyed, the Indians were able to produce healthful, balanced societies by and large. Many observers upon contacting Natives for the first time remarked about their fitness. "For sheer physical endurance Indigenous peoples of the Americas were historically without peer, attaining a level of vigour and strength that would put to shame the strength and power of civilized man" (Obomsawin, 2007, p. 6). Optimal well-being was a spiritual undertakings. Movement, strength, agility, endurance and overall vitality came from the same respect for one's own system of cells as was required for a living in harmony with the many "cells" of a society. Sport activities were sacred aspects of many ceremonies. Physical play and engaging egoless competitions were full of joy, spontaneity, generosity and good will, but they were nonetheless full tilt efforts. Such activities also connect people to their non-human relatives, whose fitness continually modeled the beauty and survival aspects of optimal performance. And everyone participated as happens today in those areas where people can live relatively free of the Western paradigm.

Such respect for fitness has a different flavor in dominant cultures. Sports have lost this sense of playfulness and spiritual obligations to all relations. Competitions instead of being constant manifestations of joyfulness have come to reflect the "winning is everything" sentiment where people are either winners or losers. As a result, many people avoid the joy of friendly competition and physical training because they fear such put-downs. Sports have largely become a show for passive observers, a vehicle for demonstrating superiority, or a money-making enterprise.[1] "They have become profane, 'unholy' in every way and have little organic connections to maintaining a healthy society. However important organized sports have become for profit, reward or spectatorship, they no longer serve to enhance the health of the population, but to the contrary. They are thus relatively sterile and no longer a true-culture-creating activity" (Huizenga, 1955, p.18).

Older readers may remember "health education" in public schools as being "P.E." (Physical Education), which usually amounted to learning games like volleyball and required participation at a given time during the day. Only in the past thirty years has a broader focus on overall health emerged as a curricular approach. Nonetheless, the subjects of fitness and overall wellness remain marginalized. Since passage of the No Child Left Behind Act in 2001, little to no funding has been available for them. Despite the wealth of knowledge concerning the benefits of programs that promote healthy lifestyles and student participation in physical activities, both in terms of general health and in terms of improved learning in all school subjects (Taras, 2005), only 3.8% of elementary schools, 7.9% of middle schools, and 2.1% of high schools provide daily physical education or its equivalent (SHPPS, 2006; Brink, 2010). Health education and physical education programs are the first to be eliminated in schools when there is a financial cutback. A number of states like Texas have removed health education entirely from high schools. School sports in high schools and universities are now largely a money-making enterprise in education as much as they are outside of education.[2]

So what is the hegemonic or corporate benefit that could possible come from a health and physical education that does not truly enhance the health of its citizens? If asking "who benefits" is a good way to expose hegemony, who does benefit from an unhealthy population? Of course, the answer is it is the healing industries with large enough profit motives and lobby force to influence curriculum, policy and budget priorities so they ignore the overwhelming evidence in support of the right ways to teach students about authentic health and fitness. Perhaps those struggling to survive and without vitality are also less likely to stand strong against structural inequalities. Before we begin to learn new values and perspectives for living a healthful life, it is important for students to try to understand why health education coursework seems to lean away from wellness and towards dependence on external care. Let us start by looking at the typical health education standards.

Today in those schools that actually even have health education courses, a typical health education curriculum covers six major themes:

1. Nutrition and physical activity
2. Growth, development and sexual health
3. Injury prevention and safety
4. Alcohol, tobacco and other drugs
5. Mental, emotional and social health
6. Personal and community health

Even when time is given to these subjects, typical syllabi are insufficient for addressing these broad topics in ways that can truly help children develop healthy lifestyles. This makes it all the easier for "sound bites" that only offer basic information about external factors that cultivate a dependence agency outside ourselves for the care of our health. Indeed, most of the books, films and curricula guidelines emphasize learning about professional services, as does Standard 3 for fourth grade health education in the *California Common Core State Standards*:

> Standard 3: Accessing Valid Health Information. All students will demonstrate the ability to access and analyze health information, products, and services.

Lessons like "Identify resources for valid information about safe and healthy foods" tend to sustain this reliance on external authority for basic things that all people should know about the food they eat. From whom do we get the information? What can we teach to students that allows them to become experts themselves in what is a safe and healthy food? What can we teach communities to help assure that the options for healthy foods are not so difficult? What can we assume about corporatism that makes certain foods suspect?

Even when standards seem logical and significant, they rely on negative extrinsic motivation to be effective for transferring responsibility for personal health to the student and community to the medical industry. How have standards that mandate "students must demonstrate" this or that. They must "meet minimum criteria as measured by a scientifically based assessment." Such academic approaches obviously are not working or current rates of obesity and diabetes among children would not be so high. The current health and physical education standards are insufficient for preventing such problems, but they do help establish dependence on professional healthcare industries. They teach students to give responsibility for their health to others in positions of authority or expertise. Meanwhile, even as students are being taught to read labels for sugar content or are receiving no health education at all, schools continue to engage in money-making vending deals with companies that sell unhealthy products laden with sugar (like Coca-Cola.)[3]

Evidence that capitalistic priorities are woven into the health education curriculum abound. They infiltrate every aspect of education policy legislation. In 2007 over $150 million was spent by "healthcare" advocates to steer legislation their way (Smith & Birnbaum, 2007). *The National Health Education Standards: Achieving Health Literacy—An Investment in the Future,* a seventy-five-page document developed by a committee of health educators who solicited guidelines from thousands of people (American Cancer Society, 1997). Endorsements listed for it include the American School Health Association, the American Cancer Society, the Association for the Advancement of Health Education, the American Public Health Association and the Walt Disney Company. The ultimate goal for this "state of the art" curriculum, one adopted by many public schools, is summarized in the opening subsection, "Health: A Key Part in Building a Solid Future":

> Educational excellence in the traditional content areas may not be sufficient to secure the future competitiveness of the country. Such a narrow focus ignores poor health status as a major threat to this nation's ability to compete economically. Alcohol, tobacco, and other drug use; low levels of physical fitness; poor nutrition; injuries; and stress contribute to lowered health status and result in loss of work or school time. Health education in schools is essential to enable students to acquire the knowledge and skills to promote health. Students who have health knowledge and skills have better health status and contribute to the nation's economic competitiveness by:
> * working more effectively;
> * missing fewer days from work due to injury and illness;
> * using fewer medical services due to prevention or delayed onset of disease; and
> * reducing use of health insurance benefits.
>
> Productivity will increase and business costs will decrease as a result of a work force whose members know how to be and stay healthy. Students who gain health knowledge and skills in school are contributing members of society and important to economic competitiveness.

This quotation emphasizes that ensuring the "nation's ability to compete economically" is the priority for the curriculum. If health education is about economic profit, it is tied to decisions about what makes for the best profit. I am all for recognizing the connection between productivity and the health of workers when it motivates businesses and industries to help their employees become healthier.[4] However, as we will see later, the focus on "economic competitiveness" as the primary goal for health and fitness in America and Canada misses many of the more motivational reasons for people to engage in healthful lifestyles.

The two examples that follow offer a sense of how systemic hegemony actually is in the field of heath education, even to the point where life's most basic health priorities, childbirth and water access, are at risk!

The Centers for Disease Control and Prevention (CDC) and Its Influence on Health Curriculum

Although beneficial studies have come from the work of this federal agency, our focus here is on its hegemonic influence on health education curriculum in public schools. The CDC's *National Health Education Standards* have been voluntarily adopted by most public schools in the U.S. These essentially relate today to what the CDC saw in 1999 as the ten greatest achievements in health education:

- Vaccination
- Motor vehicle safety and engineering
- Control of environmental hazards
- Infectious disease control from antibiotic therapies and clean water processes
- Early detection and better treatment of heart disease
- Safer foods, food fortification program
- Prenatal care
- Contraception and family planning
- Fluoridation
- Recognition of tobacco use risks

Each of the items in this list would provide students with a good topic for investigation in terms of looking at possible hegemonic or economic influences. For example, over the years there have been a number of concerns about the CDC's policies in support of the multi-billion-dollar vaccine industry and other allegations about corporate collusion. It is likely that this collusion has found its way into decisions about what is (or is not) taught in health education coursework. In her book *AIDS, Opium, Diamonds and Empire*, Nancy Turner Banks, M.D., a graduate of Harvard Medical School, alleges that the "politburo" at the CDC has intentionally misinformed the public in its "education" about AIDS "in order to keep the industry in business" (2010, p. 276). Also, according to a report by the Center for Public Integrity, there is evidence that the CDC has "lied to us in an effort to hide inconvenient truths about pollution's impact on our health" (Sturgis, 2008).

Such charges are typical of corporatism's insidious control of education (see Saltman & Gabbard, 2003). The list of financial contributors to the CDC includes the majority of the large pharmaceutical companies, a fact that also hints at the possibility of corporate influence. In 2009, 200 Harvard Medical School students confronted their school administration with the demand that it end the "pharma industry's" influence in the classroom (Mercola, 2009). No one, however, has studied what effect the industry or the healthcare industry in general has had on K-12 health education beyond its promotion of the overuse of drugs for attention deficit disorder and hyperactivity, which in itself is highly suspect and controversial. You, as the teacher, might notice in your own content standards that for every grade level there is reference to the importance of professional healthcare services. For example, the CDC's recommended national standards for grades K-2 include, "Describe why it is important to seek health care." For grades 3–5, the standards say, "Describe when it is important to seek health care." For grades 6–8, they say, "Describe how appropriate health care can promote personal health." For grades 9–12, they say, "Analyze the relationship between access to health care and personal health." Consider the ways that your teaching of these standards might contribute to the continuation of an overreliance on professional medical and pharmaceutical products and services as opposed to prioritizing preventive and lifestyle-oriented measures.

The influence of CDC's financial ideology on curriculum extends to motherhood and birth itself. Beyond the tragic impact of conservative restrictions on sex education, which require an "abstinence only" curriculum, the overreliance on professional healthcare services that is generally advocated in health education programs may also have contributed indirectly to increased maternal deaths. According to Amnesty International, the U.S. presently ranks 50th in terms of safe labor and delivery. "Deadly Delivery," a report to Amnesty International, reports that despite annual expenditures of $98 billion, 12.7 of every 100,000 American women die in childbirth. For people of color, the rates are four times worse (Amnesty International, 2011). The corporate influence of the medical industry and its educational agenda is to blame.

The same influence has caused many mothers and fathers to believe in cesarean operations as normal. In 2008 the rate of cesarean operations (C-sections) instead of natural birth was six times higher than in 1968. (They cost about twice what a natural birth in the hospital costs—$11,000 versus $6,000.) That more C-sections occurred between 5 and 6 p.m. than at any other time of day shows that besides more profit and time savings, it may simply be more convenient to recommend a C-section. "Cesareans may be attractive to providers who feel that the surgical procedures reduce their risk of being sued or help them better schedule and control their professional and personal lives."[5] Tragically, these facts are essentially hidden rather than highlighted in education and targeted for policy change. Studying the rise in maternal deaths, which tripled between 1996 and 2006, might change attitudes about cesareans and thus hurt medical profits (Gaskin, 2011, p. 236).

Using information about such hegemony and then explaining natural birth as practiced by our Indigenous ancestors for tens of thousands of years can begin a process of rethinking our overdependence on the medical model. Dr. Sarah Buckley (n.d.) agrees:

> At the time when Mother Nature prescribes awe and ecstasy, we have injections, examinations, and clamping and pulling on the cord. Instead of body heat and skin to skin contact, we have separation and wrapping. Where time should stand still for those eternal moments of first contact, as mother and baby fall deeply in love, we have haste to deliver the placenta and clean up for the next 'case.'

Of course, many more examples exist showing how we have allowed a corporatized medical model overshadow serious lifestyles that emphasize "preventive medicine," from our dependence on prescription drugs to our willingness to jump into operations before considering more natural remedies. One that is so basic to survival that it is amazing how mainstream education can avoid engaging it has to do with access to clean water. Yet, health education courses from kindergarten through university do not teach the truth about this basic necessity for survival.

Water and Educational Hegemony

Recall that hegemony works because the public buys into it and then actually supports it. Schools and teachers have to be complicit for it to be effective. The lack of appropriate education about water is no exception. Many school districts fall prey to corporate influence in selecting books, a curriculum and modes of delivery, such as corporate-sponsored Internet programs for virtual learning experiences relating to a most basic requirement for health—water. Hall (2012) describes how the ever-growing water industry is now supplying K-12 school children and community colleges with corporate materials and activities throughout the United States, Canada and Mexico. One water bottle corporation, for example, sponsors Water Education for Teachers (WET), a program delivered to more than 180,000 teachers in over twenty countries who have been trained to implement this WET curriculum. Backed by the World Bank and the World Water Council, many schools are given good deals on bottled water.

Hall's (2012) research shows that transnational corporations play a significant role in health and environmental education. Students are not exposed to a line of questioning regarding the logic or ethics of schools contracting water utility services for profit. Rather, they are taught about the good work being done by the water experts. This is the basis of hegemony's effectiveness—our belief that those in power know best and have our best interests at heart. As a result, many students do not know of the worldwide depletion of fresh water, or if they do, they have a blind faith that corporate-financed technologies will save us. (One of several excellent free Internet-based documentary films that can teach the truth about water is John Pilger's documentary, "A World without Water," first released in 2006 and available along with many other free films at topdocumentaries.com.)

I will conclude this section with a personal story about how corporatism can stifle authentic health education. Concerned that education was doing more to harm children than to help them, my daughter and I long ago co-authored the book *Happy Exercise: An Adventure into the World of Fitness for Children* (1981). In the book's fictional story, a little rabbit is rescued from a fire and while in captivity teaches healthy diet and exercise habits to the young children of the firefighter who saved it. He shakes his head when he sees a cartoon rabbit on television promoting cereal as healthy that is really 80% sugar and the children learn to be critical of television ads. Six months after the publisher of *Runner's World Magazine*, Bob Anderson, published our little book, his corporate sponsors started yelling. They did not like that we were teaching children not to believe what advertisers said on television. They were bothered by our saying that the deception was intentional. The book was taken off the market soon afterward because these corporations threatened to pull their ads from the magazine. A number of teachers who managed to get copies of the book are still able to bring it into the classroom and teach the truth. Until *Teaching Truly* is somehow banned, remember it can be brought into the classroom as well!

Real-World Outcomes

An elder of the Mic-Mack tribe named Sa'k'j has said, "you cannot be the doctor if you are the disease" (1992, p.8). If modern medicine's desire for profit is more important than an authentic concern for the health and vitality of humans, it is no wonder we have lost our health. If teachers whose own health status is significantly poor are teaching health education courses, what message is sent to the students? "Do as I say and not as I do?" If textbooks and the curriculum do little more than bore, confuse or discourage personal responsibility, then the following statistics are to be expected.

Cardiovascular disease is the number-one cause of death in the United States (Roger et al., 2012). In March 2012 the *Journal of the American Medical Association* (Yang et al., 2012) reported on a study conducted by the Centers for Disease Control involving 50,000 American adults over the age of twenty that analyzed seven essential components that determine cardiovascular health: (1) being a non-smoker for the past twelve months; (2) maintaining healthy blood pressure (120/80 or lower); (3) having healthy fasting blood glucose levels (under 100 mg/dL); (4) maintaining healthy blood cholesterol levels (240 mg/dL or less); (5) having a healthy body weight (fat versus lean body mass); (6) eating a healthy, balanced diet (adequate percentage of fruits and vegetables in diet); and (7) participating in sufficient physical activity (any activity requiring three to six METs[6] five times per week or requiring more than six METS three times or more per week). Participants who met six or more, versus one or fewer, of these cardiovascular health metrics had a 51% lower risk of all causes of mortality and a 76% lower risk of cardiovascular mortality. In addition, meeting a greater number of these metrics appeared to be associated with a lower risk of cancer mortality. The study found that only 1.2% of participants met six of the seven essential metrics connected to cardiovascular health. This is down from 2%, measured in 1994, so as bad as only 2% was, it is getting even worse!

The most enduring Western definition of health—provided by the World Health Organization (WHO) in 1946 and generally accepted by health education curriculum developers—defines health as "a state of complete physical, mental, and social well-being and not merely the absence of disease or infirmity" (p.100). Thus, in addition to physical statistics, we should also briefly look at mental and social statistics to assess how well health education is achieving the Western goal. Regarding mental health, half of Americans will experience a mental health problem at some point in their life (Reinberg, 2011). Whereas cardiovascular disease kills more people, neuropsychiatric disorders are the leading cause of disability. The total burden of disability can be measured in units called disability-adjusted life years (DALYs). DALYs represent the total number of years lost to illness, disability, or premature death within a given population. They are calculated by adding the number of years of life lost to the number of years lived with disability due to a certain disease or disorder. The World Health Organization estimates that neuropsychiatric disorders in both the U.S. and Canada are the leading contributor to DALYs, accounting for nearly twice as many DALYs as cardiovascular diseases and cancers![7]

As for social well-being, a number of different approaches to measuring this have emerged in the past twenty years, and in all of them things do not look good for even the most developed countries. For example, in 2007 a report for the U.N. Children's Fund on a study of forty factors involved in well-being, such as poverty, deprivation, happiness, and relationships, revealed that for children the United States and Britain were the worst of the top twenty-one countries in the industrialized world (Gifford, 2007). In a 2011 report entitled "Social Justice in the OECD: How Do the Member States Compare?" the United States ranked twenty-seventh among the thirty-four developed countries: "The U.S., with its alarming poverty levels, lands near the bottom of the weighted index, ranking only slightly better than its neighbor Mexico (30th) and the new OECD member Chile (29th)" (SGI, 2011). Another approach to measuring well-being is an interactive Internet project that allows users to select their priorities in life from a list of ten in order to rate how their country compares to the thirty-three most developed countries in terms of housing, income, jobs, community, education, environment, governance, health, life satisfaction, safety and work-life balance.[8]

Mainstream health education tends to ignore the environmental and ecological influences on human health. Even though the health of our planet is not specifically targeted in the mainstream goals for health education, it is reasonable to assume that health is not likely without fresh water, unpolluted oceans, clean air, uncontaminated soils, and the like. Although most diseases and health problems in the world relate to such environmental considerations, mainstream thinking tends to see us as separate from the delicate biosphere. Unfortunately, as mentioned in the Introduction, all life systems on Earth are at or are nearing points of depletion from which there can be no return. Not a single peer-reviewed scientific study in the past twenty years denies this. The claims are worth repeating here:

- Ocean acidification is now significantly higher than pre-industrial levels and is rapidly worsening. In some parts of the ocean, plastic particles outnumber plankton. Coral reef systems are dying. Fish are disappearing.
- Climate change impacts from human-caused greenhouse gasses are worse than imagined.
- Over one-fourth of the world's river systems no longer reach the ocean. Fresh ground water is drying up.
- Extinction rates are up to 1,000 times higher than at any time in recorded history, with 100 extinctions per million species per year. Among all mammal, bird and amphibian species, 30% are threatened with extinction in the twenty-first century. Two hundred species go extinct every day!
- Excessive nitrogen and phosphorous production is destroying soil fertility and causing increasing numbers of dead zones in our oceans.

- There is an overwhelming and continuing loss of rainforests.
- Chemical pollution is widespread, with nearly 100,000 human-made chemical compounds in use.

Indigenous Curricular Alternatives

A traditional Indigenous way of life envisions close harmony with the natural world. If every creature in the natural world demonstrates optimal health and fitness, why should humans be different? Physical well-being reflects spiritual life. Maintaining balance amidst the billions of cells under our skin is a microcosm for balancing the health of societies. It is this awareness of interconnectedness and appreciation for doing what one can do honor the gift of a physical life that bonds the physical to the spiritual. For Indigenous Peoples able to live in accordance with their values, this spiritual orientation is the foundation and motivation for sustaining high levels of physical, mental and social fitness. A system of physical training in concert with adherence to virtuous conduct is in accord the natural law of life. When people were not prevented from following this law, children were inspired high ideals of physical strength and agility that required self-directed control of eating, persistent exercise and respectful sexual behaviors. Fasting and strenuous sports, combined with sweat lodge ceremonies, were as intrinsic to life as breathing. This "health education" perspective assured that members of the community lived in a state of emotional, physical, spiritual and social balance that assured continual symbiosis with the rest of the natural world. How this contrasts with mainstream priorities, as one of the leading textbooks for mainstream elementary and middle-school health education concedes:

> While most elementary and middle-level teachers believe that health education is important, it is difficult to dedicate sufficient instructional time to adequately address all health education content and skill areas within their course of study or curriculum. (Telljohann, Symons, Seaber & Pateman, 2011, p. 65)

According to studies conducted by Fuchs and Havighurst (1983), such minimal, "sequential learning" is inadequate for Native students. I suggest that the sequential, paradigmatic instruction commonly used in mainstream schools is also inadequate for most non-Indian students. In their article "Joining the Circle: A Practitioner's Guide to Responsive Education for Native Students," Grant and Gillespie explain the unhealthy effects of a mainstream curriculum that contradicts Indigenous expectations:

Native students confront a dilemma. They must decide to which cultural belief system they will pledge their allegiance: the one they have learned from their community or the one promoted by the public school system. Choosing the former usually means falling further and further behind and eventually leaving school. Choosing the latter can lead to serious self-destructive behaviors of chemical addiction, violence, abuse—all typical responses of a societal group coping with cultural discontinuity. (1993, p. 4; see also York, 1989)

In this subsection, I briefly introduce some of the main ideas behind traditional Indigenous approaches to healthy living. In preparation for questions in the next section, students should consider how different these ideas are from those represented in their class's content standards and whether or not these ideas inspire a greater commitment to personal and community health and fitness. In general, as the opening quotations reveal, Indigenous health, fitness and medicine are about "energy, power, spirit, relationship…movement, balance, a way of life and an honoring of the non-human teachings" (Peat, 1994, p. 128). "Health education" is a communal responsibility that offers appropriately timed learning that encourages students to:

- honor alliances with the spiritual energies that reside in all of Nature
- realize that illness stems from disharmonious relationship with Nature, spirits, community or self
- appreciate that "disease is a manifestation of human thought because it is ideas, worldviews, and beliefs that create the conditions in which a society can be riddled with disease, strife and poverty, or can continue in health and harmony." (Peat, 1994, p. 117)

This idea of "balance" and the mandate for living in harmony with one's environment require a strong orientation toward prevention and the healthy maintenance of numerous relationships. Durie describes this approach:

Indigenous peoples' concept of health and survival is both a collective and an inter-generational continuum encompassing a holistic perspective incorporating four distinct shared dimensions of life. These dimensions are the spiritual, the intellectual, the physical, and emotional. Linking these four fundamental dimensions, health and survival manifests itself on multiple levels where the past, present, and future co-exist simultaneously. (2003, p. 510)

Durie's four dimensions of life are often found in contemporary medicine wheels.[9] When the spiritual, intellectual, physical and emotional are in balance, health and vitality result. Vitality is a foundational component of Indigenous pathways to learning. Invoking the persistence and strength that have allowed

American Indians to survive, Eber Hampton includes this concept as one of his twelve descriptors of true Indigenous education (1995, p. 41). Although this vitality[10] is an essential component of the health of all humans in our ever-changing world, it is ebbing from both Indigenous and non-Indigenous children. A number of studies have revealed a correlation between student burnout and low levels of vigor and vitality (Nowack & Hanson, 1983).

Examples of vigor and vitality in Indigenous cultures may seem extreme when contrasted with contemporary lifestyles, but they merely represent a natural striving toward one's full potential. I am amazed at how many people tell me I exercise "too much!" Yet at age sixty-six I play handball for only an hour a day and then paddle my stand-up paddle board around the islands near my home for only about an hour. This is nothing in contrast to the routine abilities of my Indigenous ancestors. We must replace this rationalizing of our sedentary lives with a motivation to live naturally, and we must base assumptions about our potential health on the realities of living more naturally. Raymond Obomsawin, of Oneida and Abenaki ancestry and a member of the Odanak First Nation in eastern Canada, spearheaded the first public sector–funded study of Indigenous knowledge systems. In his essay "Historical and Scientific Perspectives on the Health of Canada's First Peoples" (2007), he contrasts the health of people before and after conquest. Available online for review with 264 citations to support his work, Obomsawin's article offers the following examples of Indigenous fitness to inspire students and the rest of us:[11]

1. William Wood in describing early contact with the original inhabitants of the northeastern woodlands of North America spoke of them possessing "lusty and healthful" bodies which did not experience "those health wasting diseases which are incident to other countries [such] as fevers, pleurisies, calentures, agues, obstructions, consumptions, convulsions, apoplexies, gouts, stones, tooth-aches, measles or the like." He reported that most of them reached fifty before a "wrinkled brow or grey hair" betrayed their age and that they spun out the thread of their days to fair length, numbering threescore, fourscore, some a hundred years.

2. John Ross's 1830 encounter with the Inuit in the far north was typical of the many early contact reports on North American Indians. He speaks of this people as "occupying so apparently hopeless a country, so barren, so wild, and so repulsive; and yet enjoying the most perfect vigour [and] the most well-fed health."

3. Oral histories describe Elders as commonly exceeding 100 years of age.

Historical writings and present-day scientific research report that Aboriginal people of the time were able to control disease and enjoyed high levels of mental and physical health. Skeletal remains of unquestionable pre-Colombian date are, barring a few exceptions, remarkably free from disease. There was no plague, cholera, typhus, smallpox or measles. Cancer was rare, and even fractures were infrequent....There were, apparently, no [skin tumours]. There were no troubles with the feet, such as fallen arches. And judging from later acquired knowledge, there was a much greater scarcity than in the white population of...most mental disorders, and of other serious conditions.

4. Physician Eric Stone speaks of the incredible abilities of North American Indians to recover from severe wounds and accidents. All military and medical observers who came in contact with the Indians agree that they recovered more rapidly than the white from most wounds, and many recovered from wounds which would have been fatal to the white man...gunshot wounds of the bladder were invariably fatal to the white, [yet] the Indians seemed to suffer this accident with impunity. Loskiel examined a man whose face had been torn away, his rib cage crushed, limbs ripped and the abdomen disemboweled by a bear, yet [he] had been able to crawl four miles to his village and in six months had completely recovered, except for extensive scarring.

5. For sheer physical endurance the indigenous peoples of the Americas were historically without peer, attaining a level of vigor and strength that would put to shame the strength and power of civilized man. The most famous runner of ancient Greece was Pheidippides whose record run from Athens to Sparta was 140 miles in 46 hours. Seton mentions that he saw a young Cree who on foot had just brought in dispatches from Fort Qu' Appelle 125 miles distant in only 25 hours. The well-known Sioux chief Running Antelope was given this name by his people because in his youth he pursued and ran down an antelope in a "straight-away race lasting 5 hours."

6. Research also indicates that the Inca "Chasqui" relay runners were unparalleled. "At a time when Rome was boasting of an unheard speed in delivering messages at a rate of 100 miles a day, the Inca runners were putting fresh fish on the table of the Emperor at Cuzco 242 miles from the sea in one day. This was no level journey; the runners ran up their stair-step roads from sea level to 11,000 feet elevation."

Such examples could be continued almost indefinitely, as many observers recorded how impressed they were with the health, beauty, stamina and strength of Indigenous Peoples when first witnessed. In fact, I have many similar stories I could tell of the Raramuri Indians of Mexico and do describe some of them in my book *Primal Awareness: A True Story of Survival, Awakening and Transformation with the Raramuri Shamans of Mexico*. The point is that such robust health is humanity's normal condition. It is not disease but dis-ease that plagues us. We have accepted a false standard for fitness and health. For thousands of years, our Indigenous ancestors, relatives, friends and neighbors developed cultural priorities that were based on the natural vitality in Nature. A curriculum that incorporates the following Indigenous precepts for health can help students reclaim their own natural vitality. Health education classes can post this list or a modified version of it for younger children. Even if you do not teach a formal health education, these guidelines appropriately apply to other subjects because good health is essential for the optimal learning of anything!

1. The "spiritual" dimension relates not to a religion but to a deeply felt relationship to place and Nature and to the invisible energies that inform it. The absence of health is directly related to violating Nature's balance. "The harmony between the psychic and physical circulation of earth and man maintains a channel of communication, like an umbilical cord, through repeated cycles of death and rebirth" (Lawlor, 1991, p. 133).

2. Animals and plants are important teachers for living life in balance. "Indians and animals know better how to live than white man; nobody can be in good health if he does not have all the time fresh air, sunshine and good water."—Flying Hawk (Oglala)

3. When spirit is removed from food, health is also. Animals in cages, fed chemicals and slaughtered without respect for the animal's spirit, create disease when eaten.

4. "Spirit is part of the ontological existence of medicine. To approach medicine plants only in terms of biologically active molecules is to see them in only one dimension" (Peat, 1994, p.133). Ceremony, relationships, songs, trance states and beliefs are as important to healing as pharmaceutically manufactured drugs (many of which have been stolen from Indigenous healers.

5. Health status is not only a product of the healthcare system or of education. It reflects political, economic and political factors, as well as

beliefs and actions of the community, individuals and media.

6. Anti-diversity beliefs and actions, such as those related to bullying violence against people with multiple sexual orientations, are seen as forces that create imbalances that affect the health of everyone.

7. Respect for the gift of life is reflected in taking care of one's body and making sure it achieves its highest potential fitness, which is necessary for individual and group survival and for a full, balanced engagement with life.

8. The health of individuals is related to the health of communities. Therefore, generosity, reciprocity, humility, courage and attention to conflict resolution strategies that aim at maintaining and restoring community are vital to wellness.

9. Skills and knowledge about all of the above operate in concert with humorous respect for cognitive dissonance when one falls short of healthy life habits. So when someone falls short and contradicts best intentions, no one ridicules the person and the community comes to support a regaining of balance.

10. When considering health, one cannot regard physical, emotional, mental, spiritual, social or environmental factors as separate from each other.

11. Games, play and sports were an integral part of Indigenous life. Men and women played a variety of active sports with unrestrained vigor. A game might be played to heal the sick, ensure a good harvest, strengthen kinship ties, or show respect for the Creator. The winnings from gambling were shared with the community, and they were even used to resolve disputes.

12. Health comes from a respectful connection to the natural land, its rocks, trees, rivers, creatures and spirits.

Questions, Research, Dialogue, Choices and Praxis

(Note to teachers: Phrase the following to suit age and developmental levels in your class and according to what best complements your lesson plans.)

1. Go through each of the Indigenous beliefs above that represent priorities for Indigenous paths to health. Which ones need clarification? What does your intuition say about their value? How might your health education curriculum embrace them?

2. What similarities and what differences are there between the objectives of your state content standards or your course guidelines and those related to the Indigenous precepts for health listed above? In mainstream content standards there is a big emphasis on "avoiding risky behaviors." Why do you think this is not mentioned directly in the Indigenous concepts?

3. What have you learned from this chapter that you can put into action for yourself, your community and/or for Indigenous cultures whose wisdom you are tapping?

4. Name some specific new health commitment for yourself that you will make that aligns with at least one of the Indigenous concepts above.

5. Name one action you can and will do to help bring health and well-being to higher levels in your own community. For example, in what ways might you combine an act of generosity with something that would ultimately offer you and another an opportunity for improved health?

6. Since the World Environmental Summit in 1992, only four of ninety-six goals have been somewhat addressed. Instead, the so-called "green movement" has been about making a commodity of Nature. What contributions to saving our natural systems does the Indigenous health perspective offer?

7. What problems or possible contradictions do you see with the mainstream emphasis on the economic competitiveness of corporations as a major goal of health education?

8. What evidence can you find of the superior fitness and health of pre-contact Indigenous Peoples in contrast to most peoples today? For example, besides references associated with the opening quotations, one source is *The Book of Chilam Balam of Chumayel*, written by Mayan authors sometime in the 1600s after the Spanish invasion of the Yucatán Peninsula. In a section entitled "Memoranda Concerning the History of the Yucatán," the author describes the year 1519:

> Here was then no sickness; they had then no aching bones; they had then no high fever; they had then no smallpox; they had then no burning chest; they had then no abdominal pains; they had then no consumption; they had then no headache. At that time the course of humanity was orderly. The foreigners made it otherwise when they arrived here. (Roys, 1967, p. 81)

9. Find something in your curricular materials that speaks about the worldwide water crises and identify something related to this issue that seems to be hegemonic?

10. Health for its own sake, independent of its relationship to living a full life, is not a goal Indigenous Peoples embrace. Health and fitness are means to more important and satisfying activities in life. Make a list of the activities you enjoy that do not require being fit or healthy and then make a list of things you would like to do or do better that would be enhanced by high levels of health and physical fitness. Talk about whether a lack of fitness accounts for your not doing what you would like to do.

11. Study the sponsors of the 2012 Olympics, such as BP, DuPont and MacDonald's. Do you see any hypocrisy here? In what ways do these companies stand against the ideals of the Olympics? What do they specifically do that hurts people and the environment?

12. What motivated pre-contact Indigenous Peoples to stay strong, fit and healthy that has parallels in your life?

13. How can taking optimal care of one's body and mind be a spiritual endeavor?

Notes

1. The 2012 Olympics (and many preceding it) exemplify this problem. The goal of the Olympic Movement is clearly defined in the Olympic Charter: "The goal of the Olympic Movement is to contribute to building a peaceful and better world by educating young people through sport practiced in accordance with Olympism and its values" (Olympic Charter, 2011, Rule 1). However, at a cost of more than $17 billion, mostly paid for by British citizens during a great economic crisis, the 2012 Olympics benefit mostly corporations like MacDonald's and BP, whose recent histories contradict the purpose of the games, while corporatism, militarism, racism and structural inequalities are magnified despite being hidden by the worldwide television cameras.

2. Consider also the incident at Penn State University, where a coach's molestation of youth was covered up for years to protect the income from its football team. See DemocracyNow.org, Nov. 11, 2011.

3. In 1982 the USDA, under pressure from some health educators, tried to regulate the selling of soft drinks in public schools, but the National Soft Drink Association challenged the regulation, and in 1983 the U.S. Court of Appeals struck down the USDA prohibition. When hegemony is not sufficient, corporate-sponsored legislation steps in.

4. I wrote some of the first books about this, *Physical Fitness and the Fire Service* (1976) and *Getting Your Executive Fit* (1988), and realized during my research that the profit motive was the only way to get businesses to invest in fitness programs for employees. Of course, to a point, this is understandable. However, as we know from the widespread use of sweatshops and from continuing attacks on labor unions, the end result is not a healthy society—as we shall soon see.

5. See http://www.childbirthconnection.org/article.asp?ck=10285.

6. One MET (metabolic equivalent of task) is equal to the energy expenditure of the body at rest, so five METs are five times this energy, or five times the number of calories expended at rest.

7. See chart at http://www.nimh.nih.gov/statistics/2LEAD_CAT.shtml.

8. See http://oecdbetterlifeindex.org/about/better-life-initiative. The U.S. has done poorly here as well.

9. For thousands of years, medicine wheels have been used by Indigenous Peoples to symbolize and to help manifest the balancing of important ideas, cycles, goals and priorities.

10. Vitality refers to "exuberant physical strength or mental vigor; capacity for survival or continuation of a meaningful or purposeful existence; a vital force" (http://dictionary.reference.com/browse/vitality).

11. Some of his examples in this text come from volume 3 of a 1996 report of the Royal Commission on Aboriginal Peoples (RCAP).

6 | Music

The music of the Indian is the spontaneous and sincere expression of the soul of a people. No civilized music has such complex, elaborate, and changing rhythm as has the music of the American Indian.
— NATALIE CURTIS (HTTP://WWW.NATIVEVILLAGE.ORG/LIBRARIES/
QUOTES/NATIVE%20AMERICAN%20QUOTES3.HTM)

Aboriginal Music unites consciousness with the invisible laws and energy patterns of nature.
— LAWLOR, 1991, P. 290

The overseers must be watchful against innovations in music and gymnastics counter to the established order, and to the best of their power guard against them, fearing when anyone says that song is most regarded among men….For a change to a new type of music is something to beware of as a hazard of all our fortunes. For the modes of music are never disturbed without unsettling of the most fundamental political and social conventions.
— PLATO

Educational theory has become fragmented into a series of isolated and often contradictory 'findings' which, because they cannot find a place in any unified or integrated whole, are incapable of producing a coherent response to fundamental political questions about what the social purpose of education should be.
— CARR & HARTNETT, 1997, P. 9

K-16 Teacher Instructions:

Adapt and use this chapter's information according to your students' ages and cognitive levels. Use as an introduction to your standard course content or weave values, ideas or critical reflections into it throughout the course. Encourage students to carefully reflect on this information with the goal of deciding what mainstream ideas are best replaced with Indigenous ones, which ones are best as they are, and how the two might be partnered in terms of practical benefits for the students and their community (local and global). Use the questions at the end of the chapter to help with this process and to stimulate primary source research and enthusiastic, critical dialogue. Since in Indigenous ways of thinking the ideas related to this subject have relevance to all the other subjects, you may want to incorporate some of this chapter's material into the study of another subject area. As with all chapters in this section, this chapter is organized as follows:

1. Corporate and Hegemonic Influences
2. Real-World Outcomes
3. Indigenous Curricular Alternatives
4. Questions for Research, Dialogue, Choices and Praxis

Corporate and Hegemonic Influences

Just as health and fitness are spiritual priorities in the Indigenous worldview, so too are music and the other arts, such as drawing, dancing and storytelling. Music in traditional cultures heals, enlivens and connects. It is also used for hunting game, identifying plants and navigating vast land areas or oceans. Everyone sings and dances. There are no spectators.[1] Of course, music is important to all cultures, including mainstream American culture, but there are important differences that may start from how it is addressed or ignored in schooling. Alfie Kohn offers a reason why this may be:

> Putting aside for the moment the fact that reading and writing skills, too, have obvious implications for real-world success—and, conversely, that theoretical physics and "pure" mathematics do not—it's easy to see how politicians and corporate leaders would favor the fields that appear to be more directly linked to economic productivity and profit.
> Moreover, anyone whose sensibility is shaped by a zero-sum mindset, such that the goal is not success but victory, is far more likely to be drawn to STEM [science, technology, engineering and mathematics] subjects than to the humanities.
> "The nation that out-educates us today," said President Obama last month, "is going to out-compete us tomorrow." (2011)

I have previously mentioned how mainstream education can serve to pacify people into accepting the status quo ills that surround them and considering Plato's words in the opening quotes, it is worth considering whether there is some intentionality about keeping popular music away from schools. Perhaps a dissertation some day will reveal that people who emerge from such schools will be less likely to protest injustice if they do not sing. Having not practiced the spontaneity of song, they make for more obedient soldiers and workers. If such ideas seem to stretch the imagination, again we must consider the state of our world and open our minds to the role education has played in our creation of it.

Patrick K. Freer describes health and music education's common plight in an article for *Arts Education Policy Review*, entitled "Parallel Frames and Policy Narratives in Music Education and Physical Education" (2012, pp. 26–34). He observes that both subjects wrestle with gender equity and diversity, that both require constant advocacy in support of their value in an increasingly materialistic society, and that educators in both fields have long been concerned with a curriculum that emphasizes conformity or competition, two common hegemonic goals. Freer also cites a study showing that physical education, like music education, suffers from a lack of administrative support, a shortage of facilities and equipment, oversized classes, apathetic and unqualified teachers, inadequate parental involvement and difficulties in motivating students (Robinson, Zeng and Leung, 2008, p. 124). Freer describes other problems that both physical education and music share:

- No holistic perspective, as only parts of the subject are taught
- Compartmentalization of subdisciplines
- Meritocracy: high-achieving students are afforded opportunities to learn through tryouts
- Accepting only the authority of standards as valuable
- Little relevance to lifelong participation and learning
- Struggle for academic acceptance and value in spite of overwhelming evidence that physical fitness and musical learning contribute to a person's life in remarkably significant ways

Many scholars have written about the corporatization of music (Negus 1998; Neal 1997). Adorno, speaking of corporate motives, has written prolifically about "compliance through [the] commodification" of music and about "audience commericialization" (1941, p. 45), indicating that the industrialization and standardization of music are direct results of contemporary capitalism, which leaves little place for originality, a quality that is not easily marketed on a large scale. More disconcerting than corporatism, however, is the maintenance of structural inequality through music education. Van Dorston writes,

> Political and social dissent in cultural expression has always been expressed most frequently with music. As a result it is music that has often been subverted or suppressed....The dominant class chooses what music is relevant and what will be "internalized" by the subordinate class. One just has to look at the history of early rock 'n' roll during the fifties to see a functional example of Gramsci's concept of hegemony in operation. Black artists began to develop the rock 'n' roll sound. However, white artists were recognized as being the pioneers of the new sound and received all the airplay and rewards for essentially picking up on what was predominantly a black movement. (1990)

In the next section, the phenomenon of "hip hop" music is offered as a contemporary example of the continuing racism against people of color. Ironically, in a land of immigrants, it seems a part of the hegemonic agenda regarding music education relates to the goal of ensuring that everyone believes "America is the best nation in the world." The less people know about the world at large, the more they trust the decisions of their leaders to rule the world. If diverse, authentic music from various countries, cultures and classes came to be understood as equal to the carefully selected categories of music taught in schools, this might cause doubt in "America only" beliefs (Spruce 2001). Music, as Indigenous cultures have not forgotten, can enhance conscious awareness and can provide a common language that breaks down "us versus them" thinking and encourages people to question inequalities. Thus, as Plato instructed in his writings (see his opening quotation), it must be controlled.

Research shows that music education today tends to contribute to the reproduction of both social and cultural inequalities (Rose 1990). Music education is full of boundaries and exclusions. By ignoring certain kinds of music, people unconsciously reject the individuals or cultures producing this music. Of course, this has been exemplified in the extreme with regard to American Indian cultures. For example, using Christian rationales to support authoritarianism and exclusivity, European missionaries suppressed Indigenous music in the sixteenth century as part of the conquering process. Here in Jalisco, Mexico, where I live, Franciscan friars introduced European music to the Nahua Indians in the 1500s along with their missionary work. Later, in the United States between 1800 and 1925, Indian healing and ceremonial music was banned by the Office of Indian Affairs. This office also made American Indian dances illegal, such as the Sun Dance and the

Ghost Dance, which were associated with communal evens that celebrated the values and ties the government was trying to destroy. At the same time, Native children were placed in mission boarding schools (so much for the separation of church and state), where Indian children were not allowed to enjoy any of their traditional modes of expression and where non-Native music replaced Indigenous songs and instruments (Troutman 2009).

By and large, contemporary music education continues this process (Richerme 2012). Both educational hegemony and cultural hegemony still manage to control what music is allowed or "enjoyed." Following Plato's advice, the hegemons' agents cause schools to avoid music that has emotional content, such as that felt in many protest songs, since emotional content could somehow lead students to challenge those in power.[2] As we see in the next section, in spite of the ability of the Internet to break through such barriers, music is still not being used to its full, positive potential. Music teachers who realize this have an opportunity to use music's power to help us regain diversity and balance in the world.

Real-World Outcomes

A real-world contemporary example of how music is controlled to maintain structural inequality relates to hip hop music and how its origins have changed. In "The Culture Industry, Hip Hop Music and the White Perspective," Walter Edward Hart explains how the dominant class has controlled this music to maintain historically negative racial attitudes. He and others explain how early hip hop's consciousness-raising music about equality and diversity was quickly confiscated by those in power. Reflecting the local identity of artists and their communities, this music called for radical changes to American society, changes for the public good. Toward the end of the 1990s, hip hop music painted African Americans and Hispanics as embodying negative manifestations of sex and violence. Music as a social critique was replaced by "commodities of gangster, ghetto, violence, drug dealer and misogyny that attracted a wealthy, suburban, white, teenage audience" (Hart 2009, p. 6). The culture industry's intentional one-dimensional representation of hip hop music, for the purpose of attracting white consumers, played on historically negative assumptions about the black culture. "This positioning of hip hop music created an economic environment which necessitated rappers adopt the commoditized negative images" (Hart 2009, p. 6).

Aside from the fact that music education in most schools continues to maintain an illusion of inclusion while fostering exclusion and racism, it seems schools are also not achieving one of the stated goals of the music curriculum.—simply preparing the citizen to enjoy playing music and singing. According to 2009 U.S. Census data, about 8 percent of Americans play musical instruments regularly, and another 5 percent sing in a chorus or chorale.[3] Personally, I think that these figures are high and that the authors of a 2011 opinion piece in *Time* magazine are closer to the truth when they say only 1 percent play music.[4] In a 2009 Gallup survey of 1,000 people, 87 percent of those who did not play music said they wished that they had learned to play, and 69 percent said they still wanted to learn but didn't have the time. Ninety-two percent agreed that schools should offer music as part of the regular curriculum.[5] These statistics present a clear picture of the current state of music education. If participation in music is as good for people as the research claims,[6] yet very few people wind up participating, then like health and fitness education in the previous chapter, music education is failing.

There are no statistics to show how many Indigenous people sing or play instruments, but in all my years of travel and engagement with many tribes, I have never met one who did not? This is true of all art forms in Indigenous culture. Cajete writes,

> All Tribal People participated in the creation of art. Young and old, men and women, each in their own way and with their own degree of experience, created art....Art was an integral expression of life, not something separate. Everyone was an artist. (Four Arrows, Cajete and Lee 2010, p. 90)

We now turn to considering Indigenous ways to complement your current music instruction or, if none exists, ways to integrate music into other coursework. Let us find out why and how authentic music education can help all students, at long last, subscribe to the joy and power of participation in the musical experience firsthand and just what potential music has to help us all regain our lost balance.

Indigenous Curricular Alternatives

In her peer-reviewed essay "How Can Music Education Be Religious?" Estelle R. Jorgensen examines Alfred North Whitehead's claim that general education should ideally be understood as a religious experience specifically into music education. She quotes Whitehead's definition of "religious" from his essay "The Aims of Education":

> A religious education is an education which inculcates duty and reverence. Duty arises from our potential control over the course of events. Where attainable knowledge could have changed the issue, ignorance has the guilt of vice. And the foundation of reverence is this perception, that the present holds within itself the complete sum of existence, backwards and forwards, that whole amplitude of time, which is eternity. (1959, p. 43)

The model for seeing music as a truly spiritual phenomenon is in the Indigenous paradigm. Indigenous approaches to music are and have always been spiritual. Spirituality, in the Indigenous sense, embodies the idea of sacred reverence and duty that Whitehead describes. It is about giving significance to all and being intensely aware of one's personal relationship and interconnections with the universe. "It comes from the process of exploring and coming to know the nature of the living energy that moves in each of us, through us and around us" (Cajete 2000, p. 61). It is not about the individualism and consumerism that define music education today, something music educators have not sufficiently addressed but can now begin to solve.

Encouragingly, the National Art Educators Association has listed reasons why education in music and other arts is important, reasons that align well with Indigenous perspectives but that have not been adequately acknowledged by the curriculum. They are quoted in Eliot Eisner's book *Arts and Creation of Mind* (2002, pp. 66–67):

1. The arts teach children to make good judgments about qualitative relationships. Unlike much of the curriculum in which correct answers and rules prevail, in the arts, it is judgment rather than rules that prevail.
2. The arts teach children that problems can have more than one solution and that questions can have more than one answer.
3. The arts celebrate multiple perspectives. One of their large lessons is that there are many ways to see and interpret the world.
4. The arts teach children that in complex forms of problem solving purposes are seldom fixed, but change with circumstance and opportunity. Learning in the arts requires the ability and a willingness to surrender to the unanticipated possibilities of the work as it unfolds.
5. The arts make vivid the fact that neither words in their literal form nor numbers exhaust what we can know. The limits of our language do not define the limits of our cognition.
6. The arts teach students that small differences can have large effects. The arts traffic in subtleties.
7. The arts teach students to think through and within a material. All art forms employ some means through which images become real.
8. The arts help children learn to say what cannot be said. When children are invited to disclose what a work of art helps them feel, they must reach into their poetic capacities to find the words that will do the job.

9. The arts enable us to have experience we can have from no other source and through such experience to discover the range and variety of what we are capable of feeling.

10. The arts' position in the school curriculum symbolizes to the young what adults believe is important.

With these reasons in mind, the following list of values, concepts, goals and strategies related to Indigenous approaches to music can be used with whatever coursework you can connect them to and can bring the spiritual power of music into everyone's lives again:

1. Indigenous learning is holistic and tends to use "both sides of the brain." Music makes this easy. Although divisions between the right and left hemispheres in popular educational materials are often over-simplified, suffice it to say that music elicits activity in the corpus callosum. This creates a complementarity between various modes of thinking and communication. It ties emotional power to cognitive power. Singing ideas will help students remember them, so whatever course you are teaching can be an opportunity for creating song. Singing a greeting to the sun in the morning or a song to a friend should no longer seem a strange undertaking.

2. When important ideas are communicated to self or others through singing, word usage becomes more rhythmical for those who speak a mostly noun language like English as opposed to one of the verb languages of the Indigenous Peoples, which have the rhythm built in. Practicing singing can help bring students to a place where they begin to use words more carefully and with more musical flow and motion. This can help prevent the labeling and concretizing of communication.

3. A spiritual connection to music infers an awareness of how music and song connect us to our communities. What does a piece of music say about the human and non-human communities? Their strengths and needs? Some songs also connect us to invisible worlds. It is important for us to select songs and enjoy them with a sensitivity to these ideas. Analyzing them is not the goal, as music stimulates the intuitive part of our brains. Songs and a sacred awareness of them can affirm our links with the mystery of the cosmos. "Communication with the powerful and all pervasive spirits is established through the combination of sounds produced from musical instruments (most of which are believed

to be imbued with life), songs, and rituals" (Mather 2008, p. 107).

4. Use music to communicate between cultures and language groups whenever possible, either in person or via the Internet. Choose songs carefully or create your own. Sometimes music communicates best with those of different languages when you use words and sounds that have no translatable meaning in normal languages. Remember that one goal of Indigenous music is to reconnect the natural world to the spiritual world. "When Indigenous Peoples participate in music, they are aware that the rhythms, vibrations and sounds serve as a bridge between the visible and invisible worlds" (Jacobs 1998, p. 217). Reflect on the communication in terms of what was understood because of the music in spite of the differences.

5. Intentionally use music—whether songs for singing that are known or created, or sounds from drums, rattles or flutes, or combinations of these—to help heal yourself or someone or something else. This can be done whether the person, place or other entity in need of healing is able to hear the music or not. In Indigenous music, the content of the songs depends upon the occasions for which they are composed and on which they are sung.

6. Besides healing, there are other contexts for songs. What song you choose to listen to or play is best determined by context.

> Apart from communication with the spirits, the songs serve as a means of expressing intense emotions…reinstating the social order (as through the ritual of bithala), reviving the myth of origin, and accepting change in society (by composing new songs that not only make reference to the elements of change but also legitimate them as they become part of the collective memory)…[Indigenous songs] treat human beings as one of the many forms of life that are dependent on each other…Other songs, particularly the forest songs and those that accompany rituals punctuating the agricultural cycle, affirm the correspondence between trees, animals and human beings. (Mather 2008, pp. 108–109)

7. Whatever music you enjoy and/or perform with instruments or voice, keep in mind its relationship to the following:
   • Respect for self and all relationships
   • Service to others
   • Respect for diversity
   • Recognition of culture
   • Honoring appropriate traditions
   • A sense of history

- Vitality
- Sources of strong emotions
- Sense of place
- Transformation and/or tradition

Questions, Research, Dialogue, Choices and Praxis

(Note to teachers: Phrase the following to suit age and developmental levels in your class and according to what best complements your lesson plans.)

1. List examples of how music is used in American history, in movies and in the military to control or influence how we feel about what is happening. Give examples of how one might use music or song to escape from control. How do these ideas relate to Indigenous perspectives on music?
2. Study the words and music of rap and hip hop from various time periods and artists. Compare and contrast the ones that have a social consciousness with the ones that are designed to disparage.
3. When considering communication and language, do not let words alone limit your perspective. Consider silence, telepathic energy, art, dance, and music as equally valid (or more valid) ways of giving and receiving ideas or information.
4. Be selective in choosing background music because it will have an unconscious effect on you. Be conscious of how it makes you feel and share with your classmates examples of what you learn.
5. Vary the kind of music you listen to and try to be aware of the effect each kind of music has on your emotions, thoughts and attitude. Determine what kinds of music have what kinds of effects on you personally. Share your conclusions with classmates.
6. Use music as a collaborative way to share in community but not simply as a form of entertainment. Instead, listen to and participate in musical activities with a primal awareness of the joy and spirituality that community can share. Listen to each note. If the melody is sung, pay close attention to the lyrics, for the music can drive the ideas of the images portrayed deep into your psyche.
7. For one week, every morning go out and watch the morning come to life for five minutes while chanting with sounds that have no translatable meaning. Chant from your heart. Attempt to replicate the sounds of nature, even if all you can see is the sun, an insect or a plant.

8. Don't just listen to music; produce your own. If you do not already play a musical instrument, experiment with some traditional ones: play a rhythm on a drum, shake a rattle, try a flute, sing, whistle or hum. Especially sing, as the voice is the most important instrument in Indigenous cultures. Enjoy the uniqueness of your voice.

9. Visit the wilderness as often as possible and copy the songs of the birds and other animals and insects with your voice or a simple instrument. Unconsciously, you will begin to learn their language.

10. Buy plastic (PVC) Native American flutes for your class. (Tape the bottom three holes for younger children to make it easier to get solid notes.) Ask them to take their flutes outside and to create a composition about what they see. Maybe it is a landscape or the journey of a butterfly. When they return to the class, have the students guess what the other students' music is referring to.

11. There was a time when New Orleans jazz was spontaneous, before it was written down as sheet music and then played in standard ways to make the audience think it was spontaneous. It was "from the heart" and emotional in the ways Indigenous music is. Encourage students to learn music without the restraint of having to do it perfectly. I offer an example I have named the "Jacobs Thumb Method" after my Irish name. I have helped dozens of people learn how to play the piano with this simple four-step technique.[7]

    (1) Choose a favorite, meaningful melody and pick it, out hit or miss, only with your right thumb.

    (2) From a list of basic chords, choose one that sounds good with the melody and play it with the left hand as you wish until it sounds wrong for the melody—then find another one that sounds good. Often the note (A-G) will give a hint for the chord. So if the melody is playing a C, E or G, there is a good chance the C-chord, which has these notes in it, will work.

    (3) Begin a rhythm by using the left hand as follows: Play the first note in your three-note chord followed by the second two notes together (boom-cha). Now try to keep this rhythm going while you play and sing or hum the melody. (Singing along with playing is crucial, but let the piano follow, not lead, the singing.) This is a little like rubbing your head while patting your belly but can be mastered with practice.

    (4) Once you have the whole song learned this way, with the remaining fingers of the right hand, whenever you want, touch the notes you

can reach that are the same notes as in the chord you are using.

Now enjoy and share. And if this is too difficult, just play songs anyway you like on the black keys, even duets, and be amazed at how easy it is and how nice it will sound!

12. Join or start a drumming circle, and drum for peace and health for all of life.

13. Study Lakota inipi (sweat lodge) ceremonies and memorize one of the songs. If you can find someone who will invite you into the lodge who has done his or her Sun Dance vows, who knows the songs and prayers in the Lakota language and who believes your intentions are to help heal yourself and others, you will likely have a profound experience as a result of purifying while singing. (Your age and health are important considerations, as sweat lodge heat can be fatal if the person pouring the water is not sufficiently trained.)

14. Draw, paint or sculpt what you feel when listening to a song that stirs emotions in you.

15. We lose sight of the ways that people spontaneously engage in music throughout their lives and the skills that underlie personal music making, both of which could form a basis for more relevant school programs. How might instruction in music be more spontaneous and natural (Meyers 2005)?

Notes

1. I was involved in a project with the Seri Indians of northern Mexico where we recorded navigation songs that were being forgotten. Singing a song a certain way while paddling at a certain speed provides all sorts of information about underwater contours, fish, weather and location.

2. When Woody Guthrie sang his ballad about a character in Steinbeck's novel *The Grapes of Wrath* (1939) while playing his guitar, which had written on it, "This guitar kills fascists," Steinbeck jokingly cussed Woody out, saying he had written in seventeen stanzas what it had taken Steinbeck two years to write. See democracynow.org, archive dated July 12, 2012, which celebrates the 100th anniversary of Guthrie's birth.

3. U.S. Census Bureau, *Statistical Abstract of the United States: 2011*, 764, 762, http://www.census.gov/prod/2011pubs/11statab/arts.pdf.

4. The authors cite no sources. See http://www.nytimes.com/interactive/2012/03/24/opinion/20120324-opart-one-percent.html?hp.

5. http://www.namm.org/news/press-releases/new-gallup-survey-namm-reflects-majority-americans

6. As most music teachers know, there is substantial research showing numerous benefits. Looking up some of this research would be an excellent project for your students.

7. Now, before you music teachers shudder and take me to task, note that last month I competed in the 36th Annual Old Time Piano Playing Contest against classically trained musicians who performed complicated rags. (The rules required American songs published prior to 1929.) Unable to read music, I had no thoughts of placing in the top ten, but I placed fourth, using my self-taught "thumb method"! Just search for "Four Arrows Old Time Music" on YouTube to watch both my performances and those of the other top four.

7

English Language Arts

The emphasis, remember, is on making the school either part of the economy or making it into a commodity itself. The curriculum is often the textbook and textbooks are written to the specifications of what the most populous states want. Any content that is politically or culturally critical or can cause a negative reaction by powerful groups is avoided.

—MICHAEL APPLE, 2001, P. 2

Relative to a Native American oriented curriculum, holistic education means a fostering of a broader base and context for understanding, a multi-level approach that encourages understanding of many aspects at the same time and of the interrelationships involved, which, in turn, encourages involvement, ownership, and commitment. A technique for developing this holistic approach could be to encourage the dissolution of subject area boundaries.

—ROBERT W. RHODES, 1988, P. 1

Aboriginal languages reflect the cultural emphasis on experiential awareness. The intellectual and linguistic practice of reducing and generalizing characteristic of Western thought has the effect of lumping together all our different perceptions, thereby obscuring the nature of reality.

—ROBERT LAWLOR, 1991, P. 268

"The hole in the ice" is the classical way in English of describing the situation, but in Cree we say "the ice is wounded." It displays a completely different vision of the situation.

—ALAN FORD, 1992, P. 67

K-16 Teacher Instructions:

Adapt and use this chapter's information according to your students' ages and cognitive levels. Use as an introduction to your standard course content or weave values, ideas or critical reflections into it throughout the course. Encourage students to carefully reflect on this information with the goal of deciding what mainstream ideas are best replaced with Indigenous ones, which ones are best as they are, and how the two might be partnered in terms of practical benefits for the students and their community (local and global). Use the questions at the end of the chapter to help with this process and to stimulate primary source research and enthusiastic, critical dialogue. Since in Indigenous ways of thinking the ideas related to this subject have relevance to all the other subjects, you may want to incorporate some of this chapter's material into the study of another subject area. As with all chapters in this section, this chapter is organized as follows:

1. Corporate and Hegemonic Influences
2. Real-World Outcomes
3. Indigenous Curricular Alternatives
4. Questions for Research, Dialogue, Choices and Praxis

Corporate and Hegemonic Influences

So far, we have learned that corporate and hegemonic influences on education help maintain a sickness model where reliance on the medical industry is a priority. In music education, an "arts as entertainment" focus and a stifling of music expression overshadow deeper values and potential in service of the status quo. In language arts, hegemonic influences similarly stifle holistic and critical thinking and encourage the kind of superficial skills that work best for reading advertisements. Corporate influences also work toward selling curricula that call for purchasing significant numbers of instructional materials. Words are perhaps the most potent drug than mankind uses. An education that does not honor this realization makes us all susceptible to the deceptions that surround us in a never ending cycle of salesmanship. Education has the opportunity through teaching reading, writing and critical listening skills in ways that can allow people to take apart the illusions and deception that prevent understanding of contemporary reality. Or, it can make sure this does not happen!

Curriculum and pedagogy in English language arts (ELA) tend to suppress holistic approaches to reading and writing so as to diminish creativity and critical, independent thinking, keeping the masses "dumbed down," so to speak. Such goals are revealed in the text *Reading the Naked Truth: Literacy, Legislation and Lies.* The author, Gerald Coles, describes in great detail a report released by the federally sponsored National Reading Panel (NRP) in 2000 that has heavily influenced No Child Left Behind approaches to English[1] language arts and instruction in general. Coles concludes that the report favors "distinct skills" versus "holistic process" and that it strongly supports expert or direct instructional models. The report claims there is not sufficient evidence to support independent reading, reflection and discussion of books, a claim Cole easily disproves, ultimately showing that the NRP is an ideology-driven effort to support phonics and traditional dialectic learning models.[2]

Michael Apple's opening quotation is worth expanding upon here. He refers to how textbooks are used to control curricular content. Three states—Texas, Florida and California—essentially determine textbook policy because they make up about 35% of the textbook market and essentially determine the products that will be used nationwide. The school boards, especially in Texas and Florida, are strongly influenced by hegemonic agents, including the religious right, those who have bought into neo-conservative/neo-liberal ideology and those hegemons who are trying to protect their positions from a revolution of the masses. As we will see in subsequent chapters, politically or culturally critical material that might upset powerful groups or hurt sales is omitted, or material is inserted that tends to support the status quo. Literature is selected that tends to maintain feelings of white male superiority, that dismisses authentic multicultural perspectives, that puts a negative spin on labor unions and a positive one on free market economics, that shows U.S. policies as just and democratic and that fosters Christian beliefs and conservative values.

It is interesting that in the past, for these groups to maintain power, they had to compromise here and there when material seemed "too obvious." Today, the compromises are disappearing. The recent removal of Thomas Jefferson from history textbooks and the anti-ethnic-studies legislation in Arizona banning books like *Rethinking Columbus* and *The Tempest* are examples. Such problems can be countered by employing Indigenous perspectives to create a more dynamic, engaged classroom where English language arts involve place-based literatures and subjects vital to our current times. The power of words to engender change and the importance of recognizing the positive and negative aspects of this power can be taught better with this partnership as well. Reading and writing can be used with interactive storytelling approaches that allow students to "speak truth to power."

Although the ideology of hierarchy, control and "official knowledge" is surely a part of language arts hegemony, corporatism is there as well. There is profit to be made from publishing the kinds of phonics texts, multiple-choice tests and standards materials required for the implementation of the dominant state ideology. Although the current administration of U.S. president Barack Obama still seems to be a slave to these forces, it is worth noting here that a number of educators were aware of the connections between McGraw Hill, the largest publisher of such materials, and the false information used by the former administration of President George W. Bush to sell its reading and writing mandates. Jim Trelease, for example, in his article "All in the Family: The Bushes and the McGraws," cites the following account by journalist Stephen Metcalf:

> The amount of cross-pollination and mutual admiration between the Administration and [McGraw-Hill] is striking:
>
> Harold McGraw Jr. sits on the national grant advisory and founding board of the Barbara Bush Foundation for Family Literacy. McGraw in turn received the highest literacy award from President Bush in the early 1990s, for his contributions to the cause of literacy. The *McGraw Foundation* awarded current Bush Education Secretary Rod Paige its highest educator's award while Paige was Houston's school chief; Paige, in turn, was the keynote speaker at *McGraw-Hill's* "government initiatives" conference. Harold McGraw III was selected as a member of President George W. Bush's transition advisory team, along with *McGraw-Hill* board member Edward Rust Jr., the CEO of State Farm and an active member of the Business Roundtable on educational issues. An ex-chief of staff for Barbara Bush is returning to work for Laura Bush in the White House—after a stint with *McGraw-Hill* as a media relations executive. John Negroponte left his position as *McGraw-Hill's* executive vice president for global markets to become Bush's ambassador to the United Nations. (N.d.)

In light of the Bill and Melinda Gates Foundation's push for the Common Core State Standards, which are now being implemented by most states, there is a significant likelihood that the profits to be made from materials supporting the standards-based approach to learning are going to be seen as part of the reason for this approach. Whether this is true is yet to be known, but history shows that "high-stakes" standardized testing and standards-based learning are more likely to benefit vendors than students. I always find it remarkable how children, when left on their own in multilingual families, can be fluent in two, three or four languages by the time they are six years of age without the aid of "one size fits all" standards.

Indigenous languages, with far more words and concepts to master than European languages, are also traditionally learned without such formal structures. Rather, they are learned through active observation, respectful participation and interactive, engaged and relevant storytelling. Interestingly, although there is much research and support for the learning advantages of storytelling, it is seldom used to its full potential. Could this be because storytelling emphasizes personal connections that tend to cause resistance to impersonal political control and hierarchical structures? Or that it fosters collaborative communication and opens doors to realizing interconnectedness? I believe that education's history of suppressing such democratic ideals continues. Schooling is not supposed to foster the dispositions and abilities that might challenge corporatism, militarism and hegemony (Saltman & Gabbard, 2011).

Real-World Outcomes

In spite of all the rhetoric about critical thinking as an essential goal for learning to read and write, it is not a strong suit in the American citizenry. Critical thinking is about clarifying goals, examining assumptions and hidden agendas, evaluating evidence, taking appropriate action and reflecting on outcomes. As far back as 1972, the National Counsel for Teachers of English members have sought to improve critical literacy opportunities in coursework across the grade levels. They like many educators realize the importance of a population that can cope with the sophisticated persuasion techniques found in political statements, advertising and news. Unfortunately, forty years later ELA educators are still complaining about the absence of critical thinking. Because the Common Core State Standards (CCSS) are claiming to address critical thinking better in their new standards, NCTE is endorsing them, but not all of its members agree that critical thinking lessons are going to be effective. Instead, a number of educators believe the CCSS emphasis on one size fits all standards will make it less likely that students will become critical thinkers or have positive critical thinking dispositions. Donald Lazere describes this problem: "Although we continue to pay lip service to 'reading, writing and reasoning,' as the realm of our discipline, in practice that discipline has now become defined almost exclusively as writing instruction as an autonomous discipline, with reduced attention to the development of skills in reasoning and argumentation" (2011, p. 264).

In spite of the NCTE's support for the CCSS, it has also recognized that ELA instruction has been more about money making than about optimal holistic learning. For example, one member, a professor at Harvard University's Graduate School of Education, Jocelyn A. Chadwick, says that at the 2011 NCTE conference, entitled "Supporting High School ELA Instructors," someone joked that the reason everyone still uses the five-paragraph essay is because the vendors make money from it and no one really has to be engaged in critical and creative writing about things that matter:

> In response to the query: "How do we engage effectively students in the writing process?" there was an exasperated proclamation that vendors created the five-paragraph essay. Again, as we chuckled about that statement, a plethora of textbooks, assessments, and now computer-based approaches have emerged. So, yes, in a way, Alexander Bain's five-paragraph essay has evolved into a financial boon. (2012, p. 15)

It does not take much observation to note that communication between people today is not enriching the human spirit, fostering responsible citizenship or preserving the collective memory of a nation. Anger, deception, ego defensiveness, lack of humility, materialistic goals, illogic, fallacy, inadequate research skills, loss of critical thinking dispositions, closed-mindedness and the inability to argue cooperatively without trying to "win" a debate plague interpersonal and professional communication. A lack of open-mindedness seems to prevail. For years in my college courses for education majors, I asked on the first day of class for definitions of "open-mindedness." Answers typically included references to listening carefully, being polite, being willing to hear an alternative viewpoint and so forth. Rarely. if ever, did anyone say that open-mindedness required the readiness to change one's mind if the new information warranted.

With this in mind, in 2010 I invited Dr. Walter Block, a well-known libertarian professor to co-author a book with me even though we had vehemently disagreed over the years about the best approach to social or ecological justice education. I wanted to see whether we, as two intelligent people with polarized views, could actually learn to understand one another and even possibly change or modify each other's positions by communicating in ways intended to ensure mutual comprehension instead of personal victory in a debate. It was difficult for me to hear from Walter that animals have no intrinsic value, only utilitarian value for humans, and that free enterprise and the end of labor unions are the only ways to social or ecological justice. It was equally challenging for Walter, an avowed "Jewish atheist libertarian," to hear my "liberal" points of view. However, Walter and I became friends. We did learn from one another, and although neither of us budged on most of our positions, we did find common ground. After our book, *Differing Worldviews: Two Scholars Argue Cooperatively*, was published, we spoke together before a large audience at St. Louis University, and the response was overwhelmingly positive. People claimed at the book signing that they had not seen two polarized speakers communicate before with such humor, respect, and open-mindedness.

In our polarized, split world today, the importance of such real-world communication based on love, open-mindedness and critical thinking skills is at an all-time high. This especially relates to the lack of critical thinking that ultimately allows false information to continue our ignorance about climate change issues, wars and economic realities.[3] The ability to think critically would automatically counter the real-world bias in much of today's ELA materials, a bias that contributes to structural inequalities and prejudice against women, people of color, people with non-normative gender and sexual orientations, people with disabilities and other marginalized groups. Critical thinking is, according to a Wikipedia definition, about clarifying goals, examining assumptions, discerning hidden values, evaluating evidence, accomplishing appropriate actions and assessing results. Despite the importance of these skills, the disposition to use them is lacking among people, especially among teachers themselves. The California Critical Thinking Disposition Inventory, developed in 1987, is often used in psychological research, and the conclusions reveal consistently low scores for a variety of people from a variety of occupations. Study them and consider for yourself how well they are realized in the real world.

Seven Subscales of the California Critical Thinking Dispositions Inventory

Disposition	Description
Truth seeking	Measures intellectual honesty, the courageous desire for best knowledge in any situation, the inclination to ask challenging questions and to follow the reasons and evidence wherever they lead.
Open-mindedness	Measures tolerance for new ideas and divergent views.
Analyticity	Measures alertness to potential difficulties and being alert to the need to intervene by the use of reason and evidence to solve problems.
Systematicity	Measures the inclination to be organized, including focus, diligence and perseverance.
Critical Thinking Confidence	Measures trust in one's own reasoning and ability to guide others to make rational decisions.
Inquisitiveness	Measures intellectual curiosity and intention to learn things even if their immediate application is not apparent.
Maturity	Measures judiciousness which inclines one to see the complexity in problems and to desire prudent decision-making, even in uncertain conditions.

Source: From Facione, P.A., Facione, N.C., & Giancarlo, C. (2001). *California critical thinking disposition inventory.* Millbrae, CA: California Academic Press, pp. 2–3.

A number of studies using this matrix show that critical thinking dispositions are low in the United States, but it is even more appalling to realize that teachers rate among the lowest! One of my colleagues when I was at Northern Arizona University, Karen Sealander, co-authored a major study showing that of all college majors, education majors have the lowest scores (Eigenberer, Sealander , & Jacobs, 2001, pp. 109–122). In his doctoral dissertation on "Studies on Critical Thinking for Environmental Ethics," Courtney Quinn investigated critical thinking development for students in higher education regarding environmental, agricultural, and natural resource ethical issues. His literature review shows that many researchers find low levels of critical thinking skills and critical thinking dispositions, regardless of assessment methods:

> Though critical thinking is often a stated educational goal, encouragement and development of critical thinking in university classrooms is rare. Overall, the conclusion is that the university system does not consistently produce critical thinkers. Mahaffy laments the struggle of instructors who encourage students to engage in critical exploratory research beyond a cursory Google search....Rudd et al. found deficits in the critical thinking of agricultural students. Zimdahl concluded that the lack of critical thinking in environmental and agricultural university programs extends to faculty who judge agriculture's progress by technological success but disregard ethical questions raised by that success.[4] (Quinn, 2012, pp. 11–12)

One peer-reviewed article on ELA instruction in China showed that students had higher critical thinking dispositions when they were freshmen than when they were seniors. Ma Yu's article "On the Critical Thinking Disposition of English Majors" includes a number of supporting citations. I could not find a reference in any of them to American hegemony as responsible, but it is worth noting that the students did use the same American textbooks and pedagogical approaches as are often used in American undergraduate schools.

Peter Smagorinsky is one of the many ELA instructors whose writing attempts to put reading, writing and oral communication into a more holistic framework for schools, one that parallels Indigenous perspectives. In his textbook *Teaching by Design*, he says that although it is falling out of favor in universities, the dominant approach to English language arts causes the kind of polarization referred to above. "People who take an authoritative view of the world tend to take a competitive and aggressive stance toward other people. In a discussion, their goal is to win and so assert their greater authority, rather than to compromise, co-construct new knowledge, or learn more about the other people" (2008, p. 15). He also says that the current "transmission" model and the five-paragraph essay for teaching composition in most elementary, middle and high schools have resulted in a population that is missing out on the following opportunities:

1. Using reading and writing to offer incomparable experiences of shared conflict, wisdom, understanding and beauty.
2. Expressing ideas cogently and to construct valid and truthful arguments and honing the ability to express defensible reflections about literature will ensure comprehension and understanding.
3. Understanding that reading, writing, listening and speaking are not disembodied skills, but that exists in context and in relation to others. (2008, p. 4)

Indigenous Curricular Alternatives

Clearly, the relational components of communication education in the traditional ELA curriculum, which are supposed to "enrich human relationships" and make for "responsible citizenship," are not a priority. An education that focuses on only comparing and contrasting, defining, classifying, judging, measuring and strictly adhering to rigid writing structures is not likely to accomplish truth-seeking and a life in balance, the ultimate goals of Indigenous education. Schools must incorporate relevant, interactive storytelling and reflective dialogue that nurtures the natural curiosity and interests of students. Such narrative approaches and storytelling have been studied and encouraged by many non-Indian educators for a long while. Storytelling is a kind of conversation, which is part of Parker Palmer's definition of truth-seeking,[5] which he agrees is the goal of education. In his popular book *The Courage to Teach*, he writes that "truth is an eternal conversation about things that matter, conducted with passion and discipline" (1997, p. 104). Indigenous approaches to developing communication skills use storytelling as a way to teach us how to foster healthy relationships with people and the natural world. (Note that inclusion of "the natural world" adds something new to even the most ideal goals of mainstream ELA visions, which refer to only enriching the human spirit and responsible citizenship).[6]

After conducting a grant-supported study attempting to answer why storytelling is such an important way for Aboriginal teachers to teach important lessons, Melanie MacLean and Linda Wason-Ellam (2006) concluded that it:

1. Creates a dynamic of interactive shared learning and equality among learners.
2. Moves learning away from one expert opinion and toward honoring many voices with experience of how to best function in community.

3. Develops trusting relationships, a caring community and respect for others.
4. Teaches virtues like loyalty, responsibility, honesty, humility and sharing.
5. Increases listening skills and fosters interpersonal communication.
6. Makes learning relevant to our daily lives.
7. Offers multiple layers of meaning for continued and dynamic reflection.
8. Teaches that multiple perspectives are possible and may be equally valid.
9. Allows students a chance to reveal their knowledge and have it acknowledged.
10. Builds conceptual bridges between students' own experiences and new knowledge.
11. Professionalizes teaching so as to move away from scripted textbooks and pre-determined lesson plans.
12. Fosters respect for diversity and does not discriminate based on gender or non-normative gender and sexual orientations.[7]

This list may show why hegemonic education does not encourage storytelling, but more importantly, it offers educators a strong motivation to incorporate storytelling into schools and classrooms in order to counterbalance state hegemony. For Indigenous teaching and learning, this list explains why storytelling is a "fundamental communicative pattern" (Bighead, 1997, p. 81). It is fundamental because it is about analogy. According to linguists and cognitive scientists, the human mind specializes in learning through analogies (Lakoff & Johnson, 1980; Hofstadter, 2006; Pinker, 2007). Indigenous Peoples have understood this for thousands of years. To create understanding, we make sense of something outside of our experiences by holding it next to something from our experience, not as an equal substitute but to allow for meaningful reflection. Cajete writes that for Indigenous Peoples, "practice contexting information in culturally sensitive and holistic ways" (1994, p. 139) is central to making meaning.

It is vital to remember that Indigenous stories often use animals for context and learning for good reasons. From the Indigenous perspective, animals are our teachers:

> For the Oglala, no animal is insignificant. Black Elk told me that "one should pay attention to even the smallest crawling creature for these too may have a valuable lesson to teach us, and even the smallest ant may wish to communicate to a man. They also have power, or wochangi, which they will share if humans are attentive. (Brown, 1992, p. 28)

One of my former doctoral students, Sarah Olivia Garcia, did a remarkable study for her dissertation using American Indian animal stories entitled "The Influence of American Indian Storytelling on the Character and Ecological Awareness of Participating Non-Indian Children and Their Parents." She found that parent-child readings and reflections on selected American Indian stories resulted in enhanced awareness and behaviors for both parents and children as relates to ecological sustainability and to generosity and respect (2012). Beyond using your own stories as the teacher, the stories of community members invited to class and the students' stories, you can also use Indigenous stories to promote values we need in our world today.[8]

Indigenous perspectives also require ELA teachers to be aware of the fact that the English language is less able than Indigenous languages to prevent absolutes, categories and inflexible interpretations. Especially in the languages of America's Indigenous Peoples, multi-verb constructions are common and render declarations flowing and time dependent. In teaching English language arts, teachers who understand how a noun-based language like English can impede holistic learning and lead to labeling and other linguistic traps can avoid them. This can be done with more verbs, more clarifying adjectives, more caveats, clarity in general and interactive engagement with students. Rudyard Kipling said, "Words are mankind's most potent drug," and from the Indigenous perspective, words are like prayers. So take great care in how you use them. This awareness of the power of words is also important when seeking to move beyond the formulaic curricula and simplistic assessments found in typical language arts.

The importance of considering the effects of "noun-languages" like English is emphasized in the following part of a dialogue between physicist David Bohm and Sa'ke'j, a Mi'kmaq Algonquin scholar:

> Sa'ke'j: I struggle with getting the nouns. "Verb-object-noun." I don't think in English. I'm thinking in verbs. My eyes can see nouns and tracks. This is not the function of the language…not to become another pair of eyes. It's supposed to be speaking to the ear and to the heart. Language is about rhythm….Noun-people don't think they change because of their noun categories….Verbs are states of being multiplied. A verb language is very particular and very local. Because each time it is spoken there may be a root that new has new prefixes and suffixes add to delineate clearly this moment's reactions, so it is always created anew. Unlike the English language, the use of the possessive in Algonquian languages is simply to indicate the relationship between the person and the thing. Finally, it is difficult to say anything without identifying automatically that the source of information is not from the personal experience of the speaker….So we allow maximum diversity of thought because we have no form of censorship. We don't even have the noun-god to tell us "yes" or "no." So when you take away all these props of Indo-European languages you take away

the center of all the method. And the Indo-European method tried to derive God as a noun's plan for the universe and therefore your new knowledge….In a verb language you don't reason that way. All you share is knowledge and experience, and all your knowledge is, is the equivalent to your experiences, your visions, your dreams. (Peat, 1992, pp. 28–29)

Flow psychologist Sid Promak says it this way:

> Our disconnect from one another, from ourselves and from the natural world is embedded in the Western languages, which break the world into millions of discrete, manipulable pieces, called nouns. Westerners control reality through language, but they don't evoke it. Indigenous languages in contrast are verb-based, intrinsically linking speaker and object in a "flow" of motion that cannot be linguistically sliced and diced. (Promak, n.d.)

Merely being aware of this problematic in the English language will go a long way toward helping you implement the Indigenous perspective. Use words carefully and emphasize the potential for continual change. For example, we might tell someone, "Look how big the moon is," thereby confirming the illusion semantically as well as visually. A child hearing this comment from an authority figure might form a misconception about the moon. From an Indigenous perspective, a teacher would be more careful and expand the statement with something like, "Look, my eyes are showing me in this moment, while the sun is fading in the west, that the moon is bigger, maybe because it seems closer to the Earth or perhaps for other reasons we do not understand, so I do not think it is actually bigger than it was before."

Taking more care with accuracy when speaking to students will help ensure your lessons are as much about building relationships (per the lists above) as about technical structures per se. Below, note the standard goals, benchmarks and objectives that are the desired outcomes when teaching second graders an American Indian story. If you are an elementary grade teacher, reflect on how they contrast with your own ELA standards and how they can be used to complement them. Whatever grade level you teach, you can compare these ideas with your own standards to get a sense of how you can complement your content and lessons by incorporating the Indigenous perspective.

Standards:

- Students read and understand a variety of materials.
- Students write and speak for a variety of purposes and audiences.
- Students apply thinking skills to their reading, writing, speaking, listening, and viewing.
- Students read and recognize literature as a record of human experience.

Benchmarks:

- Students will use information from their reading to increase vocabulary and language usage.
- Students will read literature to understand places, people, events and vocabulary both familiar and unfamiliar.

Objectives:

- Students will create a mobile using the characters from the story.
- Students will practice creating their own version of the story as well as working on their fine motor skills.
- Students will listen to an American Indian animal story being read.[9]

The idea of students creating their own versions of stories relates to the understanding that if we do not realize our ability to create our own interpretations of words, we can become effectively hypnotized into uncritically accepting some externally induced reality.

This presentation has largely been about the relational goals and critical thinking objectives in English language arts. I have not offered specific guidelines for reading and writing beyond whole language approaches, storytelling in its various forms, and dialogue based on authentic and critical thinking because they do not exist in the Indigenous perspective apart from these goals and objectives being implemented through modeling and storytelling. Indigenous learning, as you may recall from Chapter Four, is about learning not from failure but from success. Giving children time to watch and listen until they are confident about participating is the Indigenous way. The goal here is to complement mainstream approaches, and I think the Indigenous perspectives presented here can do this well.

I also believe that people can learn to read and write well enough if they learn to communicate orally well. The Cherokee proved this when they created an alphabet and in short order began writing profusely. When a Cherokee syllabary was introduced in 1819, thousands of Cherokee learned how to write their language in a matter of days owing to their mastery of oral communication. In the 1830s they established a network in Oklahoma of over two hundred writing and reading classrooms. Tribal literacy rose by 90 percent. Journalism began in Georgia with the *Cherokee Phoenix*, which was published in both Cherokee and English. Now the Cherokee language, both oral and written, is on the verge of extinction.[10] The reason for this is suggested in a Cherokee elder's words to students: "Remember that the whites are near us. With them we have constant intercourse, and you must be sensible, that unless you can speak their language, read and write as they do, they will be able to cheat you and trample on your rights" (Nabokov 1992, p. 215). The U.S. "Indian education" policies ended the Cherokee's pursuit of optimal learning by introducing boarding schools that essentially used the same approaches to learning that are used today.

Universal language advocates like Noam Chomsky tend to agree that the Cherokee's more natural learning of language reflects the ability of infants and children to learn multiple languages rapidly and that contemporary schooling inhibits such natural learning. David Abram refers to aspects of language that are outside of systems of terminological, syntactic or semantic rules as "expressive speech." He believes that all truly meaningful speech is inherently creative and "wild." It comes from an interconnected matrix of intuitions and gestures (1996). Bringing this all the way up to what might be the most sophisticated representation of mainstream academic work, the doctoral dissertation, I refer to "out of the box" dissertation stories from around the world that honor this "wilder" approach in my text *The Authentic Dissertation: Alternative Ways of Knowing, Research and Representation*:

The dissertation stories tap into more diverse perspectives, more authentic experience and reflection, and more creative abilities than standard dissertations typically offer. They are, in essence, spiritual undertakings that:

- Honor the centrality of the researcher's voice, experience, creativity and authority
- Focus more on important questions than on research methodologies per se
- Reveal virtues (generosity, patience, courage, respect, humility, fortitude, etc.)
- Regard the *people's* version of reality.
- The goal of this book is not to replace the historical values of academic research in the Western tradition, but to challenge some of these values and offer alternative ideas that stem from different, sometimes opposing, values. (Four Arrows, 2008, p. i, original emphasis)

So let us begin to challenge the historic values that have brought us to the brink of extinction as educators. We must now offer alternative ideas in mainstream schools from kindergarten through undergraduate studies. We can begin to influence ecological sustainability priorities by being more careful with our language, and more attentive to the language of others. It is through language that we distort our understanding of the world.

Questions for Research, Dialogue, Choices and Praxis

1. Think of as many sentences as possible that answer the question "What kind of a tree is that?" This exercise works best if you can refer to a particular tree that everyone can see, but doing so is not necessary. The goal is to make the description as rich and potentially changeable as it can be. So instead of saying, "It is an oak tree," one might say, "It is a growing tree with acorns now being eaten by squirrels," or "It is in the oak tree family and currently its branches are bending from the wind and rain," and so on.

2. Randomly choose news items that can be made significant for the age of the students and determine their level of "truthfulness" by using intuition, critical thinking and research.

3. Read any selected piece of required literature and offer as many interpretations of it as the class can come up with.

4. Read a story about some individual and identify to what degree courage, generosity, patience, fortitude, humiliy and honesty were or were not demonstrated.

5. Share whether the last mainstream lesson made you uncomfortable in any way. Did it foster competition or collaboration?

6. Tell someone who writes well a short, one-paragraph story about something you like or think is important and have him or her write it down. It may be easier if you first record your story using a tape recorder or computer, but doing so is not necessary. If you change your story upon repeating it, that is fine.

7. Read a book that is above your reading level and guess what it is saying. If time permits, the teacher can talk about how close your interpretation is to the actual meaning.

8. In the next material you read, look for discrimination. Is there bias or bias by ommission against any group of people?

9. Discuss the idea that animals can be teachers to humans.

10. After you are finished your next writing assignment, write it again as a poem, as a graph, as a song or in pictures.

11. Practice telepathy and intuition with the following exercise. Have someone sit at the front of the room facing away from the others. The group will look at the person with love and respect in their hearts when the teacher quietly points to the person. It will look away from the person and try to think about something else when the teacher points

away. The objective is for the student in front to identify when the class is looking at or away from him or her. With practice, the outcome is better than 50–50.

12. Think of fears you may have and attach them to the words that you believe describe why you are afraid. Are the words really true? Have a glimpse at Chapter Thirteen, "From Fear to Fearlessness," which introduces about the CAT-FAWN mnemonic. How will realizing the hypnotic power of language, especially during stress, influence your use of words?[11]

13. There are many language tricks people use to persuade others. Recognizing them can prevent us from accepting statements uncritically. Listen to a political speech by a politician or talk show host (like Rush Limbaugh) and even without knowing the names of such communication strategies as "either-or" or "circular reasoning," attempt to identify the words and sentences that might put you on guard for possible deception.[12]

Notes

1. There is a significant body of literature about the hegemony related to pushing English-only instruction in schools as well as promoting English as superior in international circles. This section does not refer to this aspect of hegemony but only to that which helps dictate mainstream education.

2. I remember a Grade 2 teacher who believed in "whole language" and holistic instruction as a way to teach children to read. She had bought thirty or forty children's books for grade levels one through four over the years at garage sales for a dollar or less and would take them to class and dump them on the floor. The children would search through them looking for the one they wanted to "read" for twenty or thirty minutes, however much time they needed. Over the years this approach proved very successful in helping children read and comprehend. One day, with a new principal in place, the practice was curtailed.

3. Putting aside the fact that the United States ranks around fortieth in literacy worldwide, I feel that reading, writing, critical thinking and verbal communication are the priorities for English language arts.

4. Citations omitted. This dissertation is published online, so the omitted citations can be found by searching Google for the article's title.

5. Palmer is clear that truth is a multifaceted gem that one can know better after dialogue but is still not easily articulated in absolute terms. Indigenous storytelling similarly reaches for the likeness of truth that allows each participant—teller and listener—ways to insert their own aspects of the truth into the truth equation.

6. Gerald Vizenor's "Aesthetics of Survivance" (2008) does an admirable job of explaining how Indigenous narratives are expansive and diverse in perspective but local and contextualized at

the same time. Moreover, they allow memories and dreams to serve as possibilities for renewal. This prevents ideas from becoming controlled and rigid.

7. Benjamin and Irwin-DeVitis (1998) write in a peer-reviewed article entitled "Censoring Girls' Choices: Continued Gender Bias in English Language Arts" about classrooms that have identified gender bias. Other studies reveal similar problems with regard to non-normative sexual orientations such as gay and lesbian.

8. American Indian stories are easily accessible for all grade levels.

9. From Denisse Engstrom's second grade curriculum for a four-week unit on American Indian storytelling for the La Raza curriculum in Denver public schools; see http://etls.dpsk12.0rg/documents/Alma/units/AmericanIndianStorytelling.pdf. Note that it was the La Raza curriculum that was made illegal in Arizona under the "ban on ethnic studies" law described in Chapter One.

10. The syllabary consists of eighty-six letters representing all of the sounds in Tsalagi (Cherokee), and the grammar comes from oral understandings of the complex structures and tones. Here is an example of what Tsalagi looks like, followed by a rough translation:

    Nigada aniyvwi nigeguda'lvna ale unihloyi unadehna duyukdv gesv'i. Gejinela unadanvtehdi ale unohlisdi ale sagwu gesv junilvwisdanedi anahldinvdlv adanvdo gvhdi. / All human beings are born free and equal in dignity and rights. They are endowed with reason and conscience and should act towards one another in a spirit of brotherhood. (Article 1 of the Universal Declaration of Human Rights)

11. During times of stress, words, even those uttered in gest, can become fixed in the patient's mind and cause untold harm." In my book *Patient Communication for the First Responder,* I show how first responders can avoid this effect by using words and phrases in addition to standard medical care when possible to direct healing in the body with the assumption that stress makes all people hyper-suggestible to the communication of a perceived, trusted authority figure. Six months after this book was published by Prentice-Hall in 1998, it was remaindered in response to political pressure claiming that only medical doctors should be able to use the strategies I offered.

12. In my book, *The Bum's Rush: The Selling of Environmental Backlash (Phrases and Fallacies of Rush Limbaugh* (1994), I list "red flags of persuasion" and use them to identify Limbaugh's linguistic fallacies in his claims we have no environmental problems.

8

United States History

With guest author Barbara Alice Mann

What has been (deceptively and erroneously) referred to as "revisionist history" has usually been the other side of the story, setting it straight.
—FRANK T. DEANGELIS, 2001, P. 185

If you believe people have no history worth mentioning, it's easy to believe they have no humanity worth defending.
—WILLIAM LOREN KATZ

This is really a political philosophy under the disguise of Mexican American studies.
—ARIZONA SUPERINTENDENT OF PUBLIC INSTRUCTION JOHN HUPPENTHAL DEFENDING HIS BAN ON BOOKS SUCH AS *RETHINKING COLUMBUS: THE NEXT 500 YEARS* AND *PEDAGOGY OF THE OPPRESSED* ON *DEMOCRACYNOW*, JANUARY 18, 2012

Let us examine the facts of your present eruptions into our country, and we shall discover your pretentions on that ground.
—CORN TASSEL, CHEROKEE, 1991, P. 123

K-16 Teacher Instructions:

Adapt and use this chapter's information according to your students' ages and cognitive levels. Use as an introduction to your standard course content or weave values, ideas or critical reflections into it throughout the course. Encourage students to carefully reflect on this information with the goal of deciding what mainstream ideas are best replaced with Indigenous ones, which ones are best as they are, and how the two might be partnered in terms of practical benefits for the students and their community (local and global). Use the questions at the end of the chapter to help with this process and to stimulate primary source research and enthusiastic, critical dialogue. Since in Indigenous ways of thinking the ideas related to this subject have relevance to all the other subjects, you may want to incorporate some of this chapter's material into the study of another subject area. As with all chapters in this section, this chapter is organized as follows:

1. Corporate and Hegemonic Influences
2. Real-World Outcomes
3. Indigenous Curricular Alternatives
4. Questions for Research, Dialogue, Choices and Praxis

Corporate and Hegemonic Influences

As mentioned previously, the California State Board of Education has adopted the common core standards put forward by the National Governor's Association. Thus the language California uses to introduce its history and social science standards will be seen in the language of many other state's prefaces to history. The introduction in these standards for English Language Arts, similar to that in most states, begins with what might be hegemonic deception. I italicize the sentences that I assert are hegemonic. Following the quotation, I briefly explain why I make this claim.

> The California State Board of Education has worked hard with the Academic standards Commission to develop history-social science standards that reflect California's commitment to history-social science education. These standards emphasize historical narrative, *highlight the roles of significant individuals throughout history*, and *convey the rights and obligations of citizenship*.
>
> In that spirit the standards proceed chronologically and call attention to *the story of America as a noble experiment in a constitutional republic*. They recognize that America's ongoing struggle to realize the ideals of the Declaration of Independence and the U.S. Constitution is the struggle to maintain our beautifully complex national heritage of *e pluribus unum*. While *the standards emphasize Western civilizations as the source of American political institutions, laws, and ideology*, they also expect students to analyze the changing political relationships within and among other countries and regions of the world, both

throughout history and *within the context of contemporary global interdependence.*

…these standards require students not only to acquire core knowledge in history and social science, but also *to develop the critical thinking skills* that historians and social scientists employ to study the past and its relationship to the present.

Highlight the roles of significant individuals throughout history

Significant to whom? Books like James Loewen's well-known *Lies My Teacher Told Me* (1995) and Howard Zinn's classic text *A People's History of the United States: 1492-Present* (1980) reveal many significant people of America's history who are ignored or misrepresented in history books. The list is too long to replicate here, so I will refer to only two that exemplify how misleading this phrase is, beginning with the removal of Thomas Jefferson, one of the most influential philosophers in American history, from the history books by the Texas School Board, which we know from a previous chapter will cause Jefferson to be removed from books across the land. Why was he removed? Because Jefferson was a Deist and a revolutionist who coined the phrase "separation between church and state." The majority of the board are Christian right conservatives. Led by attorney Cynthia Dunbar, this group's members ensured that future history books will support their incorrect belief that the nation was founded on Christian rather than Deist beliefs, and they also cut Jefferson from a list of figures whose writings inspired revolutions. One of Jefferson's often quoted sayings is "Every generation needs a new revolution" to maintain democracy. According to an article in the education section of the *New York Times* on March 12, 2010, it was not enough to remove the significant individuals in American history who neoliberals do not like, but an accurate telling of history itself also had to be prevented:

> Mavis B. Knight, a Democrat from Dallas, introduced an amendment requiring that students study the reasons "the founding fathers protected religious freedom in America by barring the government from promoting or disfavoring any particular religion above all others."
>
> It was defeated ten to five on a party-line vote.
>
> After the vote, Ms. Knight said, "The social conservatives have perverted accurate history to fulfill their own agenda." (McKinley, 2010, p. A-10)

Such censorship in textbooks may be reaching new extremes but it is not new. One of the best examples of how official knowledge "highlights the roles of significant individuals throughout history" to suit its own agenda is what education has taught most of the world about Helen Keller. Most people know who she was and that she is a significant American hero, but few know the actual role she played in American history because it has been censored. Most remember her as an American heroine who displayed great courage in overcoming the obstacles presented by an illness that left her deaf and blind. Few will know that she was an outspoken anti-war activist and a member of the Socialist Party of America. Nor will they know she supported the radical labor union the Industrial Workers of the World or that she campaigned for women's suffrage, labor rights, socialism and other radical left causes. These were intentionally left out of most curricula because having a hero with this history is not in the interest of the growing corporatist "ruling" class, whose agenda for years has been to destroy labor unions and fight against liberal ideas they brand as "socialistic" like national health insurance or social welfare.

Ruth Shagoury, a professor at Lewis and Clark College who holds the Mary Stuart Rogers Chair of Education, exposed this problem recently on the website Common Dreams. Referring to Gare Thompson's widely used middle school textbook *Who Was Helen Keller?* (2003), she writes in part,

> Americans at large would be shocked to learn that she grew up to be an avowed socialist, a suffragette, was actively involved in workers rights, union promotion, and opposing racism. In 1912 she wrote "How I Became a Socialist." In 1920 she helped to found the American Civil Liberties Union (ACLU), and supported the NAACP. She supported Socialist Party candidate Eugene V. Debs in each of his campaigns for the presidency. Yet this book never mentions any of that. Never mentions or even alludes to her activism and political beliefs. Those are immense omissions. Any one of those things would be extremely significant, let alone for happening when and where they did. But the book is even worse, for it lies not just in omissions, but directly in its representation of specific events in her life…and hides what would be very interesting circumstances from which to draw great discussion material and topics for students….From publishers like Scholastic Teaching Resources—which uses her life events to "give children practice reading a timetable" by asking insipid questions such [as]: "How can you use the first two dates to figure out Helen's age at the time she got sick?"—to St. Aidan's Home School pages, which encourages teachers to show "the Disney version of the The Miracle Worker," the information on-line portrays the same individualistic and socially empty Helen Keller myth. (Shagoury 2012)

Perhaps the back cover of Thompson's book says all I want to say about the need for an Indigenous perspective that can complement both the objective of today's curriculum and his objective of highlighting the roles of significant people in American history. "Who Was Helen Keller?" it asks. Then, in keeping with today's emphasis on standardized tests, the book presents readers with a multiple-choice format for the answer and, as most textbooks for young people do, offers the answer:

[ ] A woman who could not see or hear
[ ] A best-selling author
[ ] A famous world traveler
[✓] All of the above!

Convey the rights and obligations of citizenship

According to the common core curriculum, the second thing that the content standards for U.S. history achieve is the teaching of the obligations of citizenship. I was curious what popular websites like Yahoo and Wikipedia had to offer in response to a search for "obligations of a citizen," and over and over this list appeared:

- Obey laws
- Pay taxes
- Defend the country
- Respond to jury duty
- Maintain allegiance and loyalty

Occasionally, "register for the draft" was thrown in. Then I looked at the content of instruction across age groups in the curriculum and saw why the above answers were so often repeated. There was little that seemed to satisfy or serve what Thomas Jefferson called for in his famous letters about the obligations of citizens:

> I know no safe depositary of the ultimate powers of the society but the people themselves; and if we think them not enlightened enough to exercise their control with a wholesome discretion, the remedy is not to take it from them, but to inform their discretion by education. This is the true corrective of abuses of constitutional power.
>
> Every government degenerates when trusted to the rulers of the people alone. The people themselves, therefore, are its only safe depositories. And to render even them safe, their minds must be improved to a certain degree.
>
> The most effectual means of preventing [the perversion of power by tyranny are] to illuminate, as far as practicable, the minds of the people at large, and more especially to give them knowledge of those facts which history exhibits, that possessed thereby of the experience of other ages and countries, they may be enabled to know ambition under all its shapes, and prompt to exert their natural powers to defeat its purposes.
>
> The information of the people at large can alone make them safe as they are the sole depositary of our political and religious freedom.

Of course, one does not have to highlight significant Americans when they are taken out of the curriculum.

The story of America as a noble experiment in a constitutional republic

In addition to Barbara Mann's presentation that follows, I suggest the reader and students of all appropriate ages watch the free online documentary *The New American Century* (2007). Also, for a short course in the truth about contemporary American history, read the booklet by the most decorated U.S. Marine in history, General Smedley Butler. His book *War Is a Racket* (1935) explains how the United States military has been all about taking down democratically elected governments around the world and putting in puppet "Al Capone"—type dictators so that U.S. corporations could rape a country's resources without resistance.[1]

We must also consider the shadow side of the otherwise "noble" experiment in light of the founding "fathers" treatment of slaves, women and Indians in early U.S. history and the widespread financial corruption operating in the system today. I cannot help but mention, too, the almost certain fraud continuing to operate in the world due to perpetuation of the official theory about what happened on 9/11. This staged event and a number of similar probable actions have been used to justify U.S. invasions of other countries (I'm thinking of "my" war, Vietnam, and the fraudulent Gulf of Tonkin resolution). For more on the intentional deception of the official 9/11 story, see my co-authored article "Classroom Silence about 9/11: A Failure of Education?" (2011). It is about the impossibility that the events of September 11, 2001, could have happened as the official story says they did and how education has failed to engage critically with the overwhelming evidence against the U.S. government's claims. I was unable to get the article published in a U.S. peer-reviewed journal and had to go to one outside the U.S.

The standards emphasize Western civilizations as the source of American political institutions, laws, and ideology

This is another unfortunate statement that represents the hegemony in the mainstream curriculum, one that can easily be rebalanced by an Indigenous perspective and more accurate historical truths. As for the most basic American institution, the U.S. government, there is significant scholarship to show that the founding fathers borrowed heavily from the democratic structures and forms of government used and practiced by the Iroquois. The Haudenosaunee (Iroquois) Confederacy is one of the oldest continually operating consensual governments in the world according to research completed by the guest author for this chapter, Barbara Alice Mann. She and her co-author Jerry Fields make a strong case that the five nations made their final agreement on the confederacy's foundational laws in 1142 (Mann and Fields 1997). For many years beginning in the 1700s, the Haudenosaunee negotiated numerous treaties with the English and until around 1800 most used the Native protocol (Johansen 2005, p. 141). American Indians and the early European colonists were in close contact, and many knew about the "great laws" of the Haudenosaunee Confederacy. The founding fathers, impressed with the confederacy's democratic values and its difference from the monarchies of Europe, borrowed significantly from the its principles to design the U.S. government's structure and constitution, starting with the Albany Plan of Union (1754). [2] Thomas Jefferson, in fact, was one of the first to write about the virtues of the American Indian government months before the first constitutional convention. These letters, which praise the Iroquois confederacy, observing that its members enjoyed 'infinitely greater degrees of happiness than those who live under European governments" (Boyd 1950, p. 49), may be another reason why he has been voted out of the history books, along with Thomas Paine.

In fact, Thomas Paine's treatment in U.S. History alone should be sufficient to make the case for educational hegemony's influence on curriculum. Paine also used the American Indian as a source for inspiring freedom. He wrote, "To understand what the state of society ought to be, it is necessary to have some idea of the natural state of man, such as it is at this day among the Indians of North America" (Foner 1945, p. 610). His book, *The Rights of Man*, was almost singularly the greatest inspiration for the American Revolution and yet continues to be one of the most banned political narrative. Instead of a celebrated part of American history discussed in classrooms across the nation, it was removed from public school libraries in 1946, and the U.S. State Department banned Paine's works from Information Service Libraries in 1953, and I have not been able to find a single textbook for U.S. History that truthfully describes it. Neither this book nor his book, *The Age of Reason*, a strong criticism of religion, especially Christianity, is used in classrooms either. Sadly, Paine's strident quest for truth led him to a pauper's funeral in an unmarked grave.

Thus a case can be made that the rhetoric of freedom and democracy that is famous in America actually stems from its First Nations whereas the reality of inequality and oppression is a product of Western influences. Recall how the American Indian has served as a foil to that of the European emphasis on property ownership as the basis of personal value and its individualist, materialist and anti-Nature ideology. We should also note that there have been other contributions of Indigenous Peoples to American culture—including goods, medicines, rubber, transportation, games, spiritual traditions and many others that can easily be found on the Internet—have ultimately been involved in creating American ways of thinking about life.

In reference to how the curriculum describes the development of law, too little describes the truth about how the "Doctrine of Discovery" and shaped the laws of the land because of the existence of the Indigenous Peoples who occupied it. As mentioned, this doctrine still determines legal considerations, yet the curriculum, by its own admission, does not address this fact and will fail to do so unless it incorporates Indigenous perspectives.

Within the context of contemporary global interdependence

This may be the most deceitful statement of all in the preface to the U.S. history content standards. The context of global interdependence is what is missing from the curriculum. Acknowledgment of global interconnections related to agriculture, politics, immigration policy, water resources, species extinction and especially climate change is all but absent. This occurs from kindergarten to graduate school. In a peer-reviewed essay for the *Global Studies Journal*, Professor Michael Karlberg says that what is lacking in the university is an integrated, coherent, and cross-curricular approach to educating students for global citizenship. He writes that "there is not a coherent set of core learning outcomes that can guide and inform curriculum development in a substantive and meaningful way across entire institutions" and that "global citizenship learning outcomes have received little attention among university educators" (2010, p. 130). The authors of the curriculum preface are correct in alluding to the importance of global interdependence, but it is not sufficiently reflected in the curriculum or in the real world. Beginning with the Indigenous perspective as a source for teaching the importance of such interdependence, teachers can foster an awareness that we all share and are affected by the same air, oceans and weather patterns. We are all affected by climate change and can no longer deny it or imagine that we exist independent of its effects. The issues of water safety, food economics and biodiversity do not stop at our borders, and they should not be ignored in our curriculum.

It is now my honor to introduce this chapter's guest contributor, Dr. Barbara Alice Mann of the University of Toledo, who lives, teaches, researches and writes in Ohio, the homeland of her Seneca ancestors. She is the author of *Iroquoian Women* and a co-editor of the *Encyclopedia of the Haudenosaunee*.

Hegmonic Influences in
Education and Real-World Outcomes

by Barbara Alice Mann

Nowhere in education is the anti-Indianism of Western hegemony more apparent than in the teaching of Indigenous American history. From the inception of the United States (and Canada) until the last quarter of the twentieth century, there was no doubt about it: Indians were "the enemy," bloodthirsty, uncivilized, and possibly not even fully human. They resisted conversion to the one, *true* religion (i.e., some sect of Christianity); they refused to acknowledge that their culture was savage; and they raised foolish objections to "pure" sciences like archaeology, anthropology and Western medicine.

The intensity with which such attitudes maintain a stranglehold on mainstream opinion are nowhere more apparent than, for example, in the furor surrounding Dee Brown's book *Bury My Heart at Wounded Knee* (1970), which details from the Navajo and Apache points of view the mayhem and murder of the U.S. conquest of the southwest desert. Coming on the heels of the Civil Rights Movement, Brown's book became a blockbuster. Nevertheless, being among the first popular works to present the Euro-Christian invasion of North America for what it was—state-sponsored, criminal theft and murder—it was destined for official disgust as "revisionist history" and subject to attacks by high-level venues that included the *New York Times Review of Books*, *New Statesman*, and *National Review*. The adjective "revisionist" was applied to any account of the seizure of the continent that did not automatically cast a rosy glow on the bloody process of Manifest Destiny or on the supposedly God-ordained right of Europeans to seize Indigenous land while killing anything pesky enough to move. As the gathering Reagan Revolution forced the country well to the right in 1979, well-placed opinion makers openly sneered at Indigenous Americans, as anti-Indianism again became ferociously fashionable and, worse, publishable as recently as 2007.[3]

Since overt racism had gained a bad name, however, new methods arose to preserve anti-Indian bias that their advocates pretended were balanced and fair. Major games here featured the pretense of writing from an Indigenous point of view while unabashedly forcing all data into a Western perspective, as the ethnographer William Fenton did in *The False Faces of the Iroquois* (1987).[4] A second dodge, this one emerging in the 1990s, condemned as "romantic" any depiction of Indigenous culture that did not show it to have been inferior to European culture.[5]

As the twentieth century yielded to the twenty-first, the new mode of keeping Indigenous folks in their place was to retool language. "Discovery" language was already fading due to the sheer lunacy of claims to the "discovery" a place already anciently inhabited by many millions, but the violence of words like "invasion" and "conquest" grated badly. These were restyled as "contact" between cultures. Literally endless lists of books now came out with the non-commital term "contact" in their titles—*Historic Contact* (1995), *Cultures in Contact* (2002), *Indian and European Contact in Context* (2004) and so on. The most recent linguistic cover seeks to pretend that, yeah, there *was* conflict during these "cultural encounters," but those doggoned "Indians gave as good as they got," by golly.[6]

The handy terms "pre-contact" and "post-contact," themselves giving way now to "cultural encounter" talk, replaced the even touchier "pre-" and "post-Columbian" terminology that prevailed until the 1970s. "Columbian" terms had been irreme-diably sullied by the realization that, between 1492 and 1496—two years *before* his third voyage to America—Columbus had been personally responsible for the destruction of 4 million Caribs.[7] In fact, mainstream elites were so repulsed by prac-ticing historians' accounts of the wanton and rapid destruction not only of the Indigenous Peoples of the Americas but also of their flora and fauna that entire cadres of elite-approved spokespersons took aim to disable the impact of these indis-putable facts of history. Although supported by mountains of primary documents containing population statistics gathered by highly respected scholars, the death toll under Columbus was targeted for sustained derision. The attacks somehow never examined the primary sources but, instead, conjured arguments out of dated stereotypes and unfriendly, unsourced speculation, as in purported "Lie #21" in *48 Liberal Lies about American History* (2009).[8] Today, the gloves are off, with bare-knuckle fisticuffs replacing any pretense of using actual data to construct history. Real American history has proven too unsavory to mainstream Americans to be allowed to go forward, even when softened by fuzzy language and amnesia.

Left untouched, probably because it is a hegemonic device still invisible to mainstream history, is the determined use of war-to-war timelines, which are imposed over Indigenous history as though they honestly express traditional ways of recording the past. In fact, using wars to mark historical periods is an entirely European approach. Following their exposure to the halcyon myths of the *Mayflower* and the Jamestown start of "American history," American students are suddenly faced with the Pequot War, King Philip's War, the French and Indian War, Pontiac's "Rebellion," and the Revolution. This list of wars (with mayhem contin-uing beyond where I stop here) actually appears in the Introduction of William Osborn's *The Wild Frontier* (2000) to explain why he accepts the notion of the "Four Century War," 1492 to 1890, which is what other historian have begun calling the post-Columbian, cultural encounter of contact.[9] Pretending that warfare is the nat-ural condition of all of humanity may work for mainstream hegemony, but peace is considered the natural condition of humanity by Indigenous Americans.

Worse, like "cultural encounter" spins on history, this view of humanity removes questions of the responsibility for and repercussions of historical crime from the mainstream viewfinder. When Japan did a similar thing in its high school textbooks on the Second World War by simply tiptoeing past what historians call "the rape of Nanking," referring to Japan's murderous assault on China in 1933, the mainstream academy happily jumped on the bandwagon, calling Japanese his-torians to account.[10] Christopher Barnard coined the apt phrase "Isolating Knowledge of the Unpleasant" to describe the tactic used by Japanese textbook writers to acknowledge the occurrence (briefly) while removing Japanese culpability from their accounts of the Japanese-managed genocide.[11] Having self-righteously shamed another nation for employing a hegemonic device that it, too, regularly used, the Western mainstream continued isolating itself from its own history of genocide against Indigenous America—from the brutal murder of the Pequots at Mystic River, Connecticut, in 1637[12] to the determined murders of the Mahicans and Lenapes at Goshochking, Ohio, in 1782,[13] the massacre of the Cheyennes at Sand Creek, Colorado, in 1864,[14] and the murders of the Lakota Ghost Dancers at Wounded Knee, South Dakota, in 1892.[15]

All of these, and a whole, shameful raft of less well-known massacres perpetrated by settlers and their governments, constitute America's "knowledge of the unpleasant," which mainstream education first isolates and then whizzes by as vigorously as Japanese education ever did Nanking. Mainstream Americans are protected from any sense that they and/or their direct ancestors had anything to do with the awful events of "cultural encounters" or that they directly benefit from them in any way today. Should past crimes in the name of Manifest Destiny come too close to being admitted, attention is quickly refocused on *battles*, preferably three-hanky actions like Custer's Last Stand at Little Bighorn, in which the settlers took a licking.

This sort of selective storytelling distorts the proportions of actual history by making the Indigenous Peoples and the invaders look evenly matched, whereas, in an overwhelming number of instances, the invaders hammered Indigenous People to dust. There is a reason why, depending on locale, 95 to 100 percent of the peoples originally in the Americas are now dead, at the same time that the invading population keeps growing and growing. It is not because the struggle was equal. However, in the interests of pretending that it was, mainstream historians have taken to focusing on the brief periods of equilibrium, when Indigenous Peoples and settlers held about equal power. Instead of openly acknowledging that they are describing a mere tipping point, before the fall, touted works like *The Middle Ground* (1991) zero in on this brief moment for extended and isolating treatments, leaving the false impression that it describes the whole of invasion and, worse, that men, mostly military on both sides, were the only players involved.

Consequently, mainstream education does not encourage students to question where all the Indigenous People have gone or just how the continent on which they now reside, even the land upon which their own family home rests, came to have been in Euro-American hands. Pertaining to more "knowledge of the unpleasant," these questions are simply glossed, with brief words about Indian reservations and treaties that fail to plumb any depths. Instead of a full sweep of unflinching knowledge, vague accounts are offered of what, say, the Indian Removal Act meant to the nations swept into its felonious maw under the administration of President Andrew Jackson. I actually had a university colleague tell me that the matter of settlers and Indians was resolved in her class once the students had felt sincerely moved by the plight of the Indians on the Trail of Tears. Students weaned on such drivel as *Cherokee Sister* (2001), a children's book about a little settler girl who is mistakenly dragged off with the Cherokees on a user-friendly Trail of Tears, are easily set up for a catharsis masquerading as critical thought. The movie *Dances with Wolves* (1990) might have improved on the "whites suffered, too" theme by showing army depredations against the Lakotas, but even *Wolves* ended before the end by allowing the two settler adoptees to peel off into the sunset. Left unexplored by the movie was the fact that, simply by removing their buckskins, changing their hair styles and putting on cotton fabrics, they could easily move back into the safety of the settler world, something that none of the Lakota friends they left behind could have done. These are classic examples of isolation, yet they exceed the deceit of the Japanese textbooks, for none of them pretended that any *Japanese* had been victimized by the rape of Nanking.

Indigenous Curricular Alternatives: How Indians Would Teach American History

by Barbara Alice Mann

Western scholars develop history based on war-to-war timelines, interspersed with intensive, great-man profiles. Nothing could be further from Indigenous notions of how to tell history. In the first place, Indigenous cultures assume that peace is the natural state of humanity, so war cannot be the focus. Second, particular stories belong to particular places and may be told only at particular times. Third, history consists of a set of cycles, in each of which the people learned something really important to community cohesion and survival. Fourth, Indigenous Peoples are communal and democratic, so what matters is the central event of any given cycle and how all the people fared under it, not how some elite individual distinguished himself or herself by wielding power over others. Finally, qualified Elders are listened to as they relay the many versions of each story that exists.

Each culture has its own geographical place, to which its stories are tied. The rivers that run through it, the weather, the plants, the animals, the people—everything is seen in terms of its spiritual connections to its locale. Thus, for instance, the Lenapes are called "the Grandfather Nation" because they were the first to arrive in Dawnland (the mid-Atlantic coast).[16] Indigenous cultures have, moreover, particular times of the year, which coincide with when particular stories are to be told. Thus the Laguna-Keres-Acoma story of Kochinnenako, or Yellow Woman (Corn), is told at the change of seasons from winter to summer, which also signals the shift of civic responsibility from one half of a clan to the other.[17]

In the eastern woodlands, storytelling is not even allowed during the summer, when all the crops are being planted and tended. Everyone loves a good story, so if the Elders told stories in the farming season, everyone would stop work to listen, and nothing would get done.[18] This is why "going *ga-ga*," or telling stories, is put off until harvest time.[19] It is interesting that settler culture in the U.S. copied the "summer is for work" notion of the woodlanders in setting up its school system. Any Indigenous teaching of history would certainly continue to respect the times of the year during which any story can be told, as well as the geographical place concepts vital to the stories.

Because the purpose of telling history is to ensure that the central lessons of the cycle at hand are understood and honored, Indigenous history would work from a consensus on what any particular story meant to the people. In this way, the Plains Peoples create what they call their "Winter Counts," officially recording the event that all agree most impacted the entire group over the previous year.[20] Many Indigenous groups have also formal cycles covering hundreds, or even thousands, of years and comprising multiple events. Thus do the Hopi People keep "Worlds" (epochs), saying that we are today living in the Fourth World.[21]

Instead of pushing the memorization specific dates, then, Indigenous history would be clear about the cycle to which any particular story belonged and where in that cycle it fell. For instance, in the epochs of the Iroquoian tradition, the creation of the clan system occurred in the First, or Creation, Epoch, whereas invasion by the Europeans occurred in the Second, or Great Law, Epoch.[22] As is obvious from the names, the Creation of Turtle Island, and the land life on it, was the main event of the First Epoch, whereas overthrowing oppression to create the Iroquois Constitution was the main event of the Second Epoch. Proper storytellers know the impact of all events recounted in all cycles on the people living today and make them clear. The community, not any individual, is the focus.

Cultural heroes about whom the people have many stories, such as Nanapush of the Anishinabe or Skunny Wundy of the Senecas, would be recognized as present primarily for their comic value, although small morals are also part of the stories. Some great actors, such as White Buffalo Calf Woman of the Lakotas or the prophet Wovoka of the Paiutes, would be mentioned, with both spiritual actors (White Buffalo Calf Woman) and human actors (Wovoka) included as real. It would, however, be the *deeds* of these actors, not the individuals themselves, that mattered. The impact of the deeds on the whole community, both at the time and in the present, would be emphasized over the biography of any one individual because communal peoples just do not see this or that specific individual as all-important. Biography is not an Indigenous genre.

Not everyone is viewed as qualified to tell the stories of their people, nor is only one version of an event viewed as "the one, right story." Instead, there are various recognized "Keepers" (historians) who belong to the particular lineages through which the stories have come. This is why there is always more than one version of even the most sacred traditions. Even though some versions may be generally considered better than others, *all versions of a traditional story are considered simultaneously true.*[23] This is because communal peoples work toward harmonious relations, not continual confrontation and sour spats. *Everyone's* point of view is respected. Consequently, Indigenous history would present all versions of every story, from all points of view, instead of imposing the view of just the most powerful or elite group on everyone.

Belonging to Elder-based cultures, Indigenous groups revere their oldest members. Youngsters do not demand stories (or anything else) from Elders. Instead, the Elders choose when and on whom to bestow a story, making the gift of history highly valuable to the recipient. Elders must be approached with great respect and humility and be asked gently to recite some of what they have "seen and heard in their travels" through life.[24] Youngsters do not despise hearing the stories, wriggling resentfully under the telling or surreptitiously playing with their iPhones, but listen intently to comprehend what is being said. They thank their teachers when the story is done. The final exam for history, Indian-style, would evaluate the competence with which any youngster was able to repeat all versions of a story, complete with the names of the lineages through which each story came.

Thus, instead of being seen as boring, irrelevant and soon forgotten, history would be seen as a vital link to the ancestors, those that paved the way for good things and those whose mistakes offer lessons for the present. History can remind us about the spirits that continue to influence and oversee our stories. History is the opportunity for truth-seeking stories and when these stop, the people cease to exist as well.

Questions for Research, Dialogue, Choices and Praxis

1. Name geographic places with which you are familiar and ask local people who have lived nearby for a long time what special histories they can share about each place.

2. Make a connection to some time in history you are studying that relates to the past ninety years or so and attempt to bring in a local Elder to talk about what he or she remembers about the time period.

3. Watch the democracynow.org news station to find out what is going on in the world today and make connections between whatever current content requirement you are studying and something that is aired in a program you watch or that you find in the archives.

4. For each event or individual you study, talk about what virtues (generosity, honesty, respectfulness, humility, patience, fortitude, etc.) were obviously expressed or absent in what you learned.

5. Watch Massimo Mazzucco's video documentary *The New American Century* (2007) or any of the films by John Pilger and discuss the positive ways you can react to learning about the horrible events that governments, including your own, have perpetrated.

6. Ask questions about labor unions and their history and discuss whether they are important to the American economy.

7. Study the Cherokee Trail of Tears and the motivations and governmental policies responsible for it.

8. What similarities are there between the Jewish holocaust, the treatment of immigrants to the U.S., the experience of blacks in the south during the 1960s, and the government polices toward the American Indians in the early 1800s. How are these policies similar or different today?

9. From the "Rethinking Schools" website, choose a topic that relates to one you are studying and compare and contrast the curriculum's information with the version given by the website.

10. Read from Thomas Paine's book, *The Age of Reason*, and study the history of his great influence on the positive aspects of creating the United States and how he was subsequently treated in the U.S.

11. In whatever subject you are studying in U.S. History, try to make a connection with causes to and influences of climate change and the human relationship to the natural world, and consider what can be done and what you can do to help face the problems.

Notes

1. See also Hans Schmidt, *Maverick Marine: General Smedley D. Butler and the Contradictions of American Military History* (Lexington: University Press of Kentucky, 1987).

2. For a thorough scholarly presentation of the facts about all of this, see Bruce Johansen's chapter "The Transfer of Ideas: Native Confederacies and the Evolution of Democracy" in *The Native Peoples of North America: A History* (Johansen 2005). For a fascinating story about how politicians, policymakers and revisionist historians have kept this out of our textbooks, see his chapter "Adventures in Denial" in *Unlearning the Language of Conquest* (Four Arrows 2006).

3. William F. Buckley Jr., *Cancel Your Own Goddam Subscription: Notes and Asides from National Review* (New York: Basic Books, 2007), 160.

4. See William N. Fenton, *The False Faces of the Iroquois* (Norman: University of Oklahoma Press, 1987), 501, where he claims to be employing "the perspective of the native culture." For my extended discussion of Fenton's and other Western scholars' interpolations of Indigenous perspectives, see Barbara A. Mann, "Euro-forming the Data," in Bruce E. Johansen, *Debating Democracy: Native American Legacy of Freedom* (Santa Fe, NM: Clear Light, 1998), 160–90.

5. See, for instance, Matthew Dennis, *Cultivating a Landscape of Peace: Iroquois-European Encounters in Seventeenth-Century America* (Ithaca, NY: Cornell University Press, 1993), 65.

6. Joyce Chaplin, "Cultural Encounters: Teaching Exploration and Encounter to Students" (n.d.), http://www.gilderlehrman.org/history-by-era/american-indians/resources/cultural-encounters-teaching-exploration-and-encounter-stu (accessed May 14, 2012). .

7. Kirkpatrick Sale, *The Conquest of Paradise: Christopher Columbus and the Columbian Legacy* (New York: Knopf, 1990); for the figure of 4 million, see David E. Stannard, *American Holocaust: The Conquest of the New World* (New York: Oxford University Press, 1992), 74–75.

8. Larry Schweikart, *48 Liberal Lies about American History (That You Probably Learned in School)* (New York: Sentinel Trade, 2009), "Lie #21."

9. William M. Osborn, *The Wild Frontier: Atrocities from the American-Indian War from Jamestown Colony to Wounded Knee* (New York: Random House, 2000), xiv.

10. Iris Chang, *The Rape of Nanking: The Forgotten Holocaust of World War II* (New York: Penguin, 1997).

11. Christopher Barnard, "Isolating Knowledge of the Unpleasant: The Rape of Nanking in Japanese High-School Textbooks," *British Journal of Sociology of Education* 22.4 (Dec. 2001): 519–30.

12. Francis Jennings, The Invasion of America: Indians, Colonialism, and the Cant of Conquest (New York: Norton, 1976), 220–26.

13. Barbara Alice Mann, *George Washington's War on Native America* (Westport, CT: Praeger, 2005), 151–69.

14. Stannard, *American Holocaust*, 129–34.

15. Stannard, *American Holocaust*, 126–27.

16. Hendrick Aupaumut, "A Narrative of an Embassy to the Western Indians," *Memoirs of the Historical Society of Pennsylvania* 2.1 (1827): 76–77; Frank G. Speck, "The Wapanachki Delawares and the English: Their Past as Viewed by an Ethnologist," *The Pennsylvania Magazine* 67 (1943): 325–26.

17. Paula Gunn Allen, "Kochinnenako in Academe: Three Approaches to Interpreting a Keres Indian Tale," in *The Sacred Hoop: Recovering the Feminine in American Indian Traditions* (Boston: Beacon, 1992), 232–34.

18. Harriet Maxwell Converse, "Myths and Legends of the New York State Iroquois," *Education Department Bulletin* 437 (December 1908): 11.

19. Arthur C. Parker, "Iroquois Uses of Maize and Other Food Plants," in *Parker on the Iroquois,* ed. William N. Fenton (1913; reprint, Syracuse, NY: Syracuse University Press, 1968), 31–33.

20. Vine Deloria Jr., "The Concept of History," in *God Is Red: A Native View of Religion* (1973; reprint, Golden, CO: Fulcrum, 1994), 98–99.

21. Frank Waters, *Book of the Hopi* (New York: Penguin, 1977), 328.

22. For the epochs of Iroquoian time, see Bruce Elliot Johansen and Barbara Alice Mann, eds., *Encyclopedia of the Haudenosaunee (Iroquois Confederacy)* (Westport, CT: Greenwood, 2000): First Epoch (Creation), 83–97; Second Epoch (Great Law), 265–84; Third Epoch (Handsome Lake), 307–12. Some Iroquois contend that we are now in the prophesied Fourth Epoch, when the Great Turtle (Turtle Island) pitches, rolls, and dives, brushing irritants off her back.

23. Johansen and Mann, eds., *Encyclopedia of the Haudenosaunee,* 266.

24. John Heckewelder, *History, Manners, and Customs of the Indian Nations Who Once Inhabited Pennsylvania and the Neighboring States* (1820, 1876; reprint, New York: Arno Press and *The New York Times,* 1971), 325.

9 | Mathematics

Continuing to accept Western math education as universal and authoritative is detrimental to creating a healthier and more humane world.
—Munir Fasheh, 1990, p. 22

Within Native America, mathematics is a sacred practice related to the dynamics of the whole cosmos. Numbers are manifestations of beings.
—F. David Peat, 1994, p. 154

A mathematician, like a painter or poet, is a maker of patterns. If his patterns are more permanent than theirs, it is because they are made with ideas.
—G.H. Hardy

In Hopi, like most Indian languages, temporal thinking is so drastically different from the ideas of Western time that there are no divisions such as hours, minutes, seconds, etc.
—Jamake Highwater, 1981, p. 67

K-16 Teacher Instructions:

Adapt and use this chapter's information according to your students' ages and cognitive levels. Use as an introduction to your standard course content or weave values, ideas or critical reflections into it throughout the course. Encourage students to carefully reflect on this information with the goal of deciding what mainstream ideas are best replaced with Indigenous ones, which ones are best as they are, and how the two might be partnered in terms of practical benefits for the students and their community (local and global). Use the questions at the end of the chapter to help with this process and to stimulate primary source research and enthusiastic, critical dialogue. Since, in Indigenous ways of thinking, the ideas related to this subject have relevance to all the other subjects, you may want to incorporate some of this chapter's material into the study of another subject area. As with all chapters in this section, this chapter is organized as follows:

1. Corporate and Hegemonic Influences
2. Real-World Outcomes
3. Indigenous Curricular Alternatives
4. Questions for Research, Dialogue, Choices and Praxis

Corporate and Hegemonic Influences

Before undertaking the research for this book, I would have guessed that mathematics instruction would be an exception to the ways educational hegemony operates in other subject areas. Especially when contrasted with Indigenous understandings about numbers, this is not the case. For example, Walkerdine (1992) argues that math curricula have a cultural, class and gender bias toward white upper-class males. Nunes's studies show that "mathematics instruction can be seen as an act of power to maintain privilege in society (1992, p. 1). Anyon has found that "a classroom culture that limits what children will consider in mathematic problems will affect the student with an eventual sense of failure and leads to an inability to apply knowledge...and brings forth a need to have immediate answers" (1981, p. 7). Becker's studies have found that gender bias is common in mathematic instruction, causing females to lose interest (1981, pp. 40–53). Atweh and Cooper, in their paper "Hegemony in the Mathematics Curricula" (1991), presented at the 15th Annual Conference of the International Group for the Psychology of Mathematics Education in Assisi, Italy, also draw these conclusions. Cooper goes on to explain that the mainstream teaching of mathematics creates a degree of "non-decision" and "negative power" in students by

> limiting the agenda of alternatives considered to be legitimate, [such] that potentially harmful issues and challenges are not raised. By virtue of control of privileges and rewards, a prin-

cipal, for instance, can wield power in a negative fashion without giving any direct instructions to staff or applying any vetoes to staff activity. Staff safeguard their present positions
and future possibilities by initiating only those actions they know are acceptable to the principal. (1993, p. 4)

Because Atweh's and Cooper's conclusions are based on numerous actual studies of young children, they are worth elaborating upon here to better explain the
hegemonic influence of mathematics education. Atweh and Cooper, citing support
from other researchers, say that effective mathematic problem solving requires a balance between "activators" and "inhibitors." Having no activators produces a com-
puter-like response based upon

insufficiency of domain knowledge inherent in a problem situation that will prevent the
child from giving any response other than to say that they do not have enough information. To have no inhibitors means that there is no control over the range of responses so
any response becomes acceptable. Children with poor activators will show a lack of creativity. Children with poor inhibitors will show over-generalisation, lack of permanence
of conclusions and inappropriate behavior. (1993, p. 6)

As a result, the emphasis on "negative power" in mathematics education results in
the following types of negative processing:

(1) conflict with previous learning—the child has different information already in memory; (2) poor example set—different meanings and actions for different types of examples;
(3) restrictive mathematics classroom culture—what is allowed and not allowed in formal
mathematics; (4) wrong teaching—deliberate incorrect instruction; (5) lack of confidence—unwillingness to even attempt certain types of problems; (6) disposition—the relation of mathematics to the learner; and (7) individual—personality traits that inhibit.

Interestingly, all of this seems to mean that mathematics offers the ultimate expression
of absolutist perceptions (especially common to American hegemony and only slightly
less common perhaps to Eurocentric and Western thinking as well), and these perceptions inevitably disempower people. Atweh and Cooper summarize their research:

Present information is lending credence to the idea that legitimising is a metacognitive activity that requires children to recognise and confront their own limitations with respect to
what they believe is legitimate. These beliefs may be deeply, yet tacitly, held and require
an act of empowerment. (1993, p. 12)

Thus the issue of children feeling a lack of empowerment in the dominant culture may be connected to the hegemonic assumptions surrounding mathematics,
or number computation. This outcome is due to subtle implications about who is

allowed to be successful and what the goals and references for learning mathematics are, as well as due to the lack of "sacred" relationships associated with it. What we take as our universal and value-free mathematics may be connected to the set of common paradigms that maintain the status quo. This means that the use of mathematics itself could be controlled by hegemony for purposes of economics, war, exploration and conquest, as well as to fulfill the continuing needs of technological inventions for a consumer society. Prison and social security numbers, computer equations and banking statistics—only the computational aspects of math—continue to enhance or rationalize hegemonic effects. Mathematics is thought of by too many as dry, abstract and dehumanizing rather than alive, real and immediate. Moreover, people accept that only the few who understand math and how it is the basis for technology and "truth" are able to rule society.

John Taylor Gatto's perspectives on educational hegemony offer a summarizing conclusion to this section. Gatto, a former New York State Teacher of the Year who renounced the government school system in his landmark book *Dumbing Us Down* (2003), writes,

> The secret of American schooling is that it doesn't teach the way children learn—nor is it supposed to. Schools were conceived to serve the economy and the social order rather than kids and families…As a consequence, the school cannot help anybody grow up, because its prime directive is to retard maturity.
> The real purpose of modern schooling was also announced by the legendary sociologist Edward Roth in his manifesto of 1906 called "Social Control." In it Roth wrote, "plans are underway to replace family, community and church with propaganda, mass-media and education…people are only little plastic lumps of dough. (p. 45)"

In spite of appeals from educators who know better and in spite of the rhetoric of national standards and the many books that refer to the importance of making real-world connections, mathematics textbooks, largely the source of the mathematics curriculum, do not help students make authentic connections.[1] Rather than cultivating math as the sacred endeavor an Indigenous perspective offers, math texts continue to foster fear of math, difficulty in comprehension, and forced applications that have more to do with maintaining social structures than with living according to the balance and harmony authentic math education would offer.

Real-World Outcomes

The concern with the "real world" here relates to (1) whether mathematics is taught in a way that makes it clearly relevant to real-world problems as the standards claim and (2) how well American students in the real world grasp mathematic operations. Beginning with the first issue, in spite the research-based claims in the math standards preface (again using California's version of the national K-12 common core standards), the importance of real-world applications is indeed touted as being the foundation for the curriculum:

> The Standards for Mathematical Practice describe varieties of expertise that mathematics educators at all levels should seek to develop in their students. These practices rest on important "processes and proficiencies" with longstanding importance in mathematics education. The first of these are the NCTM [National Council of Teachers of Mathematics] process standards of problem solving, reasoning and proof, communication, representation, and connections.

Although there are legitimate counterarguments within the National Council of Teachers of Mathematics, most of its members agree that students learn best when mathematics is connected to real-world, relevant problem solving.[2] In fact, "real-world" is mentioned thirty-five times in the K-12 math standards. However, the first mention is not until Grade 5, and thereafter teachers are instructed to find their own real-world problems to connect to otherwise typical content objectives. For example, for the Grade 7 content, one instruction reads, "Solve real-world and mathematical problems by graphing points in all four quadrants." Another example is found in the California state standards for Grade 8:

> Understand the absolute value of a rational number as its distance from 0 on the number line; interpret absolute value as magnitude for a positive or negative quantity in a real-world situation. *For example, for an account balance of -30 dollars, write $|-30| = 30$ to describe the size of the debt in dollars*….Include use of coordinates and absolute value to find distances between points with the same first coordinate or the same second coordinate.

In the Grade 12 standards, students are told, "Diagrams of various kinds, spreadsheets and other technology, and algebra are powerful tools for understanding and solving problems drawn from different types of real-world situations." Hiebert sums the problem up when he says, "I shall argue that it is the *absence* of these connections that induces the shift from intuitive and meaningful problem-solving approaches to mechanical and meaningless ones" (1984, p. 498, original emphasis).

In the next section, on Indigenous curricular alternatives, I suggest more significant real-world connections than what the above examples might offer. For now, we turn to what this section of the chapter is usually about—how well the subject seems to be taught in terms of the real world. If we look at the standardized metrics used to evaluate the knowledge of math students, the United States is not doing well. Even if mathematics were taught without hegemony influencing the curriculum, most people in the real world do not use it well. According to a National Assessment of Adult Literacy by the U.S. Department of Education, adults are terrible at solving real-world math problems ranging from calculating a tip for a waitress to determining hourly pay rates from a weekly salary. Only 13 percent were deemed "proficient" (Kutner et al. 2007, p. 8).

Using standardized evaluation metrics, American students are also near the bottom of industrialized countries year after year (TIMSS 2007).[3] However, even the Trends in International Mathematics and Science Study (TIMSS) worldwide evaluation process itself favours a more global Western hegemony in support of values that relate to Western culture versus Indigenous ones. For example, the TIMSS Index of Students Valuing Mathematics is based on four criteria:

1. I think learning mathematics will help me in my daily life.
2. I need mathematics to learn other school subjects.
3. I need to do well in mathematics to get into the university of my choice.
4. I need to do well in mathematics to get the job I want. (TIMSS 2007, p. 18)

Responses reveal many students think math is not relevant to any of these needs.

An international study on trends in international mathematics by the National Center for Education Statistics provides data on the mathematics and science achievement of U.S. students in Grades 4 and 8. It explains why the needs listed above relate to objectives that are superficial and lead to inadequate math education. According to the Core Plus Mathematics Project of the National Science Foundation, the reasons why countries like Japan do better may relate to U.S. math instruction, which it describes as follows:

1. More fragmented and less cohesive
2. Breadth is emphasized over depth (A typical American text covers 35 topics compared to a Japanese one that covers six.)
3. Skills are emphasized over problem solving and thinking
4. Skill acquisition and speed are more important than understanding
5. Deductive reasoning is virtually absent
6. More homework is given in the U.S. than in countries that outperform the U.S.
7. Most U.S. teachers spend their class time telling students how to do something, and students follow their lead. This results in students hav-

ing a very passive view of learning, quite at odds with what we know about how learning actually occurs.

None of this works very well.

Fasheh describes the results of the U.S. approach to teaching math:

> My math had no power connected with anything in the community and no power connection with the Western hegemonic culture which had engendered it. It was connected solely to symbolic power without the official ideological support system, no one would have 'needed' my math; its value was derived from a set of symbols created by hegemony and the world of education....Math was necessary for her (his mother) in a much more profound and real sense than it was for me. My illiterate mother routinely took rectangles of fabric and, with few measurements and no patterns, cut them and turned them into beautiful, perfectly fitted clothing for people. In 1976 it struck me that the math she was using was beyond my comprehension; Moreover, while math for me was a subject matter I studied and taught, for her it was basic to the operation of her understanding. In addition, mistakes in her work entailed practical consequences completely different from mistakes in my math. (Fasheh 1989, pp. 84–5, quoted in Kitchen 1995, n.p.)

These concerns and outcomes can be overcome with Indigenous values related to relationship, ecological considerations, community and the cosmos.

Indigenous Curricular Alternatives

Although Indigenous mathematics knowledge paths are seldom considered, mathematics was highly developed in ancient Indigenous cultures throughout the world (Rudman 2007). Modern mathematicians are still perplexed by the complex mathematical computations of the Mayans, such as those relating to its calendars.[4] "Real-world" associations were responsible for the deep understandings most individuals possessed, but the real world for Indigenous Peoples was more expansive. Math was used to understand, honor, predict and gamble with sacred relationships in both the visible and invisible worlds.

One small example comes to mind about how Native children perceive something as basic as adding numbers as being related to important life knowledge. While living and working on the Pine Ridge Indian Reservation as director of education at Oglala Lakota College, I observed a non-Indian math teacher[5] attempting to teach simple addition to a group of Oglala first-graders. She asked, "What is one plus one plus one? In other words, if I have three different things and I put them together, what do I have?" Most of the children were reluctant to volunteer since as we have learned Indian children prefer to be sure before answering, but a little girl whose family I knew well enthusiastically raised her hand. When called upon, she answered confidently, "You have a chord!" Unfortunately, the teacher rebuffed the answer: "What? That is ridiculous and wrong! The *correct* answer is 'three.'"[6]

The child had been taking piano lessons and had recently learned that a basic chord consists of three notes played together. This was her meaningful context for the problem the teacher posed. Although a mathematician can add two trees, two apples and two eagles to obtain a new number of "things," such abstraction does not make sense to the Indigenous mind. In the first place, the Lakota (Sioux) language, like most Indigenous languages, makes it very difficult to refer to these as "things." We cannot call a tree "it." The typical mathematic abstractions tend to ignore what gives each entity its special significance. Recognition of such significance is essentially built into the language.[7] The teacher, not referring to any objects in particular, offered no context for the child. However, music did, and music to the child was sacred. She knew what Pythagoras taught—that reality is mathematical in nature and that music is the purist expression of reality, with diatonic harmony (as found in chords!) being mathematically perfect (Fauvel et al. 2003). Without context, knowledge is empty. The most important math learning and application opportunities exist in helping students understand the environmental/ecological crises we all face.

Traditional Indigenous perspectives tend to engage math when dealing "with the whole nature of time and ceremony, with the proportions of architecture and the human body, and with the structure of the cosmos and of sacred sites" (Peat, 1994, p. 190). A number of Western math educators also grasp this deeper perspective and understand that there is power in learning numbers and their magical relationships to one another and to the universe. A notable example is Patricia Clark Kenschaft of Montclair State University, winner of the Louise Hay Award for her dedicated service to mathematics education. Trained as a functional analyst, she specializes in mathematics in K-16 as it relates to the environment, affirmative action and equity and matters important for the public good. The titles of some of her publications show a deep concern for the community, a concern fundamental to the Indigenous perspective on learning anything, especially sacred numbers. These titles include "Change Is Possible: Stories of Women and Minorities in Mathematics"; "Multicultural and Gender Equity in the Mathematics Classroom" (detailing a series of "micro-inequity skits," which are based on real-life experiences and point out in a good-natured way the sorts of small injustices that may occur daily to females in mathematics); "What Can Be Done to Bring More Blacks into Mathematics?"; "Racial Equity Requires Teaching Elementary Teachers More Mathematics"; and two books, *Mathematics for Human Survival* and *Environmental Mathematics* (co-edited with Ben Fusaro).

For traditional Indigenous cultures, this idea of learning mathematics by connecting it to significant, real-life issues for the sake of a more balanced world means that mathematics relates to almost everything. The field of ethno-mathematics,[8] which emphasizes Indigenous approaches around the world, is based on the understanding that mathematical ideas are mental constructs created by individuals and groups in response to cultural activities. Mathematics must be learned via making connections to life. For example, in the Pacific region, these activities might include the following:

- agriculture
- architecture and building
- astronomy
- barter and trade
- calendar development
- decorative arts
- design and construction of canoes, musical instruments, jewelry, and household items
- healing
- kinship relationships
- navigation
- religious practices
- sewing, quilting, and weaving
- tattooing and other body ornamentation
- toys and games, including gambling

This list shows the interplay between everyday life and mathematics that is missing from most mainstream math instruction in spite of the "real-world" rhetoric. Roberts (1997) demonstrates this Indigenous perspective in her article looking at the activities performed by an Aboriginal family during the course of a day and the related mathematics. The activities include sanding didgeridoos, making a damper, erecting a shade shelter, fuel requirements for a fishing trip, fishing, collecting mussels, identifying crocodile tracks, cooking fish, and hunting for goannas and wallabies; mathematics included two- and three-dimensional shapes in design, problem solving, symmetry, locational skills, estimating, measurement, counting, and quantification. The author also shows how mathematic knowledge is valued in Aboriginal society as an art in the same life-sustaining way other art forms such as music are honored. Veteran math teacher Paul Lockhart captures the idea of mathematics as an art form in his book *A Mathematician's Lament: How School Cheats*

Us out of Its Most Imaginative Art Form (2009). In an article on this theme, he explains,

> The first thing to understand is that mathematics is an art....By concentrating on *what*, and leaving out *why*, mathematics is reduced to an empty shell. The art is not in the "truth" but in the explanation, the argument. It is the argument itself which gives the truth its context, and determines what is really being said and meant. Mathematics is *the art of explanation*....A piece of mathematics is like a poem, and we can ask if it satisfies our aesthetic criteria: Is this argument sound? Does it make sense? Is it simple and elegant? Does it get me closer to the heart of the matter?
>
> So how do we teach our students to do mathematics? By choosing engaging and natural problems suitable to their tastes, personalities, and level of experience. By giving them time to make discoveries and formulate conjectures. By helping them to refine their arguments and creating an atmosphere of healthy and vibrant mathematical criticism. By being flexible and open to sudden changes in direction to which their curiosity may lead. In short, by having an honest intellectual relationship with our students and our subject.[9]

Understanding mathematics as an Indigenous art form, however, requires the realization that art, as presented in the chapter on music education, is not mere entertainment but a process designed to help understand and interpret life. This realization calls not only for obviously relevant applications of math computations but also for engaging with the phenomenon of math itself in an enjoyable, "musical" fashion and drawing analogies from what is learned that have substantive meaning in the real world.

Most modern students and their teachers are a long way from seeing math as sacred knowledge or from understanding how individuals who have mastered some math specialty on behalf of community are best able to pass it on. Nonetheless, that Indigenous Peoples all over the world see "numbers as symbols and manifestations of the transformations, dynamics and cycles within the world of nature and spirit" (Peat 1994, p. 154)[10] can be an inspiration to all of us. I remember watching some Raramuri Indians of Mexico as they joyfully played an ancient gambling game in the dirt with sticks and rocks and being baffled by how people were scoring wins. I wanted to understand the laws of probability that obviously informed their rapid calculations. When I found out that the probabilities they employed related to current events happening in their society, I was even more impressed.

Henry Fowler, a Navajo doctoral student at Fielding Graduate University, successfully used Navajo culture to help students overcome the typical fear of math and avoid the consequential failures. In his 2010 dissertation, "Collapsing the Fear of Mathematics: A Study of the Effects of Navajo Culture on Navajo Student Performance in Mathematics," he shows that by using cultural realities like the structure of a traditional hogan, by infusing math lessons with humor and fun while engaging in hands-on activities and meaningful experiences, and by emphasizing group work and using narrative storytelling, he was able to significantly increase student performances on all eleven of Arizona state's benchmarks for the math curriculum. He proves that a partnership between Indigenous perspectives and mainstream objectives works for Indian children, and he does so using ideas that progressive educators have been saying will work for all students![11]

In *The Spiritual Technology of Ancient Egypt: Sacred Science and the Mystery of Consciousness* (2007), Malkowski and Schwaller de Lubicz refer to this everyday use of numbers. They describe petroglyphs throughout the Americas showing evidence of numbers, counting and complex mathematical processes and astronomical observations. They make it clear with their research that humans created mathematics as a measurement system to benefit society as well as to describe the natural world, but they are not so quick to say that numbers themselves are manmade. They claim numbers are an integral part of nature and are crucial to understanding how everything is both in motion *and* connected. Their book attempts to explain Indigenous sacred numbers in ways that may help enhance the math teacher's sense of how numbers are integral to life. For each assertion I have added (in italics) the way the idea coincides with the Indigenous perspective.

> In nature, number is disguised as form and exists behind the scenes as an integral part of the system, so much so that number is a part of our natural mental faculties we take for granted. We never notice it. But it is these variations (numbers) and how they relate to each other, that mathematics and physics use to describe reality....Number is what provides the physically detectable variations in nature that provide a way to perceive. An equation states a relationship, but it is through number that the equation has meaning, because number is the source of the equation. As a perception, number is intrinsically tied to quantity, and quantity is inherent in nature. *Thus how can numbers, even with their own magic and beauty, not be a part of the "real world"?* (pp. 96–97)
>
> What is it about nature that number is an integral part of it? Nature is active. In fact, everything from subatomic particles to galaxies is in constant motion. But what is the nature of activity? The nature of activity is function. *Every function of the natural world or the universe returns some consequence (value) that we perceive.* (p. 97)
>
> Any function has a force, a method and an outcome. In nature, the force—the underlying impetus for all that is—is unknown and constant. The outcome will depend on the method *with which force is applied. If there is only one method, there would be only one outcome. Then Nature, the cosmos, would have no diversity.* This variation in method can only be described as our understanding of quantity, which is what we label as number. *Thus, number thus creates nature.* (p. 99)
>
> Numbers are very closely related to how we observe and perceive the world. Through the comparison of the things we see, we continually observe number in that a quantity

always exists. *Quantity and therefore number are somehow tied to reality.* Quality is an aspect of mind as our physical senses relate to it. Quality is the intrinsic characteristic of objects that we know as a result of experience....When quantity and quality are equal, any phenomenon achieves a harmonic state, although limited by time and mass. *This harmony or balance stems from our education when it is truly a truth-seeking enterprise.* (p. 104)
Early man must have wondered where everything came from, just as we do today. Through reflection, it would long ago have been an obvious deduction that all people eventually reduce to two. (pp. 107–120)

With this last point, Malkowski and Schwaller are referring to a deduction based on the multiplication resulting from the feminine and masculine natures that existed during the creation of life but prior to procreation. They go on to expand upon the two natures and describes the number four as containing eight natures, explaining that prior to procreation, creation at the subatomic level had to have two passive feminine natures and two more direct masculine natures, plus a nature that is defined by the term "father/mother," indicating that both natures exist simultaneously in one. Thus, the number four becomes the symbol of creative spirit: "Four can be thought of as the most fundamental source of creation—the Creative Spirit or the active principle—that fecundates and maintains the cosmos and all life" (pp.121).

It is beyond coincidence that these researchers come to the same conclusion about the number four as most Indigenous cultures, which have always embraced the number four as a sacred number. North American tribes believe there are four sacred medicines (sweet grass, tobacco, cedar and sage), each used for different but complementary reasons. They have medicine wheels emphasizing the four directions and the four seasons. The Navajo refer to four sacred mountains, four colors, four times of the day and four cardinal light phenomena. Many cultures of the Americas refer to four worlds.[12] The number four is itself about a holistic effort to come into balance with the four directions and the entities in these directions:

Four is a dynamic process in which equilibrium must be constantly renewed....Within Indigenous science the number four is not a think, it is not a mental abstraction, but a living spirit; likewise the sacred hoop is not a static diagram on a piece of paper, but an unfolding process...And so within the number four stands each of the sacred directions, each on being also a point of arrival and of departure. (Peat, 1994, p. 162)

Perhaps this intuitive understanding of number symbols that Indigenous Peoples possess can be rekindled in the math classroom for everyone. Instead of using numbers only for the typical reasons (e.g., social security identification, telephone contacts, and stand-alone math equations), students should be allowed and encouraged to think about how numbers relate to the motions and music of the universe. Perhaps they can regain the Indigenous perspective, which identifies numbers as the manifestations of Nature and spirit. Math teachers can help students explore the deeper reality of numbers "by seeking to understand sacred mathematics as being based on direct experience, which includes the whole world of dreams, visions, spirits and powers. Within sacred mathematics, a number is never abstracted from the animating spirit that gives it life, nor from the concrete situations in which it is used" (Peat, 1994, p. 161).

Students should also learn that numbers can be thought of outside the noun structure of the English language (revisit this topic in Chapter 7, on English language arts) and reconsidered from the point of view of a verb language. This means thinking of math not as static but as always changing. Numbers are beings in constant change. To play with the possibilities of this change through mathematical operations is to look into the most basic aspect of relationships: "To enter the world of numbers and sacred mathematics is not an act of abstraction but a sacred process. To understand the transformations of number is to seek a relationship with the dynamic processes of energies and spirits" (Peat, 1994, p. 163). Teachers and students can start talking about numbers in this way together from a point of unknowing and move joyfully toward new ways of seeing the world.

Questions for Research, Dialogue, Choices and Praxis

Beyond the concepts suggested above for countering hegemony and aligning math standards with the visible and invisible worlds, it is up to teachers and students to create authentic lesson plans that incorporate meaningful, fun and collective applications. I realize that implementing these ideas may be difficult given the imperative teachers face to employ standardized tests that force the more superficial memorization of formulas, but incorporating these ideas into your teaching will likely enhance students' interest in math—and test scores, ironically, will improve. They can't get much worse anyway, right?

Here are some prescriptions for implementing the Indigenous perspective:

- Allow for chaotic complexity and holistic approaches that prioritize relationships, unity and integrity in relation to whatever is being studied and move away from authoritarian, linear instruction.
- Use math to make significant connections with family, community and student interpersonal relationships with one another as possible. (For example, use the mathematics being studied to create a home gar-

den, to purchase a bus for the school, to play games common in Indigenous cultures that require mental arithmetic and probabilities, or to plan a recipe that will feed all the students' parents and guardians.)

- Emphasize cooperation and non-competitiveness in the math class, and do whatever can be done to create applications for concepts in math that might be used in life to make the world more harmonious.
- Focus on cycles whenever possible and explore how mathematics can be used to talk about ending and starting new ones. (Use birthdays, moon and sun transitions, family trees, learning accomplishments, and so forth as examples for teaching fractions, time and various calculations. The medicine wheel should be referred to so as to connect stages of learning and life to various math questions.)
- Use ecology and nature as the most important arena for mathematics.
- Allow for multiple perspectives on ways to get to the same "answers."
- Use local community members for stories that can be converted into math problems.
- Allow both critical cognition and emotional feelings to enter into mathematics teaching and learning. (Use storytelling to illicit both as often as possible.)
- Use mathematics to teach virtues like patience, courage, generosity, honesty and fortitude (see *Teaching Virtues: Building Character across the Curriculum,* Jacobs and Jacobs 2006, p. 141).
- Study diverse perspectives and approaches to math problems.
- Celebrate and encourage an absence of any gender bias during math instruction.
- Use role models from numerous cultures and emphasize relational, not procedural, understanding.
- Connection what students already know about both within and outside of math to what they know about in real life (see Hiebert and Carpenter 1992).

If teachers and students have trouble coming up with ideas for any of these connections, see the American Indian Content Standards by subject at the website of the Center for Educational Technologies.[13] And remember to refer to Paul Lockhart's book *A Mathematician's Lament* for ideas, as well as to look at the many ways to use a medicine wheel that are on the Internet.

Also, in Chapter 12 note that the sample Indian curriculum I have selected for geography is actually comprised of their mathematics lesson plans! For a Nature-based culture, learning geography is like learning to breathe, whereas the art of mathematics is married to the land and can be learned. From the website noted above, here is a sample of the American Indian Content Standards:

Standard 1: Productive resources are limited. Therefore, people cannot have all the goods and services they want; as a result, they must choose some things and give up others.

Sample Focus Areas for American Indian Students

Grade: 4

Benchmark 10: Natural resources, such as land, are "gifts of nature"; they are present without human intervention. American Indian communities have strong traditional values related to nature and its resources. These values often affect decisions regarding how natural resources on tribal lands should or should not be used in the production of goods for economic benefit.

At the completion of Grade 4, Indian students will use this knowledge to:

- Explain why a choice must be made, given a specific piece of tribal land and some alternative uses for that land (e.g., mine, farm or pow-wow camp ground).
- Identify examples of natural resources which are currently harvested or potentially harvestable on tribal lands and which could be used in the production of products, or in generating income for the tribe, if sold.
- Use a resource map of students' reservation or other tribal lands to locate examples of natural resources.

Notes

1. From extensive studies in many countries and from international comparisons, it is clear that textbooks are important artifacts in the classroom and that they strongly influence what happens in the classroom. Indeed, it can be further claimed that they are the mediators between "the intent of curricular policy and the instruction that occurs in the classroom" (Valverde et al. 2002, p. 2).

2. There is a debate among the NCTM's members about the appropriateness of such real-world connections in math education. Some math educators believe that students learn best by focusing exclusively on the operations and formulas, which in a sense encourages them to appreciate the intrinsic beauty of mathematics and numbers. Others believe that attempting to apply math to real life takes time away from teaching formulas and concepts. Many others believe that most students learn math best when it is connected to known, real-world situations.

3. Average scores rose slightly in the 2011 evaluation.

4. Numbers resonated throughout all aspects of Mayan life and ceremony and were the glue that connected the inner world to the outer. For an expansive description of the Mayans and numbers, see F. David Peat, *Blackfoot Physics: A Journey into the Native American Universe* (1994).

5. Most of the K-12 teachers on the Pine Ridge Indian Reservation are non-Indian, and many from the border towns harbor serious prejudices against the Native children. Once I observed a middle school class on the "First Americans." It was about Davy Crocket and Daniel Boone!

6. This arithmetic lesson followed another event that frustrated the teacher. She awarded another child a large Hershey's chocolate bar for having the fewest absences during the term and made a big deal of the award. Embarrassed by being pointed out in such a way, the student graciously took the award and proceeded to count the number of students in the class. She then carefully broke the bar into equal pieces, one for each child. Speechless for as long as the process took, the teacher finally exploded, saying that now the children would not be motivated to make attendance a more important priority and ridiculing the student instead of complimenting her on both the generosity and the accurate addition and division used to hand out the candy!

7. In Chapter 7, on English language arts, the problem of "noun people" versus Indigenous "verb people" is presented.

8. The articles related to how mainstream teachers can implement Indigenous approaches to mathematics are numerous and easily accessed at http://www.ethnomath.org/search/browse Resources.asp?type=subject&id=326.

9. Paul Lockhart, "The Mathematician's Lament" (n.d.), 3–10, original emphasis, http://www. maa.org/devlin/LockhartsLament.pdf. Lockhart's larger body of work is essential reading for those who wish to come closer to understanding the Indigenous perspective.

10. F. David Peat, a brilliant physicist and author of many books about science, as well as the organizer of the Fetzer Institute's Dialogues between Indigenous and Western Scientists (1992), wrote an entire chapter for his book *Blackfoot Physics: A Journey into the Native American Universe* (1994) entitled "Sacred Mathematics." Much of the following comes from his work as well as my own understandings.

11. It is perhaps ironic that this study occurred in Arizona, where the following year the Senate bill essentially banning ethnic studies was passed.

12. Some, like the Hopi, believe that our fourth world is ending and that, although difficult, we are in the midst of a transition into a fifth world that is leading us back into balance.

13. http://web.archive.org/web/20030729222625/http://www.ldoe.org/cetia/subject.htm

10 | Economics

Avarice, said to be the root of all evil, and the dominant characteristic of the European races, was unknown among Indians, indeed it was made impossible by the system they had developed.

—OHIYESA

When the most basic elements that sustain life are reduced to a cash product, life has no intrinsic value. The extinguishing of "primitive" societies, those that were defined by animism and mysticism, those that celebrated ambiguity and mystery, those that respected the centrality of the human imagination, removed the only ideological counterweight to a self-devouring capitalist ideology.

—CHRIS HEDGES, 2012, P. 4

The Indigenous inspired political economic and existential goal is balance. The wise to be wise must also be just. Western economists like to think and say economics is value neutral; a system operating separate from its surrounding environment. This in itself denies the totality of the whole. Just as the sacred whole manifests an order that unifies all life, economic development should organize the assets—human, capital and community—in accordance with that belief system.

—REBECCA ADAMSON, 2008, P. 3

Our economics does not operate as if people mattered. The Indigenous notion of wealth that comes from giving things away is strange to us.

—DAVID MAYBURY-LEWIS, 1992, P. 83

K-16 Teacher Instructions:

Adapt and use this chapter's information according to your students' ages and cognitive levels. Use as an introduction to your standard course content or weave values, ideas or critical reflections into it throughout the course. Encourage students to carefully reflect on this information with the goal of deciding what mainstream ideas are best replaced with Indigenous ones, which ones are best as they are, and how the two might be partnered in terms of practical benefits for the students and their community (local and global). Use the questions at the end of the chapter to help with this process and to stimulate primary source research and enthusiastic, critical dialogue. Since in Indigenous ways of thinking the ideas related to this subject have relevance to all the other subjects, you may want to incorporate some of this chapter's material into the study of another subject area. As with all chapters in this section, this chapter is organized as follows:

1. Corporate and Hegemonic Influences
2. Real-World Outcomes
3. Indigenous Curricular Alternatives
4. Questions for Research, Dialogue, Choices and Praxis

Corporate and Hegemonic Influences

According to Mark C. Schug in his introduction to *Economics in the School Curriculum, K-12*, published by the Joint Council on Economic Education and the National Education Association, "the goal of economic education is to foster in students the thinking skills and substantial economic knowledge necessary to become effective and participating citizens" (1985, p. 6). Social justice teacher David Seiter also writes that economic educators should see the teaching of economics "as a key to effective citizenship in a free society" (1988). These comments are consistent with most curriculum vision statements for economics instruction. The National Council for Social Studies states, "The primary purpose of social studies is to help young people make informed and reasoned decisions for the public good as citizens of a culturally diverse, democratic society in an interdependent world" (1994, p. 1).

Since educational hegemony emphasizes individual gain and materialism rather than "effective citizenship," a "free society" or the "public good," our task is to understand how exactly it influences curricula to do this. The first hint, we have learned, relates to what is omitted in the curriculum that might best be included. When judged by this criteria, economics education is indeed shown to be compromised by hegemony, for it is largely absent from K-12 schooling. In 2011 the National Council on Economic Education conducted a nationwide survey in the

U.S. and found that only 22% of public schools require an economics course in high school and that only 16% require any testing of student knowledge in economics.[1] Since testing drives curriculum and since economics is not a significant item on standardized tests, we should not be surprised to find that few social studies teachers infuse economics into history or other coursework either. If the lower priority given to economics education is due to hegemony, this might mean that there is resistance to putting status quo beliefs about economics at risk by teaching students something that could lead them to challenge the status quo. There is a risk that critical dialogue or changing values might contribute to the growing concerns about capitalism's pitfalls.

Where economics is taught, hegemony takes another form. Those in power do what they can to make sure the curriculum supports the status quo. Scholars like Michael Apple and the many contributors to both editions of *Knowledge and Power in the Global Economy: The Effects of School Reform in a Neoliberal/Neoconservative Age* (Gabbard, 2008) continue to write about the hegemonic influence on curriculum, and some economics professors continue to critique educational precepts about economics, such as John Kenneth Galbraith does in his article "Free Market Fraud: The Myth of Capitalism" (1999). More recently, in *Economics without Illusions: Debunking the Myths of Modern Capitalism* (2010), Joseph Heath, an award-winning author and economics professor at the University of Toronto, has claimed that nearly everyone has succumbed to the illusions of profit making.

The problem is that material like this is not taught in economics classes. The idea of questioning the capitalist system is not on the curricular table. Liberal blogs can eloquently offer critiques, as in Chris Hedges's piece "The Implosion of Capitalism" (2012), but such "radical left-wing" articles seem to have no place in contemporary economics courses. Certainly, there is no place for an article that calls capitalism more a religion than a science, as Hedges does in the following:

> Capitalism, as Benjamin observed, called on human societies to embark on a ceaseless and futile quest for money and goods. This quest, he warned, perpetuates a culture dominated by guilt, a sense of inadequacy and self-loathing. It enslaves nearly all its adherents through wages, subservience to the commodity culture and debt peonage. The suffering visited on Native Americans, once Western expansion was complete, was soon endured by others, in Cuba, the Philippines, Nicaragua, the Dominican Republic, Vietnam, Iraq and Afghanistan. The final chapter of this sad experiment in human history will see us sacrificed as those on the outer reaches of empire were sacrificed. There is a kind of justice to this. We profited as a nation from this demented vision, we remained passive and silent when we should have denounced the crimes committed in our name, and now that the game is up we all go down together. (2012)[2]

Even right-wing conservatives have expressed concern about free-market-based hegemony in K-12 schooling. The Thomas B. Fordham Institute is a respected, slightly right-of-center conservative think-tank sponsored largely by Walmart.[3] In 2011 it surveyed state standards for history and economics throughout the U.S. Although in previous surveys, the institute alleged a liberal bias in education, this time it expressed a concern about right-wing bias, claiming that most states were addressing history and economic education poorly. They were especially frank about the Texas School Board's adoptions for standards, standards that refer to free enterprise eighty-six times. The report states:

> Throughout the Texas standards, dozens of references (even the title of the high school economics course) offer a drumbeat of uncritical celebration of "the free enterprise system and its benefits"—resembling, in an inverted historical echo, Soviet schools harping on the glories of state socialism. Native Americans, disproportionately discussed in many other states, are almost totally missing. Slavery is downplayed and segregation barely mentioned. (Stern and Stern 2011, p. 16)

The Fordham Institute's harsh critique was prompted by pressure from the left-leaning educators of color in Texas. The institute had no such pressure in evaluating the California state curriculum. It gave a grade of "F" to the Texas curriculum and an "A" to California. However, a closer look than the Fordham Institute managed reveals that California's updated state standards for K-12 economics reflect significant educational hegemony and corporate influence. Moreover, the process starts early. In kindergarten, for example, children are to learn key economic concepts that include:

Scarcity—The condition of not being able to have all the goods and services that we want.

Choice—What someone must make when faced with two or more alternative uses for a resource, also called an *economic choice*.

Goods—Objects that can be held or touched that can satisfy people's wants.

Services—Activities that can satisfy people's wants.

Kindergarten children also learn that "natural resources" are "are aids to the production of goods and services." In the history/social studies standards for Grade 1, entitled "A Child's Place in Time and Space," standard 1.6 states, "Students understand basic economic concepts and the role of individual choice in a free-market economy." By the time students reach Grade 12, the standards instruct teachers to:

- Evaluate the role of private property as an incentive in conserving and improving scarce resources
- Analyze the role of a market economy in establishing and preserving political and personal liberty (e.g., through the works of Adam Smith)
- Explain the roles of property rights, competition, and profit in a market economy
- Explain the role of profit as the incentive to entrepreneurs in a market economy
- Understand how the role of government in a market economy often includes providing for national defense, addressing environmental concerns, defining and enforcing property rights, attempting to make markets more competitive, and protecting consumers' rights.
- Discuss wage differences among jobs and professions, using the laws of demand and supply and the concept of productivity.
- Define, calculate, and explain the significance of an unemployment rate, the number of new jobs created monthly, an inflation or deflation rate, and a rate of economic growth.

Such assignments reveal how the assumptions about free enterprise being an accepted are maintained in education. The curriculum essentially says that capitalism is the only economic paradigm to consider, that private property ownership versus the public commons is unquestionable, that natural resources serve production, that wage differences are only about supply and demand, and that the U.S. government's policies and its monetary system are good for the whole world. There is no room in the curriculum to critically consider alternatives to corporatism or even to study its profound effect on society as relates to militarization, labor exploitation, wealth distribution, destruction of habitat, wars and loss of biodiversity. More importantly perhaps, the curriculum does not stimulate authentic, relevant thinking that connects economics to the real world, as do the Indigenous curriculum examples discussed later.

In *Corporate Hegemony: Contributions in Economics and Economic History*, William Dugger states that a change in education "in the direction of countering rather than tolerating this hegemony is necessary for U.S. prosperity in the future" (1989, p. 37). In the current volume, rather than such direct encounters, I offer a third option to countering or tolerating, namely a return to the wisdom found in the Indigenous perspectives. Chet Bowers also has written that Indigenous cultures offer "the only real source of resistance to the imperialism of market liberalism" (2005, p. 123). In this statement he blames not only the free-market neo-liberal and neo-conservative forces but the liberal and progressive ones as well. Neither have embraced Indigenous perspectives, which prioritize the relationship between humans and the rest of the natural world. Bowers understands that critical and progressive educators and even activists standing against the ruling elite are perpetuating a culture that encourages people to want more in spite of the finite nature of our resources and the delicate balance needed to maintain them. He also condemns "transformative learning" as a cause of our plight because it usually emphasizes innovation, progress, technological advancement and individualism (autonomy) instead of the balance reflected in traditional Indigenous perspectives—which, as revealed in Chapter 1, have been dismissed by both conservative and progressive forces in education.

Awareness of corporate hegemony is nonetheless a prerequisite for the partnership between mainstream and Indigenous values—even though asking people to be aware of hegemony is like asking a fish to be aware of the water. We must first be sensitized to this particular phenomenon. With this in mind, I offer the following brief representative look at the insidious history of educational hegemony in economics education, which has set the stage for what is happening today. This material comes from Sharon Beder's essay "The Role of 'Economic Education' in Achieving Capitalist Hegemony" (2006).[4]

After the Second World War, the labor union movement in the U.S. was strong and offered a counterweight to corporate power. Many people were also aware of the role government played in regulating unfettered free enterprise. This was not what the capitalists wanted. Businesses began to sponsor "economics education" as a guise to enter schools and find out what students really thought about free enterprise. High school students filled out multiple-choice surveys as a sort of economics test. The results confirmed that there was an "ignorance" about economics that needed to be fixed. Questions like the following were supposed to be answered as the check marks indicate, but too often the opposite (i.e., correct) answer was given instead.

Money invested in new machinery and equipment has increased output. The workers have got some of the increase but the larger share has gone to the owners.
( ) I agree
(√) I disagree

The wealth of this county is becoming more and more concentrated in the hands of the wealthiest 10% of the families
( ) True
(√) False

Clearly such questions merely tested the degree to which high school students' opinions coincided with those of conservative ideologues. Many students thought that owners got too much profit and gained most from new machinery. Worst of all, from a capitalist point of view, over half of the students agreed with the Marxist statement "The fairest economic system is one that 'takes from each according to his ability' and gives to each 'according to his needs.'" Although most teachers disagreed with the statement, this failure of students to "see through" this Marxist doctrine was taken to be evidence of "how little high school seniors comprehend the fundamentals of our economic system."[5]

Corporations then hired public relations (PR) firms to continue this remarkable campaign to connect business interests with such concepts as national interest, democracy, freedom, social harmony, religion and patriotism. They made sure that actions by unions or government regulators in conflict with business goals "and all liberals who supported such 'interference' were associated with communism and subversion" (Carey, 1995, p. 27). One of the PR firms, a company named Psychological Corporation, incorporated language in the new marketing scheme that reframed the idea of free enterprise to include the freedom of all individuals under this system while connecting "capitalism" to "Americanism." *Fortune* magazine called the campaign the most intensive marketing ever. An unprecedented $100 million was spent on 1,600 business periodicals, 577 commercial and financial digests, 2,500 advertising agencies, 4,000 corporate public relations departments and more than 6,500 newsletters with a combined circulation of more than 70 million. Think tanks like the American Enterprise Institute were formed. The money came from large corporations, including General Foods, General Electric, General Motors, IBM, Johnson and Johnson, Procter and Gamble, Goodrich and Republic Steel. Ironically, the individualist message of competition and self-interest was sold through a campaign that sought to promote industrial harmony and the idea that we should all cooperate and work together to protect the system and achieve the prosperity it promised.

Thus it became "economic ignorance" that was responsible for any pro-labor or anti-business stance. "Correction" action targeted schools, universities, company employees and the public in general. Schools, however, were deemed a priority. School children, the research found, were the most impressionable and the easiest to change. Opinion Research Marketing also concluded that the high school emphasis on American history and government led teenagers to believe that a government-directed economy, since it was supposed to operate for the benefit of all, would best serve social and economic justice. It was determined that these perceptions would not change without the new economics instruction. If they did not change, the students would eventually vote for measures that countered corporate goals.

A number of individual corporations developed educational materials to this end. For example, Coca-Cola prepared and distributed eight units of curriculum material on "Our America" to some 30 million primary school children. International Harvester and the American Petroleum Institute sponsored educational materials on the development of the U.S. economy produced by an advertising agency and distributed them for free. General Mills decided that even primary school students were not too young to be taught free-market economics, and it sponsored materials such as silk-screen panels telling the story of marketing bread, filmstrips and a comic book on "Freedom of Choice." Other companies pumping materials into schools—texts, filmstrips, teaching kits, movies—included U.S. Steel, General Electric, General Motors, American Cyanamid, Standard Oil and many others. In fact, one in five corporations did so. In 1954 corporations were supplying about $50 million worth of free materials to schools, compared with an annual expenditure on regular textbooks in schools of $100 million. Individual corporations were not the only ones providing free-market "educational" materials to schools. There were also industry and trade associations that produced teaching aids and also teaching units consisting of printed materials, films, record sets, text books, activity books, teachers guides, wall charts and tests. They provided speakers, tours, awards programs and career conferences and programs for secondary school students and symposia, seminars, workshops and panel discussions for college students. Four million packages of *Industry and the American Economy* (an eleven-booklet package), were distributed to students and teachers all over the nation. In 1951 one study found that 89% of teachers surveyed used industry-sponsored materials in their classes. Another, a few years later, found that 77% of all films shown in schools surveyed were donated sponsored films. Teacher education was also targeted by individual corporations because of the influence of teachers on millions of children.

A second stage of the campaign, which started in 1977, involved a huge advertising program centered on the idea of an Economics Quotient (EQ)—an obvious reference to IQ. Advertisements asked, "How high is your EQ?" or "Do your kids have a higher EQ than you?" And they included quiz questions and answers so people could test themselves. The idea was to make people feel ignorant so that they would write away for the booklet and, at the same time, to make an ideological point. Corporate money also financed a television show on economics featuring a leading neo-liberal economist, Milton Friedman, and another show, *In Search of the Real America*, featuring a fellow from the conservative think tank the American Enterprise Institute. Various oil companies got involved. Phillips Petroleum Company supported the production of a series of five films entitled *American Enterprise*, which came with an accompanying teacher's guide. It cost $800,000 and reached over 8 million students. Amoco Oil Company also produced a twenty-six-minute film and teacher's guide to explain how the free enterprise system worked. The Exxon Company got together with Walt Disney Educational Media Company to produce a twenty-two-minute film for high school students about two children who go into business. The U.S. Chamber of Commerce also produced films, teaching materials and booklets on the economic system in support of right-wing ideologies and a package entitled "Economics for Young Americans," which included film strips, audio cassettes, lesson plans and a text on productivity, profits and the environment. As you can imagine, the environment hardly benefitted.

The above history of economics educational hegemony set the stage for what is happening today in economics education, such as the continued "selling" of the free-enterprise system by the Texas curriculum standards. Collectively, we have been duped into believing that everything in the world, including air, water, forests, rivers and plants, are commodities intended to serve maximum profit and that somehow this is the best way to preserve natural systems and egalitarian values. From an Indigenous perspective, one would agree that any external coercion that forces a way of being in the world ultimately results in hierarchy, greed, power-lust and structural inequalities. However, ensuring that citizens live as ideal capitalists without being forced to do so by any coercive government regulation requires the set of values fostered by economic profit and competition. In her article "Changing the Rules of the Game," Rebecca Adamson lists the characteristics of such values, which are based on the model of industrialized capitalism under which mainstream society now operates:

- Historically, wealth was often held in land, but increasingly wealth is held in the form of financial assets (bank accounts, and portfolios of stocks and bonds). Where wealth continues to be held in land, it is often the resources in the land that can be monetized and sold, that undergird the land's value.
- The Earth is viewed with a sense of scarcity. Production and investment are geared toward maximizing production and maximizing investment returns. Goods have value because they are scarce; the scarcer the good is perceived to be, the greater its value.
- Economic decisions are based on hierarchy and control; nature is adapted through conquest to serve human needs.
- Land is often used intensively; development is frequently concentrated and continuous, focused on maximizing efficient extraction (maximum yield). Once land is "used up," economic activity shifts to some other place.
- Concerns about economic security (because of fears of economic scarcity) orient production to constant expansion and distribution toward a pooling of wealth. Increasingly, economic security is seen as a responsibility of the individual, rather than the society.
- Economic success is measured by the increased production of goods and services, regardless of their impact on social well-being. A woman undergoing a nasty divorce who has a bad auto accident on her way to be treated for breast cancer is an economic dream-come-true in terms of Gross Domestic Product (GDP).
- Power, both economic and political, accrues to those who are good "hoarders," gathering great pools of wealth, far more than any person or family could ever need. (1995, p. 23)

Until the Indigenous, nature-based values of reciprocity, generosity, balance and interconnectedness can be embraced again, the illusion of a free market that can foster balance and harmony in the world will continue to create the opposite (Four Arrows and Block, 2011).

Real-World Outcomes

Returning to the two key phrases in the goal statements of the content standards for current economics education—"the public good" and "a free society"—we can briefly consider how successful economics education has been in terms of these goals versus the goals set forth by the corporations as described above. I have already addressed the repercussions on natural life systems, and although not mentioned in the most idealistic curriculum rhetoric for economics, the plight of our ecological systems is the most tragic real-world outcome. Focusing on humans only, the situation is not much better. For starters, out of 2 billion children in the world, about half live in poverty according to World Bank figures that use $1.25 per day as the poverty line. In the United States the poverty line is a little over $20,000 per year for a family of four. In 2010, 50 million U.S. citizens lived in poverty, the fourth annual increase and the largest number in the fifty-two years that poverty rates have been published (DeNava, 2011, p. 14). More than 20 million Americans live in "extreme poverty," which means they make less than half of the poverty-line figure, or about $10,000 per year for a family of four (p. 19). According to the latest U.S. government report, released in 2011, children were "food insecure" in one out of ten households! In 2010 the poverty rate increased for children under age eighteen from 20.7 percent to 22.0 percent. According to the same report, the 2010 poverty rate for Hispanics was 26.6 percent and for blacks 27.4 percent (Coleman-Jensen, 2011). Poverty among American Indians was more than double that of any ethnic group.

How these statistics stand up to the goals of balance, justice, compassion, choice and ethics is seen with some wealth distribution statistics. Still using money as the basis for poverty, we unfortunately see that balance does not exist. (Remember the 1947 survey above?) During the past several decades, the top 1 percent of the U.S. population have made an average of $27 million per year per household, compared to the average income for the bottom 99 percent of us, which is around $31,000. The richest 10 percent of Americans control 71 percent of all the wealth (Gilson & Perot, 2011). An interesting related statistic from 2001, which is probably worse today, is that 12 percent of the entire world's population use 85 percent of the water; none of this 12 percent live in developing third-world countries (Barlow, 2001).

It is easy to see from these and other easily obtained facts that the Western free-market economics taught in most schools has led to the disenfranchisement of certain groups of people, especially—as we continue to see—Indigenous Peoples and children, while enhancing the wealth of those at the top of the military-industrial-financial complex. (Military expenditures represent half of all U.S. expenditures.) Lobbying, tax breaks and political cronyism continue this process. Most Americans have accepted the hegemony that says it is fine for a businessperson or financier to make unlimited amounts of money over and above the earnings of others on whom they depend. While at Northern Arizona University, each semester I asked my students in a social studies course on K-8 methods whether anyone supported the concept of CEOs making no more than fourteen times what their lowest paid employees made. Over a number of years, only two thought that restrictions on income earning or guidelines for wealth distribution were not "un-American." It seems the work done by organizations like the Ad Council, the Chamber of Commerce and the American Enterprise Institute was successful. The real-world outcomes relating to ever increasing disparity between wealthy and poor individuals is a result. Let us now look at how an Indigenous perspective on economics might change all of this.

Indigenous Curricular Alternatives

Weaving Indigenous economic concepts into the mainstream curriculum would help shift the focus from monetary profit to living relationships. This would produce a curriculum that fostered a deep respect for all of life, an understanding of our interconnectedness and an appreciation for the reciprocity inherent to our holistic reality. In contrasting Western and traditional economies, Indigenous scholar Rebecca Adamson says that economics, "more than any single issue, is the battle line between the two competing world views." She continues,

> Tribal people's fundamental value was sustainability, and they conducted their livelihoods in ways that sustained resources and limited inequalities in their society. What made traditional economies so radically different and so very fundamentally dangerous to Western economies were the traditional principles of prosperity of Creation versus scarcity of resources, of sharing and distribution versus accumulation and greed, of kinship usage rights versus individual exclusive ownership rights, and of sustainability versus growth....The goal is balance. The goal is sustaining human kind in ways that don't threaten the lives of other beings. They harvest the surplus nature provides, timing their harvest when the species are most abundant and taking only what is needed. A stark contrast to maximum yield! (2008, p. 3)

A phrase used to describe the economies of traditional Indigenous cultures is "gift economy." A gift economy as represented by past and present Indigenous communities from around the world is not based on capital, nor is it a form of socialism, communism or racism. It is about relationships, authentic reciprocity, interconnectedness and respect for the entire natural world. This economy is based not on exchanges between buyer and seller but on a complex system in which reciprocal gift giving can occur anywhere. It is about generosity. It is not just about a kind of generosity that expects something in return, although this is part of it. It reflects a genuine understanding that authentic caring and cooperation are primary features in Nature. The giving and accepting of "gifts" are reflected in the complex symbiotic systems, a feature even Charles Darwin acknowledged, contrary to the "survival of the fittest" emphasis of his interpreters. "Ultimately one can trace the function of human generosity to the human instinct for survival perhaps, but survival when considered in Nature's terms is a symbiotic phenomenon with little room for the kind of selfishness seen in the world today" (Adamson 2008, p. 11).

This focus on generosity in the natural world is part of the culturally relevant Indigenous "economics" curriculum. In 1995 the Laguna Pueblo Department of Education, along with partners, used a $5.7 million U.S. Department of Education challenge grant (the only one offered that impacted American Indian students) to found the Four Directions project. It created a culturally appropriate curriculum for Indian students through the Center for Educational Technology in Indian America. In the following examples taken from "Culturally Relevant Lesson Plans" for teaching "economics,"[6] note the strong emphasis on "gifts of nature," critical thinking, interconnectedness, concern for the public good and relevant, real-life-oriented exercises. The following sample "benchmarks" for various grade levels address standards for teaching economics put forth by the Foundation for Teaching Economics.[7]

Economics Standards 1: Productive resources are limited. Therefore, people cannot have all the goods and services they want; as a result, they must choose some things and give up others.

Grade 4:

Benchmark 10: Natural resources, such as land, are "gifts of nature"; they are present without human intervention. American Indian communities have strong traditional values related to nature and its resources. These values often affect decisions regarding how natural resources on tribal lands should or should not be used in the production of goods for economic benefit.

At the completion of Grade 4, Indian students will use this knowledge to:

- Explain why a choice must be made, given a specific piece of tribal land and some alternative uses for that land (e.g., mine, farm or pow-wow camp ground).

Grade 8:

Benchmark 5: The evaluation of choices and opportunity costs is subjective; such evaluations differ across individuals and societies. Even in a single tribal community, there may be decidedly different perspectives and, thus, preferences about the allocation of tribal resources, the development and/or use of tribal land or natural resource holdings, etc. Choices have to be made.

At the completion of Grade 8, Indian students will use this knowledge to:

- Role play a meeting to allocate a budget of $100,000, based on the following scenario: there are several different options the Council needs to consider—buying four new police cars at $25,000 each, repairing two elder centers at $50,000 each, building a new powwow ground complex at $50,000, and setting up a tribal scholarship program with $50,000. Explain why a choice must be made, and decide on the best way to spend the money. Describe the trade-offs made, the effects of those trade-offs on the community, and identify the opportunity cost of the decision. Individually develop a solution to a problem that affects everybody in the students' tribal community and identify the opportunity cost. Compare the solutions and explain why solutions and opportunity costs differ.

Grade 12:

Benchmark 1: Choices made by individuals, firms, or government officials often have long-run unintended consequences that can partially or entirely offset the initial effects of their decisions.

At the completion of Grade 12, Indian students will use this knowledge to:

- Explain various ways in which a tribal government's decision to harvest timber on tribal reservation land could affect reservation life. Discuss what kinds of factors should be considered in making this initial choice, and what could be some of the positive and negative consequences for the community (economically, environmentally, etc.).

Standard 2: Effective decision-making requires comparing the additional costs of alternatives with the additional benefits. Most choices involve doing a little more or a little less of something; few choices are all-or-nothing decisions.

Grade 12:

Benchmark 1: Marginal benefit is the change in total benefit resulting from an action. Marginal cost is the change in total cost resulting from an action.

Benchmark 2: As long as the marginal benefit of an activity exceeds the marginal cost, people are better off doing more of it; when the marginal cost exceeds the marginal benefit, they are better off doing less of it.

Benchmark 3: To produce the profit-maximizing level of output and hire the optimal number of workers and other resources, producers must compare the marginal benefits and marginal costs of producing a little more with the marginal benefits and marginal costs of producing a little less.

Benchmark 4: To determine the optimal level of a public policy program, voters and government officials must compare the marginal benefits and marginal costs of providing a little more or a little less of the program's services.

At the completion of Grade 12, Indian students will use this knowledge to:

- Apply the concepts of marginal benefit and marginal cost to an environmental ordinance that a tribe has passed (which restricts the level of air pollution a factory can emit), and weigh it against the employment opportunities that the factory provides to the community. [Provide students with hypothetical data regarding reservation unemployment rates, the costs to the community associated with unemployment and the costs for reducing pollution produced by businesses on tribal lands.]
- Use the concepts of marginal cost and marginal benefit to evaluate the best pollution-control options for the tribe.

Standard 3: Different methods can be used to allocate goods and services. People, acting individually or collectively through government, must choose which methods to use to allocate different kinds of goods and services.

Grade 8:

Benchmark 2: There are essential differences between a market economy, in which allocations result from individuals making decisions as buyers and sellers, and a command economy, in which resources are allocated according to central authority.

Benchmark 4: National economies vary in the extent to which they rely on government directives (central planning) and signals from private markets to allocate scarce goods, services, and productive resources.

At the completion of Grade 8, Indian students will use this knowledge to:

- Compare the advantages and disadvantages of economic systems used among American Indian communities both prior to and after the arrival of Europeans; for example, examine trade and barter systems, reciprocal giving traditions. Relate these to criteria of broad social goals such as freedom, efficiency, peace, fairness and reciprocity. Compare those traditional systems with the economic systems used by Europeans from the 16th to 18th centuries.
- Understand that as a result of their special political status and relationship with the United States government, tribal governments as sovereign entities are unique. Compare the relative size and responsibilities of different tribal governments, especially with respect to the types of decisions they make regarding the provision of services to their communities and the use of their tribally owned natural and other resources.

Grade 12:

Benchmark 1: Comparing the benefits and costs of different allocation methods in order to choose the method that is most appropriate for some specific problem can result in more effective allocations and a more effective overall allocation system.

At the completion of Grade 12, Indian students will use this knowledge to:

- Examine the local tribal economic system, and the tribal government's methods for allocating resources. Assess the effectiveness of methods used to allocate tribal resources associated with, for example and as locally relevant: housing; services to the elderly; scholarships; law enforcement; courts; hunting and fishing licenses; and school attendance zones.

Standard 4: People respond predictably to positive and negative incentives.

Grade: 4

Benchmark 4: People's views of rewards and penalties differ because people have different values. Therefore, an incentive can influence different individuals in different ways. American Indian responses to incentives can be influenced by tribal beliefs and values.

At the completion of Grade 4, Indian students will use this knowledge to:

- Identify examples of current or traditional incentives that are an integral part of the students' tribal culture—e.g., traditional child rearing techniques and disciplinary procedures that the tribal culture used or still uses with children. Identify specific roles that elders play in using these incentives through their teachings, storytelling, or role modeling. Identify ways in which non-Indians or members of different tribes might respond differently to those same incentives.

Grade 12

Benchmark 2: [Governments], small and large firms...and educational...organizations have different goals and face different rules and constraints. These goals, rules, and constraints influence the benefits and costs of those who work with or for those organizations and, therefore, their behavior.

At the completion of Grade 12, Indian students will use this knowledge to:

- Compare and contrast the positive and negative incentives an individual might face in serving as a legislator, a tribal police officer, the owner of a small business on the reservation, or the director of a tribe's education department.

Standard 5: Voluntary exchange occurs only when all participating parties expect to gain. This is true for trade among individuals or organizations within a nation, and among individuals or organizations in different nations.

Grade: 4

Benchmark 1: Exchange is trading goods and services with people for other goods and services or for money.

Benchmark 2: The oldest form of exchange is barter—the direct trading of goods and services between people. Prior to the arrival of Europeans in North America, American Indian tribes had established vast trade networks which extended across North America and into Central and South America. There was no common currency supporting those trade relationships.

At the completion of Grade 4, Indian students will use this knowledge to:

- Identify historical examples of trade exchanges between their own and other tribes and explain why they think trading was done.

Grade 8

Benchmark 4: Imports are foreign goods and services purchased from sellers in other nations.

Benchmark 5: Exports are domestic goods and services sold to buyers in other nations.

At the completion of Grade 8, Indian students will use this knowledge to:

- Describe American Indian roles as suppliers (exporters) and consumers (importers) during the colonial and early American fur trade era. Examine both the fur trade's effect on North American natural resources as well as the availability of new choices in goods for those tribes who participated in the fur trade.

Standard 6: When individuals, regions, and nations specialize in what they can produce at the lowest cost and then trade with others, both production and consumption increase.

Grade: 4

Benchmark 1: Economic specialization occurs when people concentrate their production on fewer kinds of goods and services than they consume.

At the completion of Grade 4, Indian students will use this knowledge to:

- Name several adults in the school or tribal community who specialize in the production of a good or service (e.g., tribal government employee, tribal business employee, teacher, traditional artist), and identify other goods and services that these individuals consume but do not produce for themselves.

- Describe the production of goods which occurs on the students' reservation, and identify the production processes that involve specialization and division of labor.

Grade: 12

Benchmark 3: Individuals and nations have a comparative advantage in the production of goods or services if they can produce a product at a lower opportunity cost than other individuals or nations. Due to the fact that Indian lands are exempt from state and local taxes, enterprises on American Indian reservation lands are often able to produce goods at a lower opportunity cost since state and local taxes are not included in those costs.

At the completion of Grade 12, Indian students will use this knowledge to:

- Apply the concepts of opportunity cost and comparative advantage to the following problem: A large U.S. car company needs to find a new location for one of its distributor cap manufacturing plants. The company is looking at two sites: one is in a large industrial park in a small town; the other is on tribal reservation land and would afford substantial tax benefits due to the unique governmental status of the tribe. The unemployment rate is high in both the town and reservation communities. What other incentives, in addition to tax reductions, might the tribe consider offering the company to confirm the company's commitment to locate there?

Standard 7: Markets exist when buyers and sellers interact. This interaction determines market prices and thereby allocates scarce goods and services.

Grade: 4

Benchmark 3: Most people both produce and consume. As producers they make goods and services; as consumers they use goods and services.

At the completion of Grade 4, Indian students will use this knowledge to:

- Identify family or community members on the reservation who are acting as producers, and specify what they produce (type of good or service). Identify ways in which those same individuals, as consumers, are dependent on other producers located great distances away from the reservation or Indian community. Discuss the interdependencies of today's buyers and sellers.

Standard 8: Prices send signals and provide incentives to buyers and sellers. When supply or demand changes, market prices adjust, affecting incentives.

Grade: 12

Benchmark 3: Changes in supply or demand cause relative prices to change; in turn, buyers and sellers adjust their purchase and sales decisions. Because of the federal trust status of reservation land, tribes do not levy state taxes on goods sold on reservation land. This affects both buyers' purchase decisions and sellers' sales decisions, particularly in reservation border areas.

At the completion of Grade 12, Indian students will use this knowledge to:

- Predict the decisions of both reservation and non-reservation buyers, as well as decisions of off-reservation sellers given the following scenario: Reservation X has several gas stations and smoke shops on it, which are owned by tribal members; federal tax and a 1% tribal tax are included in the sale price of gasoline and tobacco products sold by those businesses. Town Y, which borders the reservation, also has several gas stations and convenience stores. All items sold there include a federal tax and a 3.5% state tax.

These examples reveal how even mainstream economic standards can be used to teach about caring for others, reciprocity, generosity and cooperation are natural economic considerations. It is logical that human economic systems should incorporate these values and vital that economic considerations include non-human "others." As mentioned in Chapter 3, anthropocentrism remains an enduring challenge to Nature-based thinking, and this is especially true when it comes to economic issues. If we scoff at the idea of learning from animals and other non-human entities, the core foundation of a gift economy crumbles. In terms of economic activity, many individuals, businesses and institutions conduct themselves as though only humans count.[8] An explicit example of this belief comes from Walter Block, an endowed economics professor at Loyola University whom I invited to co-author *Differing Worldviews in Higher Education: Two Scholars Argue Cooperatively about Justice Education* (2010). Block, who believes that under capitalism natural resources are not only unlimited but actually able to increase as well, further contends that all things and creatures non-human "do not at all have intrinsic value, only instrumental value, as a means toward human ends" (p. 89). My response to Block in the book reveals the stark contrast between the two economic worldviews embraced by the Indigenious and mainstream curricula:

The idea that everything on earth, from plants and oceans to animals and fish, are exclusively on earth for humans to exploit is to me the single greatest disagreement between us and one that colors most of the rest of our perspectives on social justice education. I don't know how slavery plays into your "human benefit only" economic theory (except that you believe African Americans are better off than those who remained in Africa, another claim I contest), but as long as we refer to "natural resources" as anything but "relatives," our white versus red worldviews will divide us on other issues. (p. 89)

Aside from the problem of anthropocentrism, another challenge facing a serious consideration of Indigenous alternatives is the sense that they would be impossible to implement in a complex society. Barbara Alice Mann offers an answer to this concern:

Is capitalism the only system ever to support large-scale, sophisticated cultures? Hell, no! Gift economies have been doing that splendidly, throughout history. Around the world, both historically and into the present, gift economies have thrived. In Native North America, they were the right-hand of our constitutional democracies, and still flourish underground. The gift economy of the magnificent Iroquois League supported five nations from the year 1142 on, adding the sixth nation in 1712, and including another sixty or so affiliated nations along the way. The Lahu, or mountain people of southern China, have survived both colonial capitalism and Maoism into the present, their gift-culture battered but intact. The Berber women in Kabylia continue to manage abundance without capitalism in the unforgiving lands of North Africa. The Minangkabau of Sumatra do just fine without capital; indeed, their gift culture weathered the Tsunami of 2005. The Sami ("Laplanders") of Finland are emerging from centuries of oppression, by both Soviets and western Europeans, with their gift economies alive. These name just *some* of the gift economies extant in the world, and the list does not even scratch the surface of the theoretical work that has been done on the economics of the gift. (2009, original emphasis)[9]

In "A Poor Man Shames Us All," a chapter in his classic illustrated book *Millennium: Tribal Wisdom for the Modern World*, David Maybury-Lewis also describes the reciprocity and gift economies of Indigenous Peoples from around the world, referring to them as "moral economies":

That is, an economy permeated by personal and moral considerations. They are productive communities, much concerned with social relations between their members, as opposed to marketplaces that are primarily concerned with economic transactions between their members. It is a system in which the economic rationality and profitability have replaced or at least superseded ideas of obligation and mutuality. (1992, p. 73)

In such a system, the "marketplace" is not impersonal. Ideas like "buyer beware" or "there is a sucker born every minute" have no place in the Indigenous perspective. The hallmark of exchange is not competition but rather complementarity and stability. It is not about "use value" but about relationships and community welfare. Such ideas are studied and encouraged by many outside Indigenous circles, although most reference the origins as being Indigenous. For example, Anitra Nelson is another scholar who studies Indigenous cultures and alternative social systems. A professor at RMIT University in Melbourne, her website at http://www.moneyfreezone.info offers numerous resources related to contemporary implementation of Indigenous gift economies and variations on them. For examples, the following resources are just the tip of the iceberg of what is available for further studies and projects:

- Mauss's *The Gift: Forms and Function of Exchange in Archaic Societies* (1925; reprint, London: Routledge & Kegan Paul, 1974)
- Gregory's introduction in *Gifts and Commodities* (London: Academic Press, 1982)
- Leahy's website at http://www.gifteconomy.org.au
- Practical examples of alternative non-monetary exchange networks include the website at http://www.freecycle.org
- Schumacher's *Small Is Beautiful: A Study of Economics as If People Mattered* (London: Blond & Briggs, 1982)
- McRobie's *Small is Possible* (London: Jonathan Cape, 1982)
- Albert and Hahnel's *The Political Economy of Participatory Economics* (Princeton, NJ: Princeton University Press, 1991) and *Looking Forward: Participatory Economics for the Twenty First Century* (Boston: South End Press, 1991)
- Vaughn's *Women and the Gift Economy: A Radically Different Worldview Is Possible* (Toronto: Inanna Publications and Education, 2007)

Some other Indigenous economic concepts to be considered when studying mainstream economics curriculum include:

- Land is not a lifeless commodity or an economic resource for financial gain but rather a sacred, living ecosystem that we depend on and relate to in a symbiotic way. Earth is not something to "outgrow," as Paul Hewitt suggests is humanity's goal in *Conceptual Physics: A High School Physics Program* (1987, p. 7). All economic considerations must take into account the effect of production and consumption on all of life on Earth, including Earth's eco systems.

- Whether domestic or foreign, trade is not merely an economic activity but also an opportunity for a network of social relationships based on mutuality.

- Food and water cannot be commodities alone but must be seen as life forces containing spirit and be treated accordingly. (See the question pertaining to this idea in the next section.)

- An economics that creates exchanges and consumes from within a small geographic radius is more likely to be done with respect and with less waste and excess.

- Every perceived thing is understood as being in some sense alive, with its own rhythm and unique vibrations. "There is no clear divide between that which is animate and that which is inanimate" (Abrams, 2011, p. 269).

- Prestige, a factor used in marketing many products for consumption, is often seen as being related to how much one possesses and how expensive are the possessions. In Indigenous economics, the idea of prestige, which itself is connected to humility, is measured by how generous a person is and by how much he or she displays sincere caring about others, even about people he or she may not like or does not know. "Gifts" include not only material items but also knowledge and cooperation. As one elder Weyewan Native says, "I'm not a rich man according to most human reckonings but I am rich in ability and I am rich in knowledge. I'm rich in favors and I'm rich in cooperation with others" (Maybury-Lewis, 1992, p. 72).

- The highest expression of courage relates to acts of profound generosity.

- Ideas of obligation and mutuality are more important than profitability.

- Gifts should be kept in circulation rather than becoming any one person's property. The gift has more than use-value, for it also helps keep people in relationship and creates social bonds when it is passed from hand to hand.

Questions for Research, Dialogue, Choices and Praxis

1. Answer the survey question given to high school students in 1947, and offer two primary source references to support your answer.

   The wealth of this county is becoming more and more concentrated in the hands of the wealthiest 10% of the families.
   ( ) True
   ( ) False

2. Males still outnumber females in leadership positions for economic industries. Why is this and what might be different if more balance between the sexes existed? Make correlations to the fact that men make higher wages for doing the same jobs as women and that there are fewer women in top corporate positions.

3. Select one or more examples from the American Indian curriculum "standards and benchmarks" above and create similar exercises related to your own local situation.

4. Why do you think the American Indian curriculum standards created by the Four Directions project include mathematics but not "economics" per se?

5. What are the "commons"? And what is wrong with free enterprise privatizing them?

6. Walter Block wrote in our book *Differing Worldviews in Higher Education* (2010) that only humans have intrinsic value and that animals have only utilitarian value for the sake of humans. Do you agree? Why or why not? How would your decision influence economic decisions?

7. What does it mean to say mutuality and obligation are more important than profit?

8. Research to see whether labor unions make employment safer and healthier for workers and whether unionized workers have higher wages and more benefits.

9. If you could make a rule that says the owner/CEO of a company cannot make more than fifteen times the money earned by his or her lowest-paid worker, would you? Why or why not? Do you know the average difference between the high and the low that exists today?

10. Describe how a "gift economy" relates to philanthropy and how Western capitalism might be able to partner with a gift economy orientation to avoid governmental interference in the "free market."

11. Has a truly free market ever really existed? Think of your own world of production and receipt of benefits for your work. Are there any rules governing it? Is there any external control or influence?

12. What are the economic benefits and consequences of war for a country?

13. What are the economic benefits and consequences for the environment that relate to various energy sources in the world today?

14. The shrimp industry, whether through farming or netting, does significant damage to fisheries, the ocean bottom and mangroves. If you confirmed this with your research, would you stop eating shrimp?

Would you encourage others to boycott shrimp as well? What other decisions can you make about what you buy that will help stop climate change or other ecological problems?[10]

Notes

1. These findings and other information can be seen at http://www.councilforeconed.org/news-information/survey-of-the-states.
2. In my own book *Differing Worldviews in Higher Education: Two Scholars Argue Cooperatively about Justice Education* (2010), I found that my invited co-author, a free-market libertarian, had such illogical views—including the notion that we should pen in whales and privatize the oceans—that I felt his claim to be an atheist was belied by his adherence to the religion of the free market.
3. In addition to Walmart's long-standing history of sweatshop practices, labor discrimination, pollution charges and the like, it is now being investigated for widespread corruption internationally. See David Barstow, "Wal-Mart Covered Up Widespread Corruption," *New York Times,* April 21, 2012.
4. I have written this short story by quoting and paraphrasing parts of Beder's article, which is published in *State of Nature* 2 (Sept/Oct 2006), http://www.herinst.org/sbeder/PR/econeduc.html. This material is covered more deeply in her book *Free Market Missionaries: The Corporate Manipulation of Community Values* (London: Earthscan, 2006) . In the online article alone, she lists seventy-nine citations for readers who wish to validate the following assertions with primary source documents. Note that the author's use of "missionaries" in her book title makes my use of it in this particular book most appropriate in light of a partnership between American Indians and Eurocentric values.
5. Opinion Research Corporation, *The High School Market for Economic Education* (Princeton, NJ: Public Opinion Research Corporation, June 1951), pp. 6–8, 11, 44.
6. The content standards and benchmarks are actually for mathematics. There is no "economics" course per se in the Four Directions project. Rather, it incorporated the economics perspectives into their mathematics section. This makes the understanding of "economics" more practical than ideological and allows students to give priority to cultural values and the functional realities of earning a living and providing for others.
7. See the national voluntary standards at http://www.fte.org/teacher-resources/voluntary-national-content-standards-in-economics/
8. If we consider the differences between the haves and have-nots, it may be that mainstream economic thought also sees some humans as counting other humans as less than others as well.
9. I have removed the references from this quotation, but it is important to note that each claim is cited. For further study, the citations can be found in the original quotation at http://www.realitysandwich.com/gift_economy_fractals. For more on gift economies, see the anthology by Genevieve Vaughn, ed., *Women and the Gift Economy: A Radically Different Worldview Is Possible* (Toronto: Inanna Publications and Education, 2007); and Rauna Kuokkanen, "The Logic of the Gift: Reclaiming Indigenous Peoples' Philosophies," *Australian Journal of Indigenous Education* 34 (2005): 251–71.
10. See Four Arrows, *The Shrimp Habit: How It Is Destroying our World and What You Can Do about It* (Vancouver: Traeger, 2009).

Science

With guest author Greg Cajete

Indigenous knowledge fills the ethical and knowledge gaps in Eurocentric education, research, and scholarship.
—MARIE BATTISTE, 2005, P. 38

Indigenous science and Indigenous languages do not seek to control or to hold on to stability within this flux with analytic ideas, laws and concepts. Instead they seek balance, harmony and relationship.
—F. DAVID PEAT, 2002, P. 278

Modern science's dazzling achievements in rationally dissecting the natural world may also be contributing to a sense of psychological, emotional, and spiritual detachment from the rest of the natural world.
—DAVID SUZUKI, 1992, P. 78.

The very concept of "scientific truth" can only represent a social Construction invented by scientists (whether consciously or not) as a device to justify their hegemony over the study of nature.
—STEPHEN JAY GOULD (C. 2000)

K-16 Teacher Instructions:

Adapt and use this chapter's information according to your students' ages and cognitive levels. Use as an introduction to your standard course content or weave values, ideas or critical reflections into it throughout the course. Encourage students to carefully reflect on this information with the goal of deciding what mainstream ideas are best replaced with Indigenous ones, which ones are best as they are, and how the two might be partnered in terms of practical benefits for the students and their community (local and global). Use the questions at the end of the chapter to help with this process and to stimulate primary source research and enthusiastic, critical dialogue. Since in Indigenous ways of thinking the ideas related to this subject have relevance to all the other subjects, you may want to incorporate some of this chapter's material into the study of another subject area. As with all chapters in this section, this chapter is organized as follows:

1. Corporate and Hegemonic Influences
2. Real-World Outcomes
3. Indigenous Curricular Alternatives
4. Questions for Research, Dialogue, Choices and Praxis

Corporate and Hegemonic Influences

A class that combines a study of mainstream science with traditional Indigenous knowledge offers unique opportunities for students to learn how to discover information about the natural world that is meaningful. Indigenous and non-Indigenous students can benefit from realizing that these two knowledge systems coexist in our multidimensional world. This combination allows students to learn at long last that science and art are two sides of the same coin. Perhaps without corporatization, militarization and ideological hegemony interfering, this partnership would have happened long ago.

In looking at corporate and hegemonic influences on mainstream education, I critique two dimensions that relate to science theory and applications in Western society. The first dimension involves the Western lens that shapes our thinking and beliefs about science. Although quantum physics, seen by some to be a bridge between Indigenous and mainstream science, is revealing that this lens is inadequate, it continues to define what makes its way into our psyche via education and media. The second dimension of misleading science education arises even when the Western lens is the sharpest and allows us to come close to important truths. I refer to the hegemons' and corporatists' control of what knowledge is presented to the masses. The list below relates to both of these dimensions. Each item represents a good reason for a mainstream-Indigenous partnership in science education.

1. Reductionism: supports continued exploitation that serves the monopolistic advantage of those in power.
2. The "myth of objectivity": empowers a false perception of scientific truth.
3. Misinformation: gives economic benefits to a minority at the expense of others.
4. A progress paradigm: overemphasizes advantages of technology, progress and social engineering to maintain consumer culture.
5. Misplaced focus on competition: dismisses Charles Darwin's perspective on cooperation and equality.

These characteristics of science education ultimately benefit the ideological, political and economic goals of the global elites, whether they manipulate things to achieve them or merely allow the historical approach to Western science to remain unchallenged. Often the agents of hegemony are to blame, whether they be politicians, scientists on corporate payrolls, well-funded and influential right-wing think tanks, right-leaning religious organizations, libertarians dedicated to free-market ideology, left-wing liberal individuals and groups that emphasize anthropocentric goals and maintain the progress paradigm or those of us who unquestioningly embrace these ideas.

Many teachers do know better. For example, teacher members of the National Center for Science Education work hard each year to undo the climate change denial or neutrality that, as we shall see, most science standards represent. Their lack of success, however, might relate to the absence of a sufficient alternative model with which to challenge or complement the mainstream curriculum. By incorporating both a more critical awareness of science hegemony and alternative and complementary Indigenous perspectives, all teachers can immediately begin to counter the five problematic characteristics of science education listed above, thus offering a holistic opportunity for children of any age to be better prepared to help reverse the downward spiral of human civilization—before it is too late.

Before turning to real life consequences and Indigenous alternatives as presented by Greg Cajete, I briefly describe the problems associated with these five characteristics of science education.

(1) *Reductionism: Supports continued exploitation that serves the monopolistic advantage of those in power*

> An old joke hints at this problem. A carpenter, a teacher and a scientist were traveling by train through Scotland when they saw a black sheep through the window of the train.
>
> "Aha," said the carpenter with a smile, "I see that Scottish sheep are black."
>
> "Hmm," said the teacher, "You mean that some Scottish sheep are black."
>
> "No," said the scientist, "All we know is that there is at least one sheep in Scotland and that at least one side of that one sheep is black."

Reductionism is central to mainstream science. By breaking complex systems down into smaller parts, researchers find out enough about how things work to create amazing technologies. One cannot be overly critical of this approach, as the miracles it has produced surround us. In some ways, an understanding of the small can lead to a better understanding of the complex. Unfortunately, frog dissections, brain scans, molecular medicine, and so on, despite having created a number of modern conveniences, have done little to prevent the destruction of our most basic life systems. Even where mainstream science is more holistically oriented, as in chaos theory, systems biology and functional magnetic resonance imaging (fMRI), reductionist assumptions still create significant problems.

The following examples offer a model for the current problems of science education and its impact on society. Although it took twenty years, after the Food and Drug Administration (FDA) encountered a relatively small number of deaths due to the otherwise non-invasive MRI machine causing metal objects in the rooms containing the machine to injure patients, the FDA finally required metal detectors at the door of the MRI room. Similarly, in 1988 the FDA permitted gadonlinium-based contrasting agents to be used with MRI procedures until a significant number of cases of nephrogentic systemic fibrosis were linked to these agents. Then in 2007 the FDA required manufacturers of the chemical to place a warning label on the product. In both of these cases, the lack of holistic thinking from the beginning caused irreparable harm.

Staying with the MRI examples, there is also the problem of diagnosis. Drawing conclusions about the whole body from images is far from dependable. Scans are easily misinterpreted and can lead to misdiagnosis and unnecessary, harmful, costly interventions.[1] For example, in sports medicine alone, MRIs are both overused and often misinterpreted. One study of MRIs showed that they had "found" abnormal shoulder cartilage in 90 percent of apparently healthy baseball pitchers and abnormal rotator cuff tendons in 87 percent of them (Kolat, 2011). Another study showed that nearly 90 percent of MRIs were unnecessary and that half had resulted in interpretations that either made no difference or were at odds with appropriate diagnosis (Kolat, 2011).

Another hegemonic influence from the MRI relates to the field of neuroscience. Here we see how the effects of hegemonic-induced beliefs on the neuroscientists themselves cause interpretations of brain scans that lead to conclusions about human nature itself that find their way into multiple subject areas. Greg Cajete, John Lee and I authored a book that exposes this problem, entitled *Critical Nuerophilosophy and Indigenous Wisdom* (Four Arrows, Cajete and Lee, 2011). The studies in this book tend to show that many of the conclusions reached by scientists based on experimental studies are questionable. Most stand in contrast to Indigenous perspectives, revealing strong Western paradigms. It is as though the scientists want to describe the whole human being in terms of the parts that can be manipulated. For instance, many neuroscientists believe that deception is an inherently valuable evolutionary phenomenon in humans. This is based on seeing a small portion of the brain that activates when someone is lying about some aspect of an artificial experiment, like cheating in monopoly. Generosity is seen as being self-serving because generous behaviors seem to activate portions of the brain related to selfishness. From an Indigenous perspective, neither conclusion holds water, and evidence from other disciplines with a broader span of reasonable associations, including animal studies, tend to support the idea that deception is not a positive evolutionary survival mechanism but the contrary and that generosity can be authentic and not self-serving.

Reductionist science is problematic from an ecological perspective as well. There are too many relevant phenomena that cannot be studied without larger systems thinking. The interconnectedness of life on many levels calls for a different approach to understanding what we must come to understand if we are to survive. We cannot continue to explain everything in terms of hierarchical structures. Such thinking seems to serve only hierarchical human structures. In her chapter in *Science, Hegemony and Violence* (1988), Vandana Shiva writes,

> Reductionist science is also at the root of the growing ecological crisis, because it entails a transformation of nature such that the processes, regularities and regenerative capacity of nature are destroyed.
>
> Since the alternative modes of knowledge which can provide solutions to these problems are oriented to social benefit rather than to personal or corporate profits, reductionist science scoffs at them as hocus-pocus. The fact, however, is that reductionist science itself often resorts to misinformation and falsehood in order to establish its monopoly on knowledge. This monopoly results in four-fold violence: violence against the subject of knowledge, the object of knowledge, the beneficiary of knowledge, and against knowledge itself. (p. 67)

As we see later when Greg Cajete offers his Indigenous science curriculum, there is an option to this reductionist perspective. I end the reductionist critique with a quotation from David Abram's work to give you a hint at a more holistic way of knowing:

> In an era when nature is primarily spoken of in abstract terms, as an objective and largely determinate set of mechanisms—at a time when eloquent behavior of other animals is said to be entirely "programmed in their genes," and when the surrounding sensuous landscape is referred to merely as a stock of "resources" for human use—it is clear that our direct, sensory engagement with the earth around us has become woefully impoverished. The accelerating ecological destruction wrought by contemporary humankind seems to stem not from any inherent meanness in our species but from a kind of perceptual obliviousness, an inability to actually notice anything outside the sphere of our human designs. In such an era, perhaps the most vital task of the sleight-of-hand magician is precisely to startle the senses from their slumber, to shake our eyes and our ears free from the static, habitual ways of seeing and hearing into which those senses have fallen under the deadening influence of abstract and overly-objectified ways of speaking and thinking. (2005)

(2) The "myth of objectivity" empowers a false perception of scientific truth

Abram's words above apply as much to the myth of objectivity as they do to reductionism. In a way they are like the chicken and the egg: it is hard to say which one came first. The goal of science is to side-step subjective beliefs as much as possible. The smaller a portion of a complex structure, the easier it is to claim the illusion of objectivity is real. Yet philosophers since Plato remind us that all information is imperfect. Richard Feynman, the Nobel Prize–winning physicist, writes, "Science alone of all the subjects contains within itself the lesson of the danger of belief in the infallibility of the greatest teachers in the preceding generation….As a matter of fact, I can also define science another way: Science is the belief in the ignorance of experts" (1999, p. 462).

Of course, a number of scientists who challenged "official knowledge" throughout history have not fared well, so Feyneman speaks too casually perhaps. Such challenges to open-minded and outspoken questioning are not a problem in Indigenous science. It appreciates we cannot deny that objectivity begins with subjectivity. To do so allows subjectivity to rule in the disguise of objective science. Understanding life requires subjectivity, humility and open-mindedness. It also calls for embracing the unknown and accepting the "feeling" of the unspeakable truths that come from lived experience. It comes from dialogue, experience and research that embraces all aspects of cognitive, intuitive, traditional and experimental learning.

Nonetheless, those in power continually claim they are telling us objective truths about reality. An example that could become classic if it ever made it into the history books would be the assertions about Iraq's weapons of mass destruction, which resulted in almost unanimous legislative support for the invasion of that country in 2003. Without belief in the myth of objectivity, more would have seen through the deceptions, outright lies and subjective assumptions responsible for the Iraq war and the devastating outcomes. Indigenous scientists understand that anything close to objectivity in science starts with subjectivity. They know that conclusions from observations must be interpreted subjectively in light of personal experience, reflections, understanding of stories and ancestral wisdom, relationships with connected subjects, and so forth. They also understand that a person's subjective belief can be so concretized that he or she will see the desired outcome even if others do not.

The myth of objectivity, along with the hegemony that supports it, is also likely to show up in the classroom when teachers dish out letter grades for work done "objectively." The more a teacher attempts such objectivity, the less learning a student probably is likely to achieve. Memorizing rather than understanding, and merely repeating "factual" information rather than applying knowledge subjectively to different situations are typical learning objectives in mainstream schooling. This helps to maintain the status quo. For example, if someone wants to talk about social/ecological justice, the dialogue can be stifled by calling for an objective, agreed-upon objective definition. The last thing the hegemons want are students who can critically and carefully consider claimed truths with honest reflection and subjective passion, for it is such passion that can lead to protests like the Occupy Movement that threaten the ruling paradigm.

Closely aligned with the myth of objectivity is the scientific fundamentalism that it fosters. There is no single scientific method or set of rules that underlines every piece of research and guarantees that it is scientific and, therefore, trustworthy. The idea of a universal and stable science is unrealistic. Scientists constantly revise their standards, their procedures, even their criteria of rationality in their research in subtle ways. In order to comply with the myth of objectivity, transparency about this is usually minimal (Feyerabend, 1978, p. 98).

(3) Misinformation: gives economic benefits to a minority at the expense of others

Misinformation and or missing information as well as misleading information are common problems in school science texts and curriculum standards. We should not be surprised, for starters, to find that their authors often do not possess credentials for condensing scientific information (Broadway & Howland, 1991, pp. 35–38). If omitting information is not an option, corporations and/or hegemons hire scholars to write what they want them to write. Some researchers sign contracts that allow them to publish only results that are favorable to the company that is sponsoring the research. However it is accomplished, information that makes its way into school curricula and textbooks is often filtered. A January 2012 press release from Texas Citizens for Science (TCS) referred to the adoption of their state's science as a product of an "ideologically-driven" and "activist Republican" effort to "edit, manipulate, censor, distort and corrupt" authentic science:

> Intimidation of teachers is the goal of those who want such topics as evolution, origin of life, age of the Earth, pollution, and excessive human population growth marginalized or avoided in public school classrooms. Also, many aspects of US history, human sexuality, and religious and economic history that reflect badly on conservatives and Republicans, unethical and dangerous business practices and companies, etc., are censored.

Even with such criticism, note that climate change is not included among the censored topics. The ability of the hegemons to suppress this subject is an example of the power of corporatist hegemony. Corporate-sponsored efforts to confuse the public about the serious problems of human-caused climate change during the past twenty years have put all of us at risk. Riley Dunlap of Oklahoma State University and Aaron McCright of Michigan State University have published their findings about the extent of this in *The Oxford Handbook on Climate Change and Society* (2011). They conclude that climate denialism exists in part because there has been a long-term, well-financed effort on the part of conservative groups and corporations to distort global-warming science. "Contrarian scientists, fossil-fuel corporations, conservative think tanks and various front groups have assaulted mainstream climate science and scientists for over two decades," Dunlap and McCright write. "The blows have been struck by a well-funded, highly complex and relatively coordinated denial machine" (p. 147).

(4) A progress paradigm: overemphasizes advantages of technology, progress and social engineering to maintain consumer culture

If the reader believes I am especially critical of the right-leaning neo-liberals in this book, know I feel that the left-leaning liberals also contribute to this particular problematic paradigm. The political and ideological perspectives of the mainstream on both sides of the political spectrum share the anthropocentric worldview and the "progress at any cost" paradigm. Chet Bowers has been writing about this for a long time:

Liberalism, with its assumptions about the progressive nature of change and of rational understanding as the source of empowerment and self-direction, is like an aura that surrounds the activities of the scientist. It also surrounds and gives legitimacy to technological innovation. (1993, p. 172)

The survival of common property, common resources including parks, creeks, clean drinking water and air, traditional cultural activities that help maintain community cohesiveness, as well as local stories and Indigenous wisdom from those who lived generations in one place all have a value that must be considered equally valid to the progress and "evolution" worldviews. Today, privatization and profit are creating a situation wherein we are about to consume the chicken that lays the golden eggs.

(5) Misplaced focus on competition: dismisses Charles Darwin's perspective on cooperation and equality

Aboriginal people, learning from their stories that a society must not be human-centered but rather place-centered, observed the natural world intensely enough to know that natural systems are essentially cooperative. Darwin came to the same conclusion, although one would never know this from looking at the science textbooks in schools. In *Lost Theory: Bridge to a Better World* (2011), David Loye carefully describes the work of academics who have distorted Darwin's theory of evolution and how social hegemons have used an incorrect emphasis on competition to further their agendas. In 1902 Peter Kropotkin made the same case in *Mutual Aid: A Factor in Evolution*.[2] He wrote this book after having been imprisoned for his subversive political activities in Russia on behalf of the commons. Because of his aristocratic background, he was given special privileges in prison that permitted him to continue his geographical work. His extensive research is summarized in the concluding paragraph of his book:

> In the animal world we have seen that the vast majority of species live in societies, and that they find in association the best arms for the struggle for life: understood, of course, in its wide Darwinian sense—not as a struggle for the sheer means of existence, but as a struggle against all natural conditions unfavourable to the species. The animal species, in which individual struggle has been reduced to its narrowest limits, and the practice of mutual aid has attained the greatest development, are invariably the most numerous, the most prosperous, and the most open to further progress. The mutual protection which is obtained in this case, the possibility of attaining old age and of accumulating experience, the higher intellectual development, and the further growth of sociable habits, secure the maintenance of the species, its extension, and its further progressive evolution. The unsociable species, on the contrary, are doomed to decay.

Real-Life Outcomes

The outcomes related to an overemphasis on competition and the dismissal of Darwin's observations about cooperation are all too obvious in our world. We seem to be doing a very poor job of "securing the maintenance of the species," whether the human species as was meant or the many other species going extinct each day. The nexus between modern science and violence seems to be a major characteristic of science in fact. In the 1980s more than 80 percent of science research worldwide found its way into military uses (Shiva, 1988). A more recent statistic directly from the National Science Foundations shows that for the past two decades the range has been from 60 to 80 percent in the U.S. During this time, an average of twice as much research and development funding has gone to the military as has gone to non-military purposes.[3] Even this figure is deceptive, for monies spent on supposedly non-military goals, such as space research and energy development, still often wind up being focused on military uses. Considering that militarism may be antithetical to the goals of science and that science for military use is subject to severe censorship, those in corporations with the most lobby power strongly influence not only science education but our social fabric and priorities as well. This is especially true if we expand the idea of violence to include the many technologies that pollute our crops and our rivers or that monopolize food production with genetically modified, sterile seeds, among other methods.

Speaking of agriculture, even when science serves the common good, such as the science of organic farming, corporatism interferes. This science and those farmers who contribute to it have proven methods that increase the lifespan of soil yield, reduce contamination runoff of pesticides and fertilizers, and allow for healthier foods while providing potentially equal economic gain compared to non-organic farming. The subject of organic agriculture is, however, not to be found in most science texts or mentioned in curriculum standards. Outside the classroom, pressures from corporate influences also prevent widespread organic farming. In a Bill Moyer's video *Earth on Edge*, a Kansas wheat farmer who uses organic methods successfully on a 10,000-acre farm says he is in the minority for three major reasons. First, corporations have arranged it so farmers can get loans for equipment only if they can prove to the bank they are using fertilizer and pesticides. Second, the advertising and one-on-one promotion by sales personnel from chemical companies tend to persuade farmers to continue a non-organic approach. Third, farmers do as their fathers did and have not learned about the organic alternative.

Climate change denial may be the most important example of a real-life outcome of science education hegemony and corporatism. Polls show that Americans' understanding of climate change is very shallow. One study by the National Center for Science Education (NCSE) found that only 54% of teens realize global warming is happening.[4] Yet the Heartland Institute, heavily funded by oil and coal companies, and others like it are working hard to bring false messages about climate change into classrooms (Samuelsohn, 2012). Neither science education, nor social studies curricula nor U.S. history or economics or literature coursework teaches the story of oil. Few students have ever even heard of "peak oil." The ways that capitalism, oil and scientific technologies for producing energy and extracting fossil fuels are connected to climate change are virtually unknown.

To some degree, the real-world outcome of all this lies in the dire scientific predictions. Bill McKibben's article "Global Warming's Terrifying New Math" (2012), for instance, offers some scary statistics. I would rather end this section with the words of Indigenous elders I have met with at several conferences in recent years. Most of the ones whose words I remember did not possess graduate degrees but were nonetheless people of great wisdom. I hope they won't mind me paraphrasing from their narratives, which, put together into one voice, sound like this:

> The Western scientists say all life systems are at a "tipping point," but what do they really know about life systems? They study them from a distance. We live amidst them. Each day depends on weather for us. We rely on signs for being safe and finding food. We must be constantly in tune with the environment. But our knowledge is not just from our attentive and consistent observations. We have the advantage of many generations of knowledge from others who also were always attentive and respectful of changes all around. This knowledge was preserved in stories, language and songs, and it was always in flux, always in context and always connected to larger circles of life. I can say that for a long time we have seen the changes in how our Mother is behaving. We have insects for which our language has no name now. Our water is disappearing and the animals grow sicker each year. Yes, the scientists say we are in trouble now, but we have known this for two hundred years. We try to teach but they do not listen. The white man's religions say there will be mercy, but this is not true. Earth is our mother, but she requires that we follow her laws. Nature shows no mercy for those who break the laws. Now she is acting strangely to us and we can imagine why. The dominant peoples on Earth have become too arrogant and have forgotten who they are. They have forgotten they are the same as the trees, with roots in the earth and a need for sunlight, clean air, fresh water and a diversity of life to stimulate growth and awareness. It may be past time perhaps for us to help them remember, but we must try. There are no leaders who can help. Each and every person must become a leader of herself. We the people are the only ones who can bring balance back. We cannot follow the lead of governments. We must make our own decisions for the sake of all. We must somehow help the "takers of the fat" remember we are all connected and soon all there will be left to eat is money, money soaked in blood and oil.

Indigenous Curricular Alternatives

I am honored to introduce this chapter's guest author, Dr. Greg Cajete. Greg is a Tewa author and professor from Santa Clara Pueblo in New Mexico. He is considered to be a pioneer in reconciling Indigenous perspectives with Western science education. He is the current director of the Native American Studies Program at the University of New Mexico in Albequerque. His text *Native Science: Natural Laws of Interdependence* (2000) exemplifies the intercultural approach to science education called for in the "Declaration on Science and the Use of Scientific Knowledge," adopted by the UNESCO World Conference on Science on July 1, 1999.[5]

A Science Curriculum Partnership

by Greg Cajete

When Four Arrows asked me to contribute to this part of the book, I was engaged in fighting fires and restoring forests in my own homeland, so most of what I say here I have said before.[6] My thoughts about what such a curriculum would look like have not changed much. Although I originally intended this curriculum to help Native students grappling with Western education, I believe the concepts that I present here can work for all children, although no doubt for a non—Native American observer, the mixture of perspectives I offer may seem paradoxical at first. Although Western scientific schooling often makes it seem otherwise, studies of cognitive development report that we are all capable of having more than one internally consistent mind-set concerning natural reality. Thus a partnership between the two distinctly different mind-sets—the mutualistic/holistic-oriented mind-set of Native American cultures and the rationalistic/dualistic mind-set of Western science, which divides, analyzes, and objectifies—is an important one.

What kinds of measures concerning science education can be implemented to decrease the confrontation of a student's cultural mind-set with that of Western science? First, the student can be introduced to the basic skills of science; through the use of familiar things or events, one can build upon students' innate interests and curiosity. Using this approach, students become involved with science as a process of observing, classifying and collecting information and making generalizations with reference to phenomena they know about. Second, once students learn to apply these basic skills, they can be presented with a comparison of the way that "science" as a thought process is exemplified in both their particular culture and that of the larger society. An analysis of symbols as they relate to the explanation of natural phenomena in both Native American culture and that of Western science should be undertaken. In no case should one perspective be presented in preference to the other.

Much of the communication concerning natural phenomena is presented in a high-context manner in Native American cultures. That is, information and communication concerning natural phenomena are presented in the context most appropriate to their purpose or through the use of symbolic vehicles such as art, myth or ritual. The actual relationships between natural phenomena are observed and symbolically coded in a variety of forms based on experiential knowledge. In contrast, Western science is learned and practiced in a low-context manner in terms of both its communication and its processing of information. That is, information concerning natural phenomena is often highly specific, parts-oriented and presented out of the context in which the phenomena naturally occurs or is observed.

Thus Indigenous perspectives for science education coincide with general systems theory, attempting to help students see parts and wholes and understand the interrelationships between them. Hologizing, learning to look at the whole while simultaneously looking at its parts, is an important tool in balancing the predominantly partialistic orientation of the Western scientific method. The Western scientific method, through its process of taking things apart, analysis, hypothesis formation and objective evaluation, has been successful in helping us to understand some components of nature. Yet this partialistic approach to real-life problem solving has not only conditioned many people to see and deal only with parts of problems but has also limited these people's ability to deal with problems that require an understanding of whole systems. From an Indigenous perspective, the relevant "science" systems are "natural systems."

Natural systems share some basic characteristics:

1. They "transact" in mutualistic interrelationships everywhere and at a huge variety of different levels;
2. They are synergistic, which means that the whole of a system is always greater then the sum of its parts;
3. They maintain their stability and continuity through a dynamic yet well-coordinated flow of information through the various levels within the system;
4. They are self-organizing, especially as they pertain to living things. All living systems are continually involved in renewing and recycling parts and in processing information in order to maintain their stability and overall structures. They achieve this dynamic state through the ability to reach beyond themselves through the creative application of

their various traits, such as the ability to adapt, evolve and learn in response to an ever-changing environment; and

5. Natural systems are characterized by a state of equilibrium commonly called "homeostasis."

These five general characteristics of natural systems can be found reflected in a variety of ways in Native American ritual, myth and social organization.

The Spider Woman myths found in many Native American cultures personify these dimensions of systems process in a metaphoric form. In Native American mythology one often finds the theme of Spider Woman and her all-encompassing web. Among many tribes Spider Woman represents a kind of creative intelligence whose web metaphorically represents the innate interrelationship between all things. Many tribes believe that when any part of the strands of this cosmic web are disturbed or destroyed, disharmony is felt throughout the web and eventually registers with Spider Woman.

Similar representations of this characteristic of systems can be found in myths pertaining to Changing Woman among the Navajo. The point to be made is that systems thinking and process are integral parts of the Native American conceptualization of the natural world. The feeling for the whole, "the People," is an integral part of the social psychology of all Native American and primal peoples of the world. This feeling for the whole permeates all social interaction within any Native American community. It is the basis for the traditional codes of ethics, political and socio-religious organization and activities, and it is the basis for Indigenous science.

To teach mainstream standards according to such a code, the development of the curriculum requires the application of several important and interdependent teaching/learning approaches. These include:

1. An understanding and application of the metaphoric thought process;
2. An understanding and application of teaching and learning strategies that address both the right- and left-brain learning styles of students;
3. Teaching for creativity;
4. The development and application of situational learning contexts where there is a specific interface between science and culture—in this case, both mainstream and Indian cultures;
5. The facilitation of opportunities for students' growth and development in their abilities to deal with and adapt to changing environmental influences; and
6. An understanding and application of interdisciplinary perspectives concerning science, culture and creativity.

(1) The Metaphoric Thought Process

In this curriculum, the strategic use of metaphor is essential in that it provides a "connective bridge" between the imagination and fantasy faculty of the right brain and the concept and reason faculty of the left brain. Metaphoric thinking stimulates the development of cognitive abilities that are higher than simply reading, writing or listening. The use and understanding of metaphor greatly enhance concept attainment, the development of insight and the ability to use imagery.

(2) Teaching To Right-/Left-Brain Learning Styles

The enormous amount of research in the past three decades concerning brain hemispheric specialization has profound implications for modern education. Educators are only now realizing the potential such knowledge forecasts for future education. Much of the prior emphasis of modern education has been on developing only the inherent potentials of the left-brain thought processes to the almost complete neglect of the potentials of the right brain. Educators must begin to address seriously the inherent potentials and characteristics of the "whole" brain. This is not a new insight. Traditional Native American teaching/learning methods intuitively employed strategies that integrated both right- and left-brain processes in the act of learning. In fact, traditional education in cultures around the world has incorporated techniques that directly access whole-brain thinking. The use of metaphor and storytelling by different world cultures is but one of the many examples of such whole-brain techniques. The characteristic duality of brain functioning can also be seen in world cultural art, architecture, mythology, religion, philosophies, medicine and science. The highly structured drill- and practice-oriented approach to science education prevalent in American schools today must be balanced with an equalizing emphasis upon right-brain teaching/learning processes.

(3) Teaching for Creativity

As students are introduced to creative thinking as it applies to science, they begin to see that for every problem they encounter, there is an appropriate level of creative thinking that can be applied. Each learner relates to this process as it reflects the intuitive understanding of growth and development that all humans seem to possess. Students learn about the creative process by being directly involved with a creative process. Once they begin to see different levels of problems and learn how to apply the appropriate level of creative thinking in search for solutions, they will have internalized one of the most important skills that science education has to offer. In the development and presentation of each unit of study, conditions of creative learning must be considered in terms of the following phases.

In phase one, emphasis must be given to the "felt" needs of the student. Teaching is geared toward motivation, discovery, perception, activity, exploration and the search for "relevant" patterns. In the second phase, analysis, verification and evaluation, followed by basic synthesis toward a more complete understanding of the content, becomes the center of activity. The enhancement and elaboration of what has been learned or created are also major activities in this phase. Teaching activity in this phase will entail the extensive use of examples supported by readings or other activities that augment and elaborate upon what has been presented. In the third phase, learning and creativity involve a high degree of synthesis, metaphoric thinking, innovation, the widening of perspectives, the creation of new grammars and symbols and the taking apart and restructuring of content toward the goal of creating something completely new. In this phase, students come to intimately understand the internal dynamics of the content and tend to develop a greater sense of motivation and commitment to what they are learning. Teaching will involve the extensive use of metaphor and analogy in the presentation of content.

In any class students will be at different levels of maturity and stages of cognitive and psychological development. Appropriate adjustments of the content and of the presentation of the curriculum to students relative to developmental needs are very much a part of this curriculum's processing. Some students need to be told everything, whereas others wish to explore possibilities for themselves. As students grow and develop, they internalize their own relationships to what is being presented at each level of the curriculum. Through their increasing awareness of these relationships, they will become more aware of how different aspects within and without science are related to one another and thereby see the need for a process perspective in science. They also grow in their cognitive ability with the science process. Students need to be encouraged to use differences of thought and perception while retaining the unique characteristics of each. Learning to combine differences resulting from cultural biases and modes of thinking increases the capacity of thought to include broader perspectives of nature and allows students to become aware of the nature of probabilities and thus more comfortable with "uncertainties" within each system of thought. The realm of possibilities is expanded, and science is no longer perceived as a closed system based on irrefutable facts that must be memorized. Rather, it is rightly viewed as an open and potentially highly creative system.

(4) The Interface of Science and Culture

Making science "real" to students requires the conscious manipulation of situations and contexts to illustrate the relationship between the students' own cultures and the science concept being presented. Modern science and technology have touched practically every corner of the earth and have affected every human cultural group. The interface between culture and science is so pervasive that it is sometimes difficult to distinguish what is science and what is culture. Situations may arise in the workplace through the purchase of the products of science or by encountering science and technology through medical treatment. Within any of these situations, modern science and technology are presented without explanations and are used as a means to an end. These various encounters with modern science and technology can provide a wealth of content for the development of culturally based science education. Science from this perspective is much more than simply a foundation for technology; it can form a basis for cultural exchange and understanding that is almost limitless because it is always expressed within a specific cultural context. Learning to recognize, understand and use these situations for the purpose of gaining a deeper understanding of science in process is a key consideration of this curriculum.

(5) Student Growth and Development through Adaptation and Change

Every system of cultural science attempts to develop a basic understanding of change while searching for patterns in natural processes and developing classifications of natural entities. These classifications and recognitions constantly change, evolve or are adapted as new information is gathered concerning the natural world. Science involves continuous exploration of the natural world as it moves through stages of growth and development. The knowledge gained from the science process evolves through each stage of development and continually transforms itself toward successively higher levels of understanding.

Numerous examples of growth and development of scientific knowledge in both Native American cultures and Western sciences should be presented as possible in classes to familiarize students with these processes and to facilitate their awareness of their own growth and development in understanding their relationships to their culture and the natural environment. All students should understand that Native American cultural sciences were characterized by adaptations to the surrounding natural environment and reflected a deep understanding of change, life-cycles and creative process inherent in nature. Creative adaptation is exemplified in Native American farming, hunting, fishing, medicine, art, myth, architecture, material technology, religion, ecological practices, astronomy and social organization. Through these examples, non-Indian students can be helped to a more comprehensive understanding of change relating to their own associations than would be possible in standardized science curricula.

(6) Science, Culture and Creativity: An Interdisciplinary View

In reality, science interfaces with a number of other disciplines. It is the understanding and creative application of this interface that is essential in widening students' perspectives of science. An interdisciplinary approach presents science as it actually appears in the day-to-day life of students. Students become aware of the influence of scientific thought processes and associated technology on their immediate environment. This awareness extends to the realization that science affects practically every interaction that they have with their world. Exploring science from the perspectives of disciplines such as art, psychology, history, philosophy and the humanities infuses it with new meanings and fosters new understandings. The interdisciplinary approach views science in relationship to the greater whole of human knowledge systems. This establishes the relevancy of science to the whole of human experience. For instance, exploring the historical evolution of the Western scientific paradigm and comparing this with the historical evolution of the scientific paradigm of a Native American group, such as the Aztec, provides a broader perspective and appreciation for both orientations than would be possible through any one discipline. Application of knowledge is gained from both disciplines bi-directionally since learning flows in both directions.

Learning, like creativity, is not a linear, single-directional process. Rather, it is cyclic, in a constant state of flux, multidirectional and multidimensional. This essential characteristic of learning is more often than not disregarded in the way teaching and learning are traditionally structured within the academic presentations of science, art, the social sciences and humanities. This tendency of contemporary mainstream education lies at the heart of the charges leveled by its critics that it lacks relevancy and that its adherents exhibit an "ivory tower" complex. The interdisciplinary approach forces a deconstruction of traditional boundaries of disciplines and their restructuring and synthesis toward the goal of more complete learning.

Final Thoughts

Curriculum implemented with these principles will have different meanings for different people, necessitating development of different grammars or ways of communicating these meanings. Students, then, are placed in a situation where they must develop their ability to respond to the different relationships that they perceive in Western and Native American cultural/scientific perspectives. Each student must develop his or her own strategy for making meaning out of the content encountered at each phase of the curriculum. There is a constant ebb and flow, an unfolding and infolding, between all of the processes and components. It is in these interactions and relationships that learning in science must be allowed to develop.

Becoming open to the paradigm of Indigenous science has some other prerequisites that need to be considered. There must be an understanding and acknowledgment of the history of exploitation of Indigenous peoples by Western culture and science. There must be a willingness on the part of the non-Indigenous teacher to view science from a perspective that is "inside out, upside down and the other way around" or, more simply put, without bias and with deep vision, which allows for a deep examination of habitual thought processes. Conflict between Western and Native American perceptions and understanding of nature arises only when one system of conceptualization is emphasized over the other. What I have attempted to show is that a bridge of understanding can be constructed even between two such strikingly different cultural mind-sets as those inherent in Native American ethno-sciences and modern Western science. Native American cultures reflect the science thought process systemically, as shown by the integration of science/technology with art, religion, ritual and myth. Western science reflects the science thought process primarily through focusing on the individual parts of natural systems. The construction of a bridge between two such mind-sets concerning the natural world affords the student of science a viewpoint and orientation that allow for a broader and more realistic perspective of science as a whole process. In doing so, it allows students a greater opportunity to develop an appreciation of science as a highly flexible and creative tool for understanding the natural world as well as their own relationship to this world.

Questions for Research, Dialogue, Choices and Praxis

Note to teachers: Remember to modify the language of these instructions and examples so as to best serve the age and learning levels of the students.

1. Study the chart below and work in teams to be sure you understand the differences between the two approaches and how each approach works in real life in good ways and in unhealthy ways. Choose a science project and talk about how these two approaches would look in real life. What in the science curriculum and textbook can the students change or add to that will reflect Indigenous "scientific" knowledge?
2. Consider what you know about some scientific knowledge relating to a modern technology (e.g., the lightbulb, an automobile, a laptop

Indigenous Knowledge	[Western] Scientific Knowledge
lengthy acquisition	rapid acquisition
long-term wisdom	short-term prediction
powerful prediction in local areas	weak in local areas of knowledge
models based on cycles	linear modeling as first approximation
explanations based on examples, anecdotes, parables, metaphors	explanations based on hypothesis, theories, laws
Classification: • a mix of ecological and actual use • non-hierarchical differentiation • includes everything natural and supernatural	Classification: • based on phylogenic relationships • hierarchical differentiation • excludes the supernatural

Source: Alaska Native Science, http://www.nativescience.org/html/traditional_and_scientific.html.

computer). Using a traditional medicine wheel with the four quadrants representing the "social, physical, mental and spiritual" dimensions, have students write something about the technology or its use that fits into each quadrant.

3. Have students study the science of deep-ocean oil drilling and make a list of ten serious negative consequences. Then have them do a creative illustration, sculpture, song, dance or other art form to describe one of the consequences.

4. Watch the free online documentary *The Superior Human?* (http://topdocumentaryfilms.com/superior-human). After watching it, talk about or draw images to express what you learned. Why do you think humans believe so strongly in our superiority over animals?

5. Have older students watch the video of Robert Newman's classic comedy presentation, *Robert Newman's History of Oil* (http://video.google.ca/videoplay?docid=-8957268309327954402), and stop it often to discuss what points he makes and how they relate to science and society.

6. Consider these released questions for the California science standards test. What do you believe the correct answer is and why do you think so? Draw the three items, and using the ideas Greg Cajete presents above, come up with other things they have in common.

What do water, aluminum, redwood trees, and valley quail all have in common?

    A. They are all pure elements.

    B. They are all made of cells.

    C. They are all living creatures.

    D. They are all made of atoms.

7. For the next question, thinking of Cajete's recommendation to use different disciplines of study when researching scientific ideas, see whether you can think of another place that digestion begins besides the mouth.

The digestion process begins in which of the following?

    A. large intestine

    B. mouth

    C. small intestine

    D. stomach

8. For each of the following problems with Western science and with hegemony and corporate influence, give one example of a related outcome that is not healthy for the world.

    i. Reductionism: supports continued exploitation that serves the monopolistic advantage of those in power.

    ii. The "myth of objectivity": empowers a false perception of scientific truth.

    iii. Misinformation: gives economic benefits to a minority at the expense of others.

    iv. A progress paradigm: overemphasizes advantages of technology, progress and social engineering to maintain consumer culture.

    v. Misplaced focus on competition: dismisses Charles Darwin's perspective on cooperation and equality.

Notes

1. MRIs cost from $1,200 to $2,000 each in the U.S., about 280 in France and even less in Mexico but are routinely advised for numerous patient complaints in light of the potential profit.

2. Kropotkin's entire book can be read for free online at http://www.calresco.org/texts/mutaidc.htm

3. http://www.nsf.gov/statistics/seind12/c4/c4s6.htm.

4. See http://ncse.com/climate-change/ncse-tackles-climate-change-denial.

5. See http://www.unesco.org/science/wcs/eng/declaration_e.htm.

6. In essence, this material is a condensation of several chapters in my text *Igniting the Sparkle: An Indigenous Science Education Curriculum Model* (Asheville, NC: Kivaki, 1999).

12 Geography

Our history cannot be told without naming the cliffs and mountains that have witnessed our people.

—Ruth Benally, Diné (Navajo) traditionalist

A worldly cultural geography can play a critical role in enabling a democratic dialectic. Mapping the utopian imagining of spaces of resistance as they keep proliferating horizontally around the world, we can thereby connect the catachreses of 'worldly' and 'cultural' with the local geographic imagination of global justice.

—Mathew Sparke, 2012, p. 27

I gradually became aware that my interiority was inseparable from my exteriority, that the geography of my city was the geography of my soul.

—Aleksandar Hemon

Personality is the substantive embodiment, the unique realization, of all the relations and power emergent in a given place.

—Vine Deloria Jr., 2001, p. 76

K-16 Teacher Instructions:

Adapt and use this chapter's information according to your students' ages and cognitive levels. Use as an introduction to your standard course content or weave values, ideas or critical reflections into it throughout the course. Encourage students to carefully reflect on this information with the goal of deciding what mainstream ideas are best replaced with Indigenous ones, which ones are best as they are, and how the two might be partnered in terms of practical benefits for the students and their community (local and global). Use the questions at the end of the chapter to help with this process and to stimulate primary source research and enthusiastic, critical dialogue. Since in Indigenous ways of thinking the ideas related to this subject have relevance to all the other subjects, you may want to incorporate some of this chapter's material into the study of another subject area. As with all chapters in this section, this chapter is organized as follows:

1. Corporate and Hegemonic Influences
2. Real-World Outcomes
3. Indigenous Curricular Alternatives
4. Questions for Research, Dialogue, Choices and Praxis

Corporate and Hegemonic Influences

A joke I recall goes, "It is ironic but I have a friend who majored in geography and he can't find a place to work!" It is similarly ironic that for a topic so many scholars say is vital and "fundamental" to our lives, education has kept authentic and relevant learning about geography at bay. If geography is "everything and everywhere," as geography instructors often say, why is it almost nowhere in the curriculum? Today, unlike all the other core academic subjects, including history, civics, economics, foreign languages and the arts, there is no dedicated federal funding channel in support of geography education. Most students have negative attitudes about it (Page, 1994), and especially in the United States, we seem to be essentially geographically illiterate.

Geography offers a great opportunity for indigenizing because it offers engages one of the most important considerations in the Indigenous paradigm-place. Geography is defined by the Australian Academy of Science's National Committee for Geography as "the study of the interaction between people and environments…by investigating the spatial dimensions of topics and issues, students analyze the impact of the interaction between people and environments, and consider appropriate responses" (2011). The Association of American Geographers is specific about the importance of studying this relationship, asserting "Geographers were in fact among the first scientists to sound the alarm that human-induced changes to the environment were beginning to threaten the balance of life" (Bonnet, 2008, p. 86).

The history of geography education, however, does not reflect this sense of importance but rather a corporate and hegemonic influence that has stifled a serious study of earth-human relationships as described above. The 1965 Elementary and Secondary Education Act (U.S.) identified geography as a core subject. This bipartisan legislation was passed only because "the economic stature and competitiveness of the United States requires increasingly sophisticated levels of geographic knowledge and mastery of geographic tools." As geography was a core subject at the time, many educators expressed concerns about the superficial ways it was being taught. This did not sit well with the status quo hegemons, who wanted no part of such "political ideology" in the curriculum. Under the administration of President Ronald Reagan, their opposition led Congress to pass the Education Consolidation and Improvement Act of 1981, which reduced federal regulations and gave more curricular autonomy to the states, and geography as an educational priority fell off the charts. During the 1980s prestigious geography departments were closed at the University of Michigan in 1982, Columbia University in 1986, Northwestern University in 1986, and the University of Chicago in 1987.

The passion of geography teachers, however, did not go away. They asserted that geography is more than just naming the location of places and that people are formed by geography and must understand it in order to connect with and understand others. In 1987 the National Commission on Social Studies in the Schools was formed to make recommendations on curricular reforms. As we can see from the following segment of a 1989 report, a more liberal or "left-wing" perspective than that generally reflected in conservative or neoliberal ideas about competition and profit emerged:

> The Commission's Curriculum Task Force recommends the following goals for social studies education: (1) development of civic responsibility and citizen participation; (2) development of a global perspective through an understanding of students' life experiences as part of the total human experience, past and present; (3) development of "critical understanding" of the history, geography, and the pluralistic nature of the civil institutions of the United States; (4) development of a multicultural perspective on the world's peoples through an understanding of their differences and commonalities throughout time and place; and (5) development of students' capacities for critical thinking about "the human condition." (Mullins, 1990)

Further cuts to funding and requirements for geography curricula came in 1994 with the Improving America's Schools Act. The last major control of curriculum, which seemed to seal the fate of geography, was the No Child Left Behind Act of 2001. Focusing only on the subjects covered by high-stakes testing and the multimillion-dollar companies profiting from them, this act did not mention environmental studies of any kind. Then in 2005 a number of education associations, led by the National Commission on Social Studies in the Schools, the National Academy of Sciences and the National Geographic Society, managed to get legislation introduced via Senate bill 1376, entitled the Teaching Geography Is Fundamental Act. The legislation was intended to improve and expand geographic literacy among kindergarten through Grade 12 students by improving professional development programs via higher education. The bill died and was reintroduced as Senate bill 727 in 2007, but it died again. It came back as House of Representatives (H.R.) bill 1240 on February 26, 2009, which also died. On March 2, 2011, it came back as H.R. bill 885 and has been referred to committee, where it still seems to be. We can only speculate, but there is not much hope that the results will encourage learning about the deeper social, political and environmental aspects of geography, as progressive educators demand.[1] The two usual hegemonic reasons for the legislative failure to support adequate geography studies seem obvious: enhancement of corporate profits and maintenance of the status-quo ideologies and hierarchy. Starting with the corporations and their influence on legislation, we remember the ultimate hegemonic question: who directly benefits economically from superficial geography lessons? The answer: the testing companies. Creating maps and other geographic graphics that pertain to locations and stereotypes of peoples residing in those locations is a big business, but the addition of mandatory tests that measure such information has resulted in an even more significant publishing enterprise. In her 2005 report for Fair Test, Angela Engel writes,

> Standardized testing benefits the four major testing publishers: McGraw-Hill, Houghton-Mifflin, Pearson Assessments (formerly NCS), and Harcourt General, and allows for complete control over curriculum resources, teacher training, and other assessment tools, creating a monopoly over the "public education marketplace." McGraw Hill, publishers of CSAP [Colorado State Assessment Program], reported profit[s] of $49 million in 1993 before high stakes testing; in 2004 with contracts in 26 states, profits exceeded $340 million. Standardized testing really isn't about competition between students, it's about financial gains and competition over economic targets. The question of who benefits from school competition and the high-stakes testing craze grows increasingly clearer.

The kinds of things the National Commission on Social Studies in the Schools called for in the teaching of geography and that the National Geographic Society and others have advocated for decades are not so easily condensed into curricular materials and standardized tests. So the profit motive and the lack of power educators have over legislation once again give way to the corporate lobbyists and hegemonic gatekeepers. However, as we have seen with other subjects, the ideological hegemony continues to be powerful as well. As with the millions of dollars poured into "economics education" to turn the tide against pro-labor sentiments (described in Chapter 10), the ruling class does not want education to take a "liberal" stance that challenges the current state of affairs. From all the writing about the new geography, there can be no doubt that a more pro-environment attitude would emerge from the way most of the experts want to see geography taught. How could teaching geography correctly not engage students in serious concerns about climate change, loss of species, ocean depletion and the like? Yet opposition to learning and acting on such information is still in the interest of the hegemons in spite of the overwhelming scientific evidence that our survival as a species is at risk owing to the ecological problems. In 1994 I wrote *The Bum's Rush: The Selling of Environmental Backlash (Phrases and Fallacies of Rush Limbaugh)*, in which I exposed the anti-environment rhetoric continually being expressed by neo-liberal and neo-conservatives. Just as authentic environmental education is virtually non-existent from kindergarten to graduate school, so too may geography as a "fundamental" subject suffer this fate until teachers themselves awaken to the hegemony and partner with Indigenous perspectives to teach what we know is most important for the future generations.

In his doctoral dissertation, "Critical Geopolitics: The Social Construction of Space and Place in the Practice of Statecraft" (Syracuse University, 1989), Gerard Toal attempts to understand which part of "a hegemonic world order of militarism, nuclear terror and pervasive structural violence" is responsible for refuting deep geography and geopolitics. He argues that geography constructs a world that is projected as a copy of a supposed natural world. He refers to this in his dissertation abstract as "the writing of spaces and places to compose a world (or worlds)." In other words, whoever controls the geography curriculum, controls what the world will look like. I submit this control is ultimately in the hands of classroom teachers, who in partnering the curriculum with Indigenous constructs to produce authentic, borderless, fearless geographies can bring balance back into reality.

Mathew Sparke, a professor of geography at the University of Washington, Seattle, speaks specifically of the role of fear in the hegemony of geography. A prolific author, he writes about fear and hope in the imaginings of those in power who are creating the geographic realities to which Toal refers. He writes about "geographies of dispossession" created by neo-liberalism. He explains how geography can expose fears produced by policies so that we can all learn about how our global connectedness has been falsely obscured. In his article "Geopolitical Fear, Geoeconomic Hope and the Responsibilities" (2007), he refers to the imagined future geographies of neo-liberal American hegemony, referring to a National Intelligence Council report entitled "Mapping the Global Future," and writes, "It is not disconnection so much as a dispossessing form of connection" (p. 28) that is causing the fears that have led to our instability" (p. 24). Noting that more and more geography specialists are claiming the responsibility to question hegemonic geography, he also says we can learn from the dispossessed about their hope-filled struggles to create geographies of repossession too. Doing this, however, requires a partnership between authentic spirituality based in Nature and a radical geography curriculum that stimulates critical awareness and praxis.

Another scholar who speaks of the hegemony that prohibits a truly sincere study of the non-anthropocentric relationships between place and people is Chet Bowers. In *Education, Cultural Myths and the Ecological Crises: Toward Deep Changes* (1993), he explains that the cultural priorities related to concepts and language like success, progress, individualism, technology and science ignore cultural wisdom that reminds us of our connections and responsibilities to Earth. He refers to school textbooks as presenting only "an image of the individual as an autonomous agent engaged in social and technological activities" (p. 125).

> Cultural beliefs that influence how human wants and needs are worked out in technological practice, and influence how humans understand their relationship to their habitat, are the wellspring for the demands humans place on the environment. Yet this connection, which might involve at some point a recognition that the profit motive, personal vanity, and other sources for these demands might be the basis of decisions that have an adverse effect on the environment, is never presented in textbooks. Instead, the anthropocentric myth is sustained by referring to the environment as a natural resource (for humans) and ecological problems as merely indicators of bad technological practices. (p. 148)

So far, geography education has not come close to achieving the outcomes Bowers, Sparke and others envision, and with the growing influence of neo-liberal and right-wing groups, it is difficult to be hopeful. Australia has come close with its adoption of a new national curriculum, but the following letter from John Roskam, the executive director of the Institute of Public Affairs (IPA), reveals the same kind of backlash described above, which could lead to challenges. According to Source Watch, the IPA is a "right-wing, corporate funded think tank" whose "key policy positions include: advocacy for privatisation and deregulation; attacks on the positions of unions and non-government organisations; support of assimilationist indigenous policy and refutation of the science involved with environmental issues such as climate change" (Source Watch, n.d.). In an open letter to the Australian minister for school education, Roskam complains about the new national curriculum's stated need to "tackle complex environmental, social and economic pressures, such as climate change." He also complains about its goal of helping to create a "socially just world." He writes, "Many Australians would find it remarkable that the N.C. should attempt this and that this attempt has gone largely unnoticed. Our ideas about human rights are grounded in Christian theology." Such is the rhetoric of corporate-sponsored think tanks that influence educational policy.

Real-World Outcomes

A number of surveys conducted by National Geographic and Roper in 1989, 2002 and 2005 reveal that worldwide young people do not do well in basic geography and that those in the United States are near the bottom (Humphrey, 2011). In 2002 Mexico was last out of seven countries, and the U.S. was second to last. Because the surveys were multiple-choice, they barely touched the deeper social-political-economic-environmental issues to see how well people understood land-human relationships. One of the questions asked whether the disappearance of coastal marshes had anything to do with the damage of Hurricane Katrina. Nearly half of the respondents did not think it did. (And, of course, it was a major factor!) Here are some other examples:

- Only 13% of American students could pick Iraq, Israel or Iran out on a map of the Middle East.
- 58% knew the Taliban and al-Qaeda were based in Afghanistan, but only 17% could locate the country.
- 34% knew a season of the *Survivor* television show was located in the Marquesas Islands in the eastern South Pacific, but less could locate New Jersey.
- Only 51% could find New York.
- Only 14% thought speaking a language other than English was important; 75% incorrectly said English is the most widely spoken language.
- Only 3 in 10 felt being able to know where countries are was important.
- 2/3 did not know that an earthquake that killed 70,000 people the year of one survey (2005) occurred in Pakistan.

- 30% thought the most heavily fortified border in the world was between the U.S. and Mexico.
- 15% thought the Mississippi River empties into the Atlantic. (Imagine how many would not have known about the dead zone at the mouth of the river where it empties into the Gulf of Mexico or its cause.)
- Very few students understood basic environmental problems.

Being able to locate places on the other side of the world may not be all that important in contrast with understanding global impacts and relationships between events and policies. Perhaps place location is to geography as formula memorizing is to mathematics. Yet even with reading maps and charts, there are deeper critical possibilities students could learn. Maps and charts contain much information that if viewed uncritically can create serious deceptions. For example, most people are unaware of the long history of using basic cartography for deceptive purposes by simply creating bias in the drawing. We are taught to trust maps as being authoritative, objective measurements of places. However, maps have often been used to create false positive or negative impressions about an area to promote some particular viewpoint, whether the goal is to sell or steal land or start a war. Land areas can be minimized or exaggerated. Controversial sites can be omitted. Borders can be revised incorrectly (Monmonier, 1991). Here are just a few samples from Library and Archives Canada (Collections Canada, n.d.):

> When countries covet territory claimed by others, governments will often turn to their mapmakers for help in moving boundaries. It is much easier to assert sovereignty by drawing lines on paper than it is to take physical possession of land belonging to somebody else. Published at the beginning of the Seven Years' War, this map claims the territory around the Great Lakes for Britain by colouring the region "British red." A reduced New France is squeezed into an area along the north shore of the St. Lawrence River between Montreal and Tadoussac, plus Anticosti Island, Île Saint-Jean (Prince Edward Island), Cape Breton and the north shore of Newfoundland, all of which are shown without colour.
>
> Nowhere is the map a more powerful weapon than in disputes over territory and Canada has seen its share of such disputes. During much of the Klondike gold rush, for instance, Canada's boundary with Alaska was unsettled and open to interpretation (it was not formally settled until 1901). The Americans wanted to place the boundary further east than the Canadian claim, which would have sliced off a large portion of present-day northwestern Canada, and they prepared maps to this effect. "Every Canadian newspaper," wrote an indignant columnist in an 1897 issue of *Toronto Saturday Night* on seeing some of these American maps, "should keep drumming it into the ears of the Canadian people…that an attempt is being made, through a multiplicity of incorrect maps, to fasten the United States contention upon the world's mind as the correct and tacitly accepted one."

We can only imagine the indignation that the Iroquois Confederacy might have felt if it had an opportunity to view the map published by the Society of Anti-Gallicans. It extended British sovereignty over a large part of the North American interior, a country that had been under the influence of traders from New France for more than a century. The British claim projected into the lands of the Iroquois Confederacy solely on the basis of England's friendship with the Iroquois nations.

Returning to the deeper issues pertaining to geography and understandings about relationships between place and people, it is important to consider the broader meanings of "borders" than just their physical placements. We live in a time when socio-political "borders" are being set up all around us. Just now I received a piece from *Truthout* written by Mark Karlin that uses geography language to make us realize the importance of studying "border issues":

> Free trade, such as NAFTA, is a way of exploiting labor without national boundaries and ravaging the environment in pursuit of higher corporate profits. Borders only exist for poor migrants seeking money to keep themselves and their families alive. The victims of this trade policy—and its synergistic companion, crony capitalism—eke out an existence on both sides of the Mexican-United States border....There is no border wall for economic injustice. (July 2012)

Perhaps this is the most crucial real-life outcome to consider—that we still live in a world where our sense of community is defined by state- or corporate-determined boundaries. In spite of the Internet and the flow of monies and products across official boundaries, we seem to live in fear of what is outside our perceived borders while remaining satisfied with limited relationships within them. Next to the filtered pieces of rhetoric and deception vibrating out from corporate-sponsored media, education has also become a social, political and cultural space where geography's call for understanding relationships between people and place is unheeded. Geography, when it is still taught at all, misses the idea that "where it is at" is literally "where it is at." The central questions of importance, says Miron, must move from ones of conception to ones of place, where "democratic practices such as dialogue, coaltion, building, negotiation and consensus" are happening and where "transnational, national and indigenous racial subjects meet as they move ontologically from the periphery to the borders" (2008, p. 559).

Our curriculum and the textbooks offer students little or no opportunity to study significant global issues or even local affairs of consequence. A study by the McCormick Tribune Freedom Museum found that 22 percent of Americans could name all five family members from the *Simpsons* television show but that only one in a thousand could name all five First Amendment freedoms and that only one in four could name more than one.[2] If Thomas Jefferson was correct when he said that ignorance and freedom are an impossible combination, we are in trouble. If authentic geography education is about relationships between place and people and about the influence of the latter on the former and visa versa, then we are uneducated.

A surprising number of citizens from all walks of life are expressing more and more concerns about various oppressive activities like NAFTA and are relating them to "borders"—whether land, economic, social, political, legal or psychological—that affect spaces and places in the world. The low scores on the various geography surveys and the realization that a collective illiteracy about the real interactions between places and the people in them is allowing a few powerful people to control the world have increasingly prompted calls to improve geographic education. In 1984, responding to the growing geography education issues, the Joint Committee on Geographic Education of the National Council for Geographic Education (NCGE) and the Association of American Geographers (AAG) compiled five fundamental themes to help people learn geography. Endorsed by the NCGE, the AAG and the National Geographic Society, these five themes include:

- Location: People and places are positioned variously on the Earth's surface. Where in the world are places located?
- Place: Physical and human characteristics distinguish one place from other places. What makes a place special?
- Relationships within Places: The interactions of humans with their environments shape the characteristics of both people and the environment. How do people change the natural environment and how does the environment influence the activities of people?
- Movement: Human interactions on the Earth—people, products, and information—affect the characteristics of places. What are the global patterns of movement of people, products, and information?
- Regions: The Earth can be divided into regions to help us understand similarities and differences of peoples and places. How do regions form and change?

A decade later, in 1994, the National Council for Geographic Education, in collaboration with the National Geographic Society, created a 272-page book entitled *Geography for Life*, which elaborates on eighteen standards that are divided into six essential elements. Rather than focusing on how to locate places on a map, this publication emphasizes relationships and the idea that Earth is our home. Here are the eighteen curricular objectives:

The World in Spatial Terms

1. How to use maps and other geographic representations, tools, and technologies to acquire, process, and report information.
2. How to use mental maps to organize information about people, places, and environments.
3. How to analyze the spatial organization of people, places, and environments on Earth's surface.

Places and Regions

4. The physical and human characteristics of places.
5. That people create regions to interpret Earth's complexity.
6. How culture and experience influence people's perception of places and regions.

Physical Systems

7. The physical processes that shape the patterns of Earth's surface.
8. The characteristics and spatial distribution of ecosystems on Earth's surface.

Human Systems

9. The characteristics, distribution, and migration of human populations on Earth's surface.
10. The characteristics, distributions, and complexity of Earth's cultural mosaics.
11. The patterns and networks of economic interdependence on Earth's surface.
12. The process, patterns, and functions of human settlement.
13. How forces of cooperation and conflict among people influence the division and control of Earth's surface.

Environment and Society

14. How human actions modify the physical environment.
15. How physical systems affect human systems.
16. The changes that occur in the meaning, use, distribution, and importance of resources.

The Uses of Geography

17. How to apply geography to interpret the past.
18. To apply geography to interpret the present and plan for the future. (Boehm and Bednarz, 1994, pp. 14–15)

Neither the 1984 nor the 1994 curricular agendas for geography have made much headway in the real world of education, but they are out there and some teachers use them when they can. They make a good start for legitimate categories of study. In the next section, I offer some perspectives about place, like those in the opening quotations, that put flesh on this bare-bones list of objectives and perhaps give it soul as well. I conclude with examples of an American Indian geography curriculum that uses these eighteen points as well. I hope teachers will realize how easy it is to incorporate these spiritually based geography concepts into other subjects. Elementary, high school and university teachers can individually succeed in their classrooms where curricular policies and official textbooks have failed. Taking this step with the ideas that follow may be our last hope.

Indigenous Curricular Alternatives

Traditional Indigenous communities would not separate "geography" (as the study of relationships between places and people)[3] from everyday life. Living in relationship with all aspects of the land is what it means to be indigenous to the specific lands on which Indigenous Peoples have dwelled for hundreds, if not thousands, of years. For all students, geography, even "world geography," is best studied if it begins with local relationships. I am not advocating isolationist policies but saying that our power is greatest and will grow stronger when we commit ourselves first to the place we live while remaining conscious about the global realities. An indigenized mainstream geography curriculum therefore must be about seeing the world in terms of relationships between people and places in the most personal sense. This begins with a sense of personal relationship with the natural world. Because the natural world is ethical and internally harmonious and because virtues such as courage, patience, generosity and honest originate among the creatures in it, this relationship is foundational for all others. To make this point, I often quote a famous passage from D. H. Lawrence's classic novel *Lady Chatterly's Lover* (1928) that many environmentalists also quote, as Michael Cohen does in his book *Connecting with Nature* (1990):

> Oh, what a catastrophe, what a maiming of love when it was made personal, merely personal feeling. That is what is the matter with us: we are bleeding at the roots because we are cut off from the earth and sun and stars. Love has become a grinning mockery because, poor blossom, we plucked it from its stem on the Tree of Life and expected it to keep on blooming in our civilized vase on the table. (p. iv)

Cohen, an eco-psychology researcher, uses this passage to explain how it is possible that humanity can be so irrational in its relationship with the planet. He writes that we subconsciously elect to know the world as a dangerous place in order to explain away the pain we feel due to our separation from Nature (1990, p. iv). Oglala Lakota scholar Vine Deloria Jr. also speaks to this idea of personal relationship with place in a book he co-authored with Daniel Wildcat entitled *Power and Place: Indian Education in America* (2001). Because he agrees that relationships in the natural world are always "ethical," Deloria says that appropriate action by humans

> requires careful discernment of nature's messages as well as subsequent behavior that considers all possible consequences and ensures relationships are completed. An indigenized educational practice thus begins with the explicit aim of establishing personal relationships with the natural world, through living experience in a particular place. The exploration of such experiences becomes the source of both personal and communal identity, as well as the knowledge and wisdom for how to live ethically and well—"attentively, respectfully, and responsibly"—in the world. (p. 76)

It is admittedly a challenge for non-Indian teachers and students to grasp the idea that the land is literally the Mother and that all of the creatures and geographic features, from rivers and lakes to rocks and trees, are our relatives. However, all of us can imagine the different way of being in this world that would arise if we called a local mountain, forest, creek or animal a relative instead of a resource. From an Indigenous perspective, geography is not learning *about* land but learning *from* it. Manulani Aluli Meyer says this beautifully:

> Land is more than a physical place. It is an idea that engages knowledge and contextualizes knowing. It is the key that turns the doors inward to reflect on how space shapes us....Land is more than just a physical locale; it is a mental one that becomes water on the rock of our being. (2008, p. 219)

Students can reflect on natural settings that have informed their own way of being in the world. Maybe it was a garden in the backyard or a humming bird that came every morning to the kitchen window. Perhaps someone will remember a woods played in or hills climbed. Even now, I am being shaped by my new stand-up paddle board. Each day, I cruise around islands, contemplating my life and purpose as reflected in the mirror of the ocean or in my encounters with mating sea turtles. Each day, we all engage with *some* aspect of the natural world, even in the heart of a big city. How does breathing the air affect you? What plant is forcing its way up through a concrete sidewalk that teaches you determination? Why do some places make you feel good and others less so? Understanding such personal relationships with the land is a prerequisite for understanding all other relationships, many that we should attend to but do not. Establishing or re-establishing a personal relationship with the natural world requires a conscious break from technologies (e.g., video games, television and the Internet) that make our lives literally groundless and leave us without a sense of geography to connect us in more multidimensional ways to our roots. Only with this connection to our roots will the potential for world-wide interconnectivity be realized and result in authentic relationship building.

The reasons for our groundlessness and the absence or superficiality of geography education, aside from the hegemony, began with Greek philosophy. Aristotle's ideas about the importance of community were largely on target, but he incorrectly defined "community" because he did not include wilderness and other-than-human creatures. Socrates, the father of Western philosophy said, "I'm a lover of learning, and trees and open country won't teach me anything, whereas men in the town do" (Plato, 1982, p. 479). Such anthropocentrism has nourished our materialism and technological advancements, but our separation from Nature and from its ethical, balanced teachings has led us in unethical, imbalanced directions. Thus the first mandate for any geography class is to go outside. The average American spends far too much time indoors, and children are no exception. Collectively, we spend less than one day per person per lifetime truly experiencing an authentic connection with the natural world (Cohen, 1990, p. 8). An article in the *New York Times* cites the National Park Service's report that the number of recreational visits to U.S. national parks was lower in 2010 than a decade earlier—lower even than in 1987 and 1988. There were 35 percent more backcountry campers in the national parks in 1979 than in 2010 (Schulten, 2011). A National Academy of Sciences study, led by Patricia Zaradic and Oliver Pergams of the University of Illinois, gathered data on seventy years of various nature activities. They found that since the late 1980s, nature recreation had fallen by 18 to 25 percent on a per capita basis (2008).[4]

If we are spending little or no time creating a personal relationship with other than human-made environments that best allow us to reflect on our own natures, we will have a more difficult time showing ethics, compassion, empathy, understanding, courage and integrity in our human relationships.[5] A practical consideration for teaching, then, is how to turn whatever standard may be required for whatever course that is being taught into a local project that requires learning about connections between landscape and people. Indigenous perspectives provide the paradigm for this. Indigenous philosophy about human interactions with Nature provides lessons that can help mainstream society reconnect with nature and establish mutually beneficial and reciprocal relationships. "In the drive for a new ecological ethos, Aboriginal epistemologies can provide a framework for engendering an ethic of stewardship and sustainability" (Beckford, 2008, p. 55). Clinton Beckford, a professor of geography at the University of Windsor, in collaboration with Russell Nahdee, the director of the Aboriginal Education Center there, offers a list of key tenets that can be used for partnering Indigenous perspectives with mainstream geography instruction. If students realize the following as truths, they may start to gain geographic wisdom.

- There is an inseparable relationship between people and the natural world.
- Respect for all aspects of the environment—everywhere, not just in the community—is vital.
- Recognition that we are dependent upon Earth's complex life systems flows into all subject areas.
- Landscape is viewed as sacred.
- Responsibility for future generations is assumed.
- Respectful and responsible use of natural resources (a.k.a. "our relatives") is an imperative.

It is understood that quality of environment relates directly to quality of life. Admittedly, most schools will not have an ethic such as the Indigenous one attached to their study of the relationships between humans and land in geography coursework. In fact, most school vision and mission statements avoid even mentioning the importance of the connection. My own university, noted as being one of the most progressive in the country, has struggled for years to incorporate "ecological" language into its vision and mission statements to accompany its commitment to social justice. I have attempted to share the growing scholarship that supports the claim that social and ecological issues, especially as relates to justice, are inseparable. Interestingly, a few minutes ago, along with all faculty, students and administrators at my school, I received a request to fill out a survey related to our thoughts about the university's current vision, mission and values. Sharing what I wrote may help explain how difficult it is for schools to embrace this primary Indigenous perspective but how relatively easy it is, at least as a start, to change the hegemonic language in order to formulate a more appropriate vision for education.

Dear Provost,

Thanks for taking on this important project. Below in underlined type are my edits to the vision, mission and values statements. In most ways, the phrases and ideas are typical of most university vision, mission and values statements. I believe the edits suggested, or others that might work better, can put us back on track with the intentions that most, not all, of us have and that were intended by the university founders. To explain the edits I offer the following four brief paragraphs. After these are the edited statements.

1. I have clarified the use of the word "transformation." As it stands, this word can keep us in the cyclone of individualism, globalism, "progress" and unlimited technology and "innovation" at any cost. Red Cloud offered a simple option long ago: "Just decide what is good to take with you and what you should leave behind." In light of our dismissal of traditional Indigenous science, for one example, this has been a potentially dangerous concept in progressive education. My simple modification of the term minimizes interpretations that likely stand in opposition to the intended vision.

2. I have also blended "ecological" with "social" in the references to the statements about a commitment to "social justice." I have previously submitted scholarly arguments and citations in support of the idea that it is impossible to really separate the social from the environmental when considering structural inequalities of any kind.

3. My edits related to the reference to "community" simply reflect the contention that in addition to "collegiality, respect and compassion," we must mention our commitment to the greater good of the community as per the social/ecological justice vision. Too many of our courses and dissertations, as pointed out in previous co-authored research, do not make this connection.

4. Finally, referring to only the worth of human individuals without adding a reference to non-human creatures, as I have done below, keeps us in the anthropocentric hole that prevents authentic engagement with social/ecological issues.

The global crises we are all facing beg the question of what we all must do as educators at this moment. A good start is to address these issues in our vision, mission and values.
Saludos,
Four Arrows

Current Mission: Fielding Graduate University serves a community of scholar-practitioners dedicated to transformational learning (as defined below)* and social/ecological justice.*

Current Vision: In pursuit of a more just and sustainable world, Fielding Graduate University sets the standard of excellence as a global network of lifelong learners engaged in ~~innovative~~ scholarly practice and research that makes a unique and positive contribution to the world.

Current Values: Academic Excellence: a commitment to the highest quality academic performance that embraces the vision.*

• *Transformational Learning: a fundamental re-evaluation of one's vision, rules, goals, and priorities that results in knowing and acting on which approaches to life and learning are in balance and which are not.

• Community: an appreciation for a lifelong learning environment built on understanding our interconnections, collegiality, mutual respect, compassion and a commitment to serving the greater good.

• *Sociality and ecology are inseparable concepts, and as they relate to justice both must be considered.

- *Human Diversity, Dignity, and Worth: a respect for the dignity and worth of all individuals, <u>human and non-human</u>, within an inclusive environment that celebrates openness and diversity in the service of <u>social/ecological justice</u>.

- *Truth, Integrity, and Meaning: <u>we stand for</u> a willingness to serve others as ethical change agents in our search for truth in learning, in our work and in our lives.

Questions for Research, Dialogue, Choices and Praxis

With all of the aforementioned concepts in mind respecting how to incorporate the Indigenous perspective so that geography can be taught and learned in more meaningful ways, I offer the following opportunities for classroom research, dialogue, choices and praxis. These are actual examples of geography standards, benchmarks and lessons from the Four Directions Project. These were the result of a five-year federally funded grant project to create culturally relevant curricula. The primary sponsor of the project, which began in 1995, was the Pueblo of Laguna Department of Education, located on the Laguna Indian Reservation, west of Albuquerque, New Mexico.[6] I have selected random examples of benchmarks for multiple age groups. Many, if not most, of these ideas can be easily modified to fit whatever students are in the non-Indian class being taught. Notice how the skills addressed are especially relevant to the students' real world—how they encourage active engagement and a respect for community and sustainability. Note that these benchmarks essentially use the National Geographic Society themes listed above.

- Use symbols to identify on a map features of the local community, such as hospitals, schools, and so forth.
- Draw a sketch map of the local community from memory, showing the route to and from school and to one or more of the homes of the students' extended family members.
- Mark and label locations of places discussed in history, language arts, science and other school subjects and attempt to describe how the location may have affected the ideas being discussed.
- Write a short description from memory of the physical and human characteristics of the state in which you live, emphasizing sites of special importance to your community.
- Analyze the locations of places and suggest why particular ones are used for certain human activities.
- Create a model of agricultural development, livestock grazing and timber harvesting, identify connections among places and explain the causes and consequences of spatial interaction.

- Identify cultural characteristics that originated in various places and their impact on different regions.
- Use wood, clay or other materials to make a model of a place that shows items of special importance to the people who live there.
- Make a model of a community that shows its human characteristics (i.e., places that people use).
- Draw maps to show the distribution of the American Indian population in a region and include landforms, climate, vegetation, resources and human characteristics to suggest factors that affect settlement patterns.
- Develop a set of questions to ask tribal elders about regional change during their lifetimes, and write a summary of the answers.
- Write a historical account of the changes in a community as seen from the students' own perspective.
- Use role playing to demonstrate differences between American Indian and European views about uses of the land.
- Conduct interviews to collect information on how people of different ages, genders or cultures view the same place.
- Identify and describe the physical components of Earth's atmosphere, lithosphere, hydrosphere and biosphere.
- Use the medicine wheel to describe the water cycle in an area.
- Explain how the length of day can influence human activities in different regions of the world.
- Discuss traditional American Indian views about the elemenets of creation and their relationships to one another.
- Write descriptions of groups of plants and animals that include where they live and why they live there.
- Write a short play describing the reasons why a family might move from one area to another.
- Use interviews to explain how the roles of women affect life in a community.
- Describe how technology has changed recreational activities in your community.
- Use primary source documents to compare the ways that American Indian tribes historically satisfied their basic needs and wants with how Europeans typically do.
- Discuss important economic activities in your community and their positive and negative impacts.
- Take an item you have purchased and make a map that follows it from

its origins to you.

- Use graphics to identify voting districts in your area.
- Explain how and why people compete for control of Earth's surface by preparing a series of maps to describe how the United States reduced Indian control of lands.
- Research, write and illustrate a geographic history of a state that focuses on how the state got its present boundaries.
- Identity a local issue that has been a point of conflict between American Indians and non-Indians and that illustrates ideas of cooperation and conflict.
- Describe ways that humans alter their physical environment by listing examples of changes in land use, and create graphs to illustrate changes in physical environments and the introduction or loss of species.
- Classify various resources in your community as either renewable or non-renewable, and use charts to present your conclusions.
- Prepare a timeline illustrating changes in the vegetation and animal populations in a region.
- Draw cartoon strips to illustrate ways that resources can be managed for future generations.
- Describe how differences in perception affect people's views of the world by using a data retrieval chart to organize information on how distinct groups of people perceive the same place differently.
- Describe the essential characteristics and functions of maps.
- Use a map to decide the best place to build a restaurant in your community.
- Assess how variations in technology and perspectives affect human modification of landscapes over time.

I think this sampling serves to give teachers ideas for how to indigenize geography coursework. These activities require active and intimate associations between community and place.[7] They use a variety of skills from art to thinking and reveal a way to empower students to take control of planning relationships with the land that will be necessary for future survival.

I close with the following poem by Big Thunder (Bedagi), a late-nineteenth-century Algonquin, to help inspire teachers and students to remember the truly important geographic instruction goal of emphasizing the human-animal-earth relationships we have forsaken:

The Great Spirit is in all things, is in the air we breathe. The Great Spirit is our Father, but the Earth is our Mother. She nourishes us; that which we put into the ground, She returns to us...

Give us hearts to understand;

Never to take from creation's beauty more than we give;
never to destroy wantonly for the furtherance of greed;

Never to deny to give our hands for the building of earth's beauty;
never to take from her what we cannot use.

Give us hearts to understand

That to destroy earth's music is to create confusion;
that to wreck her appearance is to blind us to beauty;

That to callously pollute her fragrance is to make a house of stench;
that as we care for her she will care for us.

We have forgotten who we are.

We have sought only our own security.

We have exploited simply for our own ends.

We have distorted our knowledge.

We have abused our power.

Great Spirit, whose dry lands thirst,

Help us to find the way to refresh your lands.

Great Spirit, whose waters are choked with debris and pollution,
help us to find the way to cleanse your waters.

Great Spirit, whose beautiful earth grows ugly with misuse,
help us to find the way to restore beauty to your handiwork.

Great Spirit, whose creatures are being destroyed,
help us to find a way to replenish them.

Great Spirit, whose gifts to us are being lost in selfishness and corruption,
help us to find the way to restore our humanity.

Oh, Great Spirit, whose voice I hear in the wind, whose breath gives life to the world,
hear me;
I need your strength and wisdom. May I walk in Beauty.

(http://www.indigenouspeople.net/greatspi.htm)

Notes

1. There is some hope perhaps that two primary supporters of the Teaching Geography Is Fundamental Act, the Participatory Politics Foundation and the Sunlight Foundation, are working hard to make transparent the continuing hegemony against the proper teaching of geography.
2. They are freedom of speech, religion, press, assembly and petition for redress of grievances.
3. Note that the term "people" includes not only the two-legged people but the plant, insect, fish, bird and mammal people as well.
4. See http://www.cnaturenet.org/news/detail/researchers_discuss_nature_conservancy_study
5. I am reminded by the song I think Ike and Tina Turner sang called "Proud Mary" where a line says, "People on the river are happy to give." It seems that people closer to nature do possess more of these traits.
6. To view the entire curriculum, see "Pathfinders for Four Directions: An Indigenous Educational Model," http://www.eric.ed.gov/ERICWebPortal/search/detailmini.jsp?
7. Some Indigenous instructors would encourage us to conduct all geography lessons outside the classroom in human and non-human communities. In a piece entitled "Coyote Teaching for Geography Instruction" for the *Journal of Geography*, Michael DeMers introduces this idea to non-Indian teachers (2010, p. 104).

THE SOUTH

The Color White

Spiritual and Emotional Awareness

From Fear to Fearlessness
(Religion/Psychology and Spirituality)

With guest authors Ed McGaa (Eagle Man) &
R. Michael Fisher

The first peace, which is the most important, is that which comes within the souls of people when they realize their relationship, their oneness with the universe and all its powers, and when they realize at the center of the universe dwells the Great Spirit,[1] and that its center is really everywhere, it is within each of us.

—BLACK ELK[2]

Fearlessness is the first requisite of spirituality. Cowards can never be moral.
—MOHANDAS GANDHI

Courage has gone out of our race. The terror of society, which is the basis of morals, the terror of God, which is the secret of religion—these are the two things that govern us.

—OSCAR WILDE

A teacher's primary task is to help students overcome their fears and discover they can do more than they think they can.

—KURT HAHN

A Different Approach to These Subjects

Psychology and religion are two important mainstream subject areas that I did not include in the previous section with its four-part structure for a number of reasons. First, neither appears in state standards until high school, and even then they are rarely offered electives. Second, for these subjects, identifying hegemony in curriculum and instruction is problematic. For the study of religion, listing hegemonic aspects would require a book in itself. I could have mentioned the ways Judaism and Christianity are typically taught, how they tend to maintain status quo systems such as those that discriminate against homosexuality and women, and how they sustain authoritarianism, punishment and rewards. One could also expose how, by omission, the required teaching "about" religions helps support U.S. foreign policy, such as relates to Israel's oppression of Palestine.[3] There is little room in the curriculum standards for critical thinking since federal law does not allow such discourse in teaching religion, stating that it must be taught in a neutral and secular way. Finally, the role of religion, especially Christianity, as a major force contributing to anthropocentrism and the ecological crises has been a topic of academic discussion since Lynn White first brought it up in his now famous article "This Historical Roots of the Ecological Crises," published in *Science* back in 1967.[4]

I did not include the subject of psychology because the typical curriculum is so selective, shallow and fragmented in contrast to the vastness of the topic and in consideration of time available for teaching it. As for hegemonic influences in psychology, Greg Cajete, John Lee and I authored a book that clearly identifies the wrong-headed propositions about human nature that come from seeing brain science through the Western lens and according to the needs of profit-making industries. To understand the hegemony in neuroscience, see this text entitled *Critical Neurophilosophy and Indigenous Wisdom* (2011).

As for real-world problems related to both of these topics, volumes would be needed to describe the negative outcomes relating to religious practices and psychological well being stemming from what education teaches about these subjects. Also, studies about the negative consequences of religion on societies and about the poor psychological health of a large percentage (and correlations between the two) of the population are numerous and especially for older students would be worth studying. It would also have been difficult to offer comparable Indigenous alternatives to the standards because Indigenous cultures really do not have what might be considered religion. Spirituality, as we have learned, pervades the entire scope of daily life in traditional Indigenous cultures, and although they have ceremonies and rituals, there are no parallels of substance for major religions such as

Christianity, Judasim and Islam. What might have been a source of even more con-fusion if I had attempted to look at religion and psychology as I did the other sub-jects is that from an Indigenous perspective, Indigenous spirituality and the mental processes and behaviors that relate to the psyche are inseparable.[5]

Finally, I did not use the same approach to talking about psychology and reli-gion courses because most of the Indigenous material presented for the other sub-jects represents Indigenous spiritual and psychological conclusions about life. Attempting to complement a specific curriculum or standard for religion and psy-chology would have been redundant.

Instead, in this chapter I talk about religion, psychology and spirituality as they relate to courage and fearlessness, concepts that play a fundamental role in Nature-based Indigenous belief systems, thinking and behaviors. An understanding of the Indigenous path to fearlessness may serve the same goals the highest ambitions for school coursework in religion, spirituality or psychology. Any religion or psychol-ogy curriculum that does not significantly focus on cultures of fear and proven approaches for cultivating courage and fearlessness[6] is inadequate in our era of crises. Traditional Indigenous wisdom best serves as a model for teaching such lessons, as Noam Chomsky writes in his classic text on American cultural hegemony, *What Uncle Sam Really Wants* (1992). Referring to American Indians, he states, "The courage they show is quite amazing. It's a very moving and inspiring experience, and brings to my mind some contemptuous remarks of Rousseau's on Europeans who have abandoned freedom and justice for the peace and repose they enjoy in their chains" (p. 100).

Indigenous spirituality/psychology refers to the common truths traditional Aboriginal cultures embrace that stem from an intimate relationship with the nat-ural world, thus teaching Indigenous spirituality in classrooms does not violate con-stitutional policies about separating church and state in education.[7] A few ideas about Indigenous spirituality help support this assertion. Greg Cajete writes that "Spirituality comes from the process of exploring and coming to know the nature of the living energy that moves in each of us, through us, and around us" (2000, p. 261). Similarly, Vine Deloria Jr. defines "Indigenous spirituality"[8] as being comprised of "complexes of attitudes, beliefs, and practices fine-tuned to harmo-nize with the lands on which the people live" (1994, p. 70). He says that these com-plexes are involved in every facet of life. Eagle Man, in his presentation later in this chapter, speaks of Indian spirituality as being about living in accordance with the laws of Nature with a sacred sense of being related to all. Teaching and learning about these ideas as they relate to standards and coursework should never be any-thing but appropriate for the classroom?

The Indigenous writer who has provided what I believe to be the most open-minded, fearless and scholarly reflections on the connection between Indigenous spiritual wellness, social justice, ecological sustainability, psychological health and Christianity is George E. Tinker. Son of an Osage father, Tinker espouses a "theology" that follows a traditional Indigenous worldview, and he never separates environment from his scholarship. The title alone of his 1993 book reveals the nature of his investigations and how crucial the question about compatibility really is— *Missionary Conquest: The Gospel and Native American Cultural Genocide*. More than a decade later, Tinker's reflections in his text *American Indian Liberation: A Theology of Sovereignty* (2008) are relevant here to contemplations about compatibility possibilities between Christianity and Indigenous spirituality that expand on Lynn White's 1967 essay, discussed above, which refers only to the ecological crises:

> While I am very sympathetic to Indian reluctance to invest themselves into any type of Christology, an argument could be made for an Indian Christology that would respond effectively to the resurgence of right-wing racist, oppressive theologies in the U.S. and the renewed threat to Indian people today. A serious Indian reflection on christology could provide new energy and creativity to confront the new round of colonialism which we call internal colonialism. (p. 91)

The idea of internal colonialism to which Tinker refers is important to the indigenizing education agenda. It refers not to colonizing people in countries invaded by the colonizer but to colonizing people within the same nation. Until recently, this has related mostly to structural inequalities for minority groups, but as the Occupy Movement is revealing, the power and wealth of ruling elites and large multinational corporations have made it so that all of us are at risk for being colonized. This is why our present discussion points are doubly important. Everything about colonialism starts and ends with fear and it can only be prevented or conquered with courage and fearlessness.

When students of religion and psychology begin to ask questions about whether a religion causes more divisiveness than unity or more destruction than sustainability, they can begin to decide on how religion, spirituality and psychological approaches to health and happiness best serve them. This requires frank dialogue and scholarly research that can and should be done from the earliest grades on. Are their risks for teachers to allow for such critical dialogue and research? Of course. The risks to our world, however, are far greater for not having done it.[9] This is an important goal for teaching these subjects whether in designated courses or by weaving the investigation into other social studies subjects, such as U.S. history.[10] To help with this, we now turn to Eagle Man's perspectives on Indigenous spirituality.

Indigenous Spirituality vs Organized Religion

by Wanblee Wichasha (Eagle Man), a.k.a. Ed McGaa, J.D.

Eagle Man is a member of the Oglala Lakota Nation (OST-15287) and a respected elder. He has participated in six Sun Dances under Chiefs Fools Crow and Eagle Feather. As a Marine Corps officer and pilot, he flew F-4 jets in 110 combat missions over Vietnam. He is the author of nine books on American Indian spirituality, with a three-book series coming out on Kindle in 2012 entitled "Spirituality for America, the British Isles and Spain." One of his books, *Mother Earth Spirituality*, printed by Harper Collins, is in its forty-fifth printing.[11]

Since most of the readership likely knows little to nothing about Native American spirituality, I find it best to utilize a comparison between it and "organized religion." Spirituality is based on Nature (Creator's Creation). Organized religion is human-based. As an American Indian who has experienced years of forced indoctrination from organized religion, I believe that I know quite a bit about human-based organized religion. I also know something about our Native spirituality I wish to share with the reader. First, I want to briefly set the historical record straight about organized religion's invasion of our spiritual lands.

The invaders came into this land primarily because their own land had many inhospitable social and religious aspects that severely curtailed the natural freedom that is inherent to all living beings, not just the so-called "reasoning" entities—we humans. Those of the animal world—*Wamaska skan* to us Sioux—always strive to be free and are our teachers. Put a wild, free animal in a comfortable cage with abundant food and water, and it will pace back and forth seeking to escape back to its own realm. Many will refuse to eat. Perhaps European immigrants were escaping from their cages, except there they were not even fed adequately. "Nobility" owned all lands surrounding the local villages inhabited by the majority of the European populace, which was teeming with wild game mainly because of the restrictive hunting laws laid down by the controlling nobility. Any huntsman found in the deer-abundant forests would have his bow fingers severed. Hence very little protein-bearing meat supplemented the average European's meal, which consisted mainly of a gruel-like porridge. No beans, corn, or potatoes—foods rich in protein—grew in Europe until Columbus brought them back from the Americas. Consequently, the European was small in stature. English knight armor would fit a five-foot-four-inch person or a small woman of today. Europeans were thus much smaller than the average plains Indians. Chief Red Cloud (Sioux/Lakota) was close to six-foot-two, and most Sioux warriors were in the six-foot range, as were the Iroquois.

So natural spirituality is about true freedom, not the rhetoric of freedom. It is also about Reality-Nature. Everything is created out of a Mysterious Force that has designed the world and all that is in it to maintain a balance among its complex and often chaotic relationships. It is a Mystery to us, which we readily admit—indescribable and actually beyond total comprehension to us. We pride ourselves for being honest with such admittance. And any talk about such subjects, even as I am doing now, comes from a suppositional "attitude," unless referring to a reality actually observed. Otherwise, we respect spirituality as an incomprehensible Mystery.

Originally, religions began from a spiritual base, but soon human intervention put people out of touch with this base. For example, there is nothing left of the Celtic Way (European Nature-based spirituality) from what I have directly observed in travels through Europe. It has been thoroughly obliterated by organized religion. Celtic Peoples followed basic Earth principles like the original inhabitants of this land. All Indigenous cultures that I have met practice a spirituality that is Nature-based which includes both Earth, our solar system and the entire cosmos. [12] Religion is generally based on human beliefs. Often it even vilifies, deprecates Nature. Religion often disagrees with the findings of observable science, whereas spirituality more often is in alignment with it. Quantum physics is more and more coming to realize the conclusions that Indigenous Peoples drew from their observations of Nature.

A point I am trying to make is that Nature is All and that humans as part of Nature cannot change it to something it is not. This is what religion tries to do. Spirituality does not invent morals and ethics. Nature created it, and the animals taught us how to live accordingly long before humans came along. Idiotic humankind has traversed widely in its attempts to "know" what is actually impossible to truly perceive and has successfully used religion to fabricate knowledge. Man has established a religious hierarchy that controls by using fear and false promises that are endangering all of life on Mother Earth today. Through religious-based fear rather than spiritual fearlessness, people are programmed and medicated to exist as if we were not a part of the Great Mystery.

What will it take for "religious" people to recognize the imbalance and unhappiness caused by organized religions? Take one example related to the religious source for homophobic hatred of some individuals. Many Christian churches are against other gender orientations, as are Muslim ones. They deny that Nature and its complex design, stemming from the Force of the Great Mystery, allows for such variety. Indigenous Peoples always understood this. For example, the Lakota believe that a *winkte* (one born as a non-heterosexual) should be treated as everyone else. This contrasts of course with the teachings of many religions such as Christianity.

And this is just one item on a list of many religious interpretations causing unnecessary harm in the world, not to mention those ideas that have led to the current ecological crises, with every life system on Earth at a tipping point.

Another difference between natural Indigenous spirituality and organized religion relates to the latter's claim that the "Devil/Satan" exists and preys upon humankind to detour our journey away from a rewarding afterlife and on into a fiery, quite unpleasant "Hell," where one can expect eternal torture and so forth. Traditional tribal cultures often believe that beyond this life there exists a Spirit World that all humans will eventually enter. They do not profess to know the details, but *believe* we are judged by those whom we have offended as well as by those we have honored. This is supposition, of course, as we admit. We just think it makes sense that there is reciprocity and reflection on how dutiful we are in this life to the higher path. It is a simpler, pragmatic supposition, however, in my opinion. It is difficult for us to understand Nature's need for a white man's Satan, yet they call us superstitious. We are not afraid of the dark.

Indigenous spirituality is then simply about honest observation of Reality, based on a time when we lived amidst Nature and were able to observe it. It is looking clearly at what Nature reveals to us along with an awareness of civilization's deceptions and fears. (Coyote stories warn us about our own susceptibility to these things.) Of course, honest observation also holds a cautious respect for Nature's power but not for escape from it. To regain the Natural Way, we must be honest, courageous and generous. This requires making sure that we pay attention to what man is doing to our environment. We should consider how our actions relate to future generations. Spirituality tells us to mind the laws of Nature and seek balance. Religion tells us to "multiply and subdue the Earth." Natural spirituality tells us to live according to the natural balance between the masculine and the feminine. Religions say man is superior. We learn about balance, such as the truth about woman's power, from the animal world. Observations teach us how the female leads the hunt, as when the matriarch elephant leads the others to water, grasslands and so on. That is the way it *is* in Nature. Among the Sioux, the Iroquois and many other Indigenous Peoples, including the ancient Celts, woman and man live according to different ways than most of the world's religions advocate.

The Natural Way of spirituality is a matter of living your beliefs according to what you know, understand and feel in the presence of that which is Nature. It is a lifetime of moral and ethical application of integrity and caring for others. It is not about personal salvation but about the continuation of place and community. The more advanced you develop yourself from direct observation, the more advanced your mind and your spirit and the more prepared your soul for what Spirit

World may be next. This *supposition* also means one must unclutter and remove clogging superstition, harmful appetites, greed, ego and ignorance from the mind. The more truthful you keep yourself and the more knowledge you seek—especially Nature-reflected knowledge,—the more God-like you become. It is all about how much you live life every day with respect for all relationships. It is about the common sense knowing that something great and beautiful is responsible for the gift of life and Mother Earth but that it is too mysterious for human understanding. It is about the virtues that all cultures claim to cherish, such as honesty, generosity, courage, fortitude and respectfulness. Notice how the Lakota ideas below reflect the real-life application of such virtues:

Wowaunsila—compassion and pity for all creatures
Wowascintanka—thoughtful reflection
Wolokokiciapi—peacefulness within oneself and with all others
Woksape—wisdom[13]
Wohetike—courage[14]
Wowahwala—humility[15]
Wacante Ognake—generosity
Wowayuonihan—to have respect and give significance to all creations

Quite simple isn't?

Reflections on Eagle Man's Words

The primary concepts of Indigenous spirituality that Eagle Man describes are not mandates from on high, nor are they goals for salvation. They require no "black books" for implementation. Rather, they are inherent in daily life on all levels and in all manner of education. The gift of American Indian spirituality to contemporary education is thus its ability to move educational theory beyond classroom doors and literally into the light of day and the mystery of night. Non-Indians do not need to change religions or participate in unique tribal ceremonies and rituals to benefit from this enlargement. If given their due, however, these spiritual assumptions force us to recall forgotten realities. With this memory, we are more likely to do what we can to break down the concrete walls protecting the destructive institutions that surround us.

Eagle Man refers to fear and courage in his piece and did so without knowing what the title of this chapter was going to be (for at the time I did not know myself). This is not surprising because Indigenous cultures use fear as a character builder, as opposed to a controlling device, in ways that lead to courage and fearlessness.

Daniel Wildcat, in his book co-authored with Vine Deloria Jr., entitled *Power and Place: Indian Education in America* (2001), refers to this plague of fearfulness and the cultures of fear that now plague our world:

> It is difficult to say exactly why experience in the world became so frightful to civilized Western humankind. [Deloria's book] *God Is Red* made a good case: the problems ensued shortly after the life of Jesus was no longer seen as the life of a single community member in a very specific place on the planet, but as the outline for an abstract, worldwide, theology-based religion. (p. 54)

In the co-authored text *Critical Neurophilosophy and Indigenous Wisdom* (2010), Greg Cajete underscores Wildcat's, Deloria's and Eagle Man's assertions about the use of fear in the dominant culture:

> Ultimately, such cultures have made humans afraid of nature, giving us comfort in safety and conveniences instead. I'm considering your idea, Four Arrows, that Natives used fear as a catalyst for practicing a virtue, so any frightening stimuli in nature, a bear or lightening, could well have served as a catalyst to remain one with nature....Native games might illustrate the courage to become one with the great mysteries and powers in Nature. Everything in Native games moves in a circle toward or away from a real or imagined center. Such movement has great metaphysical meaning in mimicking the circumbulating movement of celestial bodies in the cosmos. So finding the center and creating dynamic balance are achieved through reverent play associated with Native games. Playing the game 'with all one's heart' facilitates the players in finding their heart and finding their face while integrating body, mind and spirit. Playing with all one's heart usually requires a level of courage to face all sorts of fears. Ego attachment and the many fears relating to ego are overcome as a result of the player's full involvement with the game. They "forget themselves" and thereby become one with themselves, the other players and the dynamic process of the game. (Four Arrows, Cejete and Lee, 2010, p. 25)

Integrating mind, body and spirit is the proper subject matter for psychology curricula because psychology is ultimately about living the "good life." Cajete views a healthy psyche as being about "thinking the highest thought," meaning "thinking of one's self, one's community, and one's environment 'richly'—essentially, a spiritual mindset in which one thinks in the highest, most respectful and most compassionate way, thus systematically influencing the actions of both individuals and the community" (2000, p. 276). He sees the process of learning such psychological well-being as essentially described by five steps (pp. 277–279), which I condense as follows:

1. One has to come to terms with where one physically lives. This is the beginning of the extension and integration of connections with Nature and others in the community.

2. We must learn to experience and understand the differences and similarities among the spirit in ourselves, in other living things and in other entities of the natural world. It is about relationships.

3. Students must learn to think things through completely and make wise choices, to speak carefully and responsibly and to act decisively in order to produce something that is useful and has spirit.

4. Thinking the highest thought comes from a complex state of knowing founded on accumulating and reflecting upon experience.

5. It is important to attain a multisensory consciousness that embraces the sacredness of life with all of one's senses.

Each of these psychological/spiritual processes emphasizes the importance of virtues and character. Indigenous views in this regard are vital complements to Western approaches to "character education." This is because most character education programs in K-12 schools today stand in contrast to the Indigenous approach. In their book *The Discourse of Character Education: Culture Wars in the Classroom* (2005), Peter Smagorinsky and Joel Taxel present their study of proposals for character education funded by the U.S. Department of Education's Office of Educational Research and Improvement (OERI). In addition to the character education programs funded, they also look at one that was not funded. It was based on a program presented in my co-authored book *Teaching Virtues: Building Character across the Curriculum* (Jacobs and Jacobs-Spencer, 2001), which instructs teachers on how to weave courage, generosity, patience, fortitude, honesty and humility into all coursework as a priority focus, with subject content serving as context. This unfunded program stood "in relief" to all of the other programs studied, which leaned toward either liberal or conservative ideologies according to their conclusions. Referring to my book's approach, they conclude:

> Permeating the entire process is one's sense of spirituality. Character education is the process of formal pedagogy designed to promote this complex process by constantly looking for teachable moments to weave virtue awareness into the daily curriculum and by emphasizing intrinsic motivation over rewards and punishments for acting in virtuous ways.
>
> Such facts of character as feeling humility, being at peace, being spiritual, seeing generosity as the highest expression of courage, and feeling connected with all life forms are absent from Western conceptions of character. As we will review in subsequent chapters, they are not surprisingly absent from proposals funded by OERI for character curricula."
> (Smagorinsky and Taxel, 2005, p. 58)

Although courage and ultimately fearlessness are fundamental to Indigenous spirituality, they are not unique to it. Consider, for example, the words of Mohandas

Gandhi quoted at the outset of the chapter. The next section, by guest author Michael Fisher, offers a perspective grounded in more than two decades of studying fear and fearlessness outside of Indigenous cultures. Then, in the closing section, I present a relatively simple way to teach how fear can turn into fearlessness when we adhere to the Indigenous view that fears serve as a catalyst for practicing a virtue.

The Sacred Ground of Fearlessness

by R. Michael Fisher

R. Michael Fisher, PhD, is a curriculum philosopher-designer, public intellectual, counselor and self-professed fearologist living in Carbondale, Illinois. He is the founder and director of the Center for Spiritual Inquiry and Integral Education (http://csiie.org).

My vision for more than twenty-five years has been to combine philosophy, spirituality, psychology and education in order to help create a liberated world no longer ruled by fear but rather infused with fearlessness. I imagined that my text *The World's Fearlessness Teachings* (2010) would provide educators everywhere with a tool for realizing this vision. I was wrong, of course. The thick walls surrounding the culture of fear are far too great for a collection of the world's great teachings to penetrate easily. I continued with my work in fearlessness studies until a voice recently came to me saying, "Take your book to the sacred ground of fearlessness." I was puzzled. Then, while reflecting on this directive, I saw a storyline that maps a way to understand how we can move from fear to fearlessness.

Shortly afterward, Four Arrows invited me to tell my story in this book. He knows that in some ways my work complements his own as relates to indigenizing education. And yes, my work also calls upon people to act and think differently from ever before, not just for oneself but for the world and future generations.

My story/map begins with information and knowledge that have accumulated on the "culture of fear." Over a period of twenty-one years, 211 authors and educators have used this phrase. The peak number of occurrences was forty-one per year in 2006. Ninety percent occurred between 2001 and 2011 (Fisher, 2011), revealing the powerful repercussions of the events of 9/11. Still, only forty-one occurrences is nothing, especially since many of them were mine! People in fear do not want to talk about the topic. In Western culture generally, there appears to be no place—and no sacred ground—where we can actualize enough embrace of fearlessness to face our fears in radical and transformative ways. And yet there is! Only it has been dismissed, neglected or intentionally maligned. *Fearlessness*[16] as a primary virtue exists only in those places where traditional Indigenous Peoples and some Eastern traditions[17] still nurture it. The question is, what can we do to regain this sacred ground and what has happened in our Western history that has caused us to lose it?

I offer an answer related to two great forces, fear and love, which exist ontologically in a dialectical tension of duality (i.e., as opposites). Imagine these forces not as feelings or emotions, as psychology does, but rather as energies with particular designs/patterns that prefigure opposing worldviews. When these two forces are not blocked from communicating with each other or when one is not favored too much while the other is repressed, they flow in a balanced, self-regulating manner. When this happens, there is no pathology that feeds the dynamics of a *culture of fear*.[18]

If all flows well as one lives his or her life or as a culture organizes itself, people and communities learn from each other, and both grow as love heals fear and as duality is eventually transformed into non-duality (i.e., fearlessness). In other words, we do not have to worry about love not existing even if fear dominates and temporarily overshadows love's light, causing insidious destruction. Rather, our concern is how to get the balanced flow started again *while the fear is dominating*. Learning to embrace fearlessness, as Indigenous cultures have over thousands of years, is the path to such sacred ground.

Indeed, this is the Natural Way[19] of the world of human experience. Fearlessness offers the opportunity to integrate something into the real world that is not fully fear or fully love. It adds a third synergizing energy that helps move us back into proper action and being. As this experience of regaining balance by transcending fear occurs over and over again, one matures and feels less and less motivated by fear and more and more motivated by a radical trust in the universe. Such trust makes it difficult for an external force to coerce or disrupt our lives in ways that cause our sense of sacred interconnectedness to be lost. The culture of fear, of course, maintains violence and normalizes it so that it spreads like a virus. The practitioner of fearlessness, like the natural animal in the wilds, knows fear and is sensitive to danger signals but never succumbs to the pathological side of fear itself. This may be why Indigenous Peoples say they learn their fearlessness from the animals, as Four Arrows has stated in his book *Primal Awareness*: "To survive and thrive, wild animals must be experts in Fear. Humans who wish to express their positive potentiality must also be connoisseurs of this great motivator" (Jacobs, 1998, p. 156). This idea of knowing and respecting fear is expressed by the eminent human geographer Yi-Fu Tuan, who writes:

In the heart of ancient Sparta was a temple dedicated to Fear.[20] Other societies may not acknowledge the role of fear so explicitly [and sacredly], but nonetheless it is there in the midst of all human groups. Society as a whole dreads the capricious will of the gods, natural calamities, wars, and the collapse of social order; rulers fear dissension and rebellion; the ruled fear punishment and the arbitrary powers of authority. Although all societies know [about] fear, its prevalence varies strikingly from one to another: some seem remarkably free of fear, others appear to live under its aegis. (1979, p. 35)

My own research tells me, as does my vision, that Western society is largely and stubbornly blind to knowledge about fear and fearlessness. Going from fear to fearlessness requires rites of passage and ritual expressions not typically available. I have designed the cultural ritual pilgrimage presented below for students and their teachers to consider practicing in part or whole. Here's how to proceed:

1. Create a sacred ground of fearlessness on which to erect (in some form) a temple dedicated to fear. Create it in a place where you live (e.g., your home) *and* in a place to which you would have to walk that is beyond the normal circle of your territory (e.g., in Nature, or a community park, or the center of a city). It does not have to be permanently marked; that is up to you. If a site you pick doesn't have "power" for you and for fear, leave it and find another that does.
2. Decide when you will go to the temple. You may make it a structured time or not, but it ought to be significant at least as a marker in your day or week.
3. Walk the path of fear as you travel to the temple. Walk it slowly, as a pilgrim traditionally does, stopping often along the way and remembering why you are doing this ritual journey to the temple. Before arriving at the temple, you ought to have thought through, even recorded in a notebook, all the most important fears that have come into your life (affecting both yourself and others around you) during the day or week. Assess how you handled the fear in this world and inside you, and walk, walk, walk. Be discerning but not judgmental in thinking about your management of fear, and remember that choosing to walk the path of fear is all about learning from both your successes and mistakes in relationship to fear(s).
4. Set up your sacred ground and temple, and then give all your learning and fear(s) to the Great Spirit of the Temple of Fear. However you can imagine it, let go of your fears cognitively and emotionally. You

may even perform a dance or a song, or you may draw your fears on the ground, being as creative as you like. Let go of your fears until you feel lighter yet grounded.

5. Give thanks to the great mysterious energies and spirits of the temple, and then lie on the sacred ground of fearlessness and remember that *all* of the past great practitioners of fearlessness are there to offer assistance and will always be there as long as you remember them and honor them. Fearlessness now has a place in your world and in the culture you live in—you are rebuilding, in small steps, the lost culture of fearlessness.

6. Having absorbed the fearlessness of all ancestors, human and animal, proceed to dismantle the temple, or not, and say good-bye, giving gratitude and perhaps a gift to all.

7. Walk back the same way you came to the temple, but now see it as the path of fearlessness. Offer the gift of fearlessness and your learning to others on the path, taking responsibility for rebuilding a culture of fearlessness, but expect nothing from them in return. Most importantly, learn how to not be afraid of fear itself so that the culture of fear will dissolve. As well, pay heed to what the Dalai Lama preaches to the West: "Don't fear fearlessness" (quoted in Ferguson, 2005, p. 14).

This offering actualizes my vision. I believe it reflects the teachings of many of the great individuals who—first with courage and then with experience and wisdom—have walked the path that brings one from fear to the more powerful and sacred ground of fearlessness. It offers non-Indian readers a perspective that can help them understand the importance of three great forces—love, fear, and fearlessness—and implement them in the classroom as a means to indigenize education.

The CAT-FAWN Connection

Connecting Eagle Man's and Michael Fisher's perspectives, I wish to offer a mnemonic for helping teachers and students use Indigenous "psychology" and spirituality to overcome misdirected paradigms in mainstream education. Shortly after a near-death experience while kayaking the Rio Urique in Mexico's Copper Canyon, I had a vision that culminated in what I refer to as the "CAT-FAWN Connection." In my book *Primal Awareness: A True Story of Survival, Awakening and Transformation with the Raramuri Shamans of Mexico* (1998), I describe both the journey and the vision, along with details about the experiences that ultimately led to the vision. After many years of seeing people use it effectively, I believe in the usefulness of this teaching tool, especially as it relates to this chapter's focus on fearlessness as a foundational idea for teaching psychology and for living an authentically spiritual life according to Indigenous spiritual understandings. It is also a tool that can significantly help the reader effectively take on the project to indigenize mainstream education.[21]

CAT-FAWN is a mnemonic for helping to remember that transformational learning is primarily connected to a processing of information that represents collaboration between the right and left hemispheres of the brain. When various brain waves involved in predominantly right-brain hypnotic states of consciousness interact with brain activity related to left-brain cognitive reasoning, truly transformative learning is most likely to occur. "CAT" refers to this process of "concentration activated transformation"—that is, transformative learning that stems from a balanced integration of both hypnotically acquired ideas and rationally considered ones. Any psychology course that does not address hypnotic phenomena is insufficient and any religion that does not reveal how its practices can elicit or play upon hypnosis is deceptive. Ignorance about human susceptibility to trance logic or hypnosis has largely led to the uninvestigated and irrational behaviors in our world today because during times of stress people become hyper-suggestible to the communication of perceived authority figures (Jacobs, 1998).[22]

Indigenous Peoples have understood this phenomenon of learning for thousands of years. Their coyote stories, use of images and art, experiences with Nature, ceremonies, rights of passage and so on both warn of the potential problem of being hypnotized by others and teach the importance of intentionally using hypnosis or trance states to help direct deep learning. Such an understanding is crucial for undoing the hypnosis of Western hegemony, religion, materialism and anthropocentrism that continues to be a cause of the increasing fear and stress in our world.

The second part of the mnemonic, "FAWN," describes four major forces that play upon the spontaneous or intended states of hypnosis that are part of the CAT phenomenon. "FAWN" refers to "fear, authority, words and Nature." Whether the outcomes of a CAT experience are negative or positive, and thus whether transformative learning is constructive or destructive, depends on whether our thinking about these four forces is informed by a dominant Western cultural worldview or by an Indigenous perspective. All four forces are interrelated.

For example, in mainstream Western cultures, the first force, fear, is something to be avoided at all costs. People do not like to experience fear and go to great lengths to avoid it or escape from the emotion and its antecedents. We do not realize that when we are afraid we become hyper-suggestible to the signals or words of a perceived, trusted authority figure. Thus we unconsciously allow others to hypnotize us into believing in and acting according to wrong information. Indigenous views about fear are quite different. First, we do not let go of any critical faculties and are aware of the potential of hypnotic influence. Second, once the emotion of fear stimulates awareness and physical avoidance of a danger, fear becomes a catalyst for practicing one of the great virtues such as generosity, courage, patience, fortitude, humility or honesty. If a person has been working on becoming more authentically generous, for instance, fear triggers a significant opportunity to learn generosity. Imagine coming across a grizzly bear while looking for berries. Fear hits you, but there is no escape. The bear is right in front of you. Aha, well, what a chance to be generous! "Grandmother Bear, I cannot believe I did not realize this was your territory in which I was seeking berries. I see I have no escape from you, so I will take this opportunity to practice my generosity. Look, if you need my flesh more than I want these berries, I offer both to you." The bear, sensing fearlessness, moves on.

The second force that interacts with CAT is the concept of authority. In Western tradition, authority stems generally from external sources. Often we unquestioningly accept the authority of our books, our teachers, our preachers, our parents, our leaders and so forth. Such authority, especially when coupled with fear or stress, literally hypnotizes us into believing the messages of the authority figure, no matter how incorrect. When the frightened student who does not understand the math equation is confronted by the teacher who says, "You will never amount to anything!" this pronouncement sticks throughout the student's life. In contrast, Indigenous wisdom teaches that the only true source of authority is personal and honest reflection on lived experience in light of the spiritual understanding that everything is connected.

The third force is words. Words from others are always carefully, respectfully and critically considered. Words are powerful and must be used with care, as is discussed in Chapter 7, on English language arts. Western culture seems to be famous for its deceptive use of words. Social neuroscience even wants us to believe that deceptive language is a key aspect of human existence. Studies in this field, as summarized in *Critical Neurophilosophy and Indigenous Wisdom* (Four Arrows et al., 2010), often conclude that deception is a higher-order brain function that evolved to help humans survive. For example, the back cover of David Livingstone Smith's text *Why We Lie: The Evolutionary Roots of Deception and the Unconscious Mind* (2004) says, "Deceit, lying and falsehoods lie at the very heart of our cultural heritage." He tells us "Mother Nature has seen to it that the conscious mind is relatively blind to the nuances of social behavior" (p. 146). In Indigenous ways of thinking, we learn to observe and listen carefully in order to understand physical reality and experience, not to find ways to misrepresent it! There can be little doubt that deception has become common today, but could this not be "de-evolutionary"? Cooperation and honesty are more useful for survival than deception. Indigenous Peoples have always believed that it is important to see what is real about a situation, a thing or an entity. When Europeans began to make false promises, the American Indians initially thought they were mentally ill, unable to clearly understand reality consistently. Indigenous cultures the world over see words (and music) as sacred vibrations. Great care must be taken to make sure they reflect one's best understanding of "truth."

Although each of the forces in the CAT-FAWN concept are vital, I want to elaborate here on words because our denial about the state of ecological affairs in the world is, in one way or another, due to our use of deception, and we have much to learn from Indigenous wisdom about changing this. Indigenous thinking honors the reality that there are always two sides to the two sides, that there are realities and there are realities. Learning how they interact is real understanding. Our knowledge comes from our stories, which mirror the way the human mind works. They echo a truth lived and remembered because their roots go beyond the context processes of the brain. They stem from the heart of the human psyche. Thus understanding what is true is a matter of heart and mind, and this also helps one know what cannot be comprehended or articulated. If it were otherwise—if deception, not right thinking and remembering, were tools for social cohesions, as studies in social neuroscience seem to conclude—it seems that survival would be compromised, not enhanced. Moreover, Nature is the first and foremost teacher of how things are in the world. This is why we believe that the animals and plants are our teachers. Neither Nature nor animals lie about reality. Animals may have instinctive ways of hiding food or playing dead or stalking prey, but these are not examples of misrepresenting reality in the ways human deception does. I think deception is not a cultural adaptation for survival and social cohesion but rather a moral failing.

In the development of early human societies, a single isolated individual had no chance at long-term survival. Of course, this perspective, as we have seen, stands in opposition to the view of many Western academics that deception is necessary for survival. Still, it was the "group mind" that developed first among human beings. This "group mind" was rooted in interdependence and mutual reciprocal behavior, which paralleled the symbiotic relationships found in natural communities. The dynamic process of human adaptation to ever-changing environmental conditions that is so much a part of the "genius" of human evolution is based on our singular ability to evolve social environments conducive to the needs of our group. Honesty is both a value and a way of behavior that is required for the development of "trust" within a group. Honesty reinforces "trust" between members of a community, which in turn fosters the cooperation necessary to sustaining the group. Human adaptive values are those that encourage individual and family relationship, love, honesty, cooperation, collaboration, compassion, generosity and selflessness. These are the values that keep a group working and living together for mutual benefit. Pre-agricultural humans cultivated these values of group cohesion because the survival of the group was the first and foremost priority. For our pre-agricultural ancestors, belonging to a group mattered and belonging to a place mattered. Values that reinforced belonging to a group form a deep part of human consciousness. Psychologically, pre-agricultural people did not see themselves as separate from their group or from the natural place in which they lived. The community or group mind and its affective orientations of belonging, interdependence, mutuality and reciprocity characterize all tribal societies. Some sociobiologists would refer to this deeply embedded need for belonging as an expression of our human instinct for "biophilia," the predisposition to affiliate with other living things, particularly other humans. This instinct might be said to be the biological basis for socialability, relationship and community.

In his wonderful book *A Time before Deception: Truth in Communication, Culture and Ethics* (1998), Thomas Cooper writes about how Native Peoples' first reaction to Europeans' habitual lying was to believe that the invaders must have been insane because in their cultures only insane people who had lost touch with reality spoke in ways that misrepresented it. His research also shows that lying can become a deviant strategy. The strategy may, like the use of weapons of mass destruction, lead to some temporary benefits for a small number of individuals, but in the long run, they are not an evolutionary boon to humankind at all. Cooper also details a research project where Indigenous individuals and Western individuals suggested and ranked various cultural values that might have an impact on integrity. In this project Native Peoples ranked "respect" above all else, but it did not even make the Western list. He shows how the concepts of appreciation for life and the recognition of spirit in all things pervaded traditional Indigenous thinking and that such perceptions informed all communication in ways that were incompatible with deception.

Finally, the fourth concept in the CAT-FAWN mnemonic is Nature. Here, I have little more to say about the difference between Western and Indigenous views than previous chapters have said. Mainstream education continues to be anthropocentric—human-centered—and to view Nature as existing only to be utilized by humans in some way. As we have learned throughout the pages of this book, Indigenous perspectives see humans as a part of Nature, without placing us in a hierarchy, (although I do recall one Native person saying humans are somewhere between the ant and the mountain.). This perspective sees sentient beings existing on the planet before us as teachers. It sees the importance of Nature and our part in it in ways that honor the Earth and its life systems as "Mother" and the larger cosmos as "Father" in ways that demand respect for them and encourage learning from them.

Like the many other resources, ideas, paradigms, lists and exercises presented in this book, CAT-FAWN offers a chance for students to compare and contrast a knowledge path that is very different from that of the mainstream. There can be no denying that a different approach is necessary. Indigenizing mainstream education is long overdue and is not an imperative for all educators everywhere. Beginning with courage, and moving toward the trust in what you are doing in ways that foster fearlessness, each of you can start now by indigenizing every class you teach in some way. This book can continue to give you the resources and directions to complement every subject and should be referred to often. You will soon see how the Indigenous perspectives contained in it will resonate with your own deepest, intuitive feelings and how sharing the Indigenous ideas with your students will cultivate a love for learning and a respect for all not seen often enough among the children. Notice also how it can develop authentic honesty, courage, patience and generosity. Consider honestly and then guide your students to consider and question mainstream ideas that are not in synch with reality and are not in alignment with "higher thinking." Let this be your legacy for future generations.

A Chapter Epilogue

Any critical presentation about Christianity can stir emotions in a Christianized nation in the same way that any suggestion that non-Indian teachers offer Indigenous spiritual concepts, generalized from the distinctively unique Indigenous cultures can do the same in "Indian country." Religion and spirituality are forces in our world that must be included in education in ways that allow both reason and faith, not hypnotic programming, to guide beliefs. I realize it may be asking too much for classroom teachers to boldly offer such instruction or even that they themselves might be able to do this. I only can hope that many will consider it and that all will not let related concerns prevent them from implementing most of what is required to indigenize education. I also hope my Indigenous brothers and sisters will do similarly with their considerations about this long overdue partnership between the red and white peoples.

Although in Chapter Four I addressed the legitimate concerns about appropriation of Indigenous spirituality and offered ways to minimize it, I want to go deeper here in discussing this concern especially as it relates to the subject of Christianity and its influence on Indigenous Peoples, more and more who are moving away from their traditional beliefs into accepting Christian doctrines. Understanding the complexity of Indian identity, the fears of those who would defend it, and the irrational attacks that it endures can help us all better understand the emotions associated with protecting our religious/spiritual traditions so that we do not abandon the indigenizing project, fearful of stepping on someone's toes. Knowing which concerns are legitimate enough to modify what is or what is not taught can help assure program effectiveness. Although I concur with most of the concerns Native academics have with the problem of the appropriation of Indigenous knowledge, I also believe that fear—logically stemming from colonizing forces that include Christianity and other monotheistic religions (Lewis, 2004)—has caused unnecessary and fear-based interpersonal conflicts and concerns that ultimately stifle constructive efforts to share Indigenous wisdom.

In this "post script" to the material just offered, I attempt a sensitive narrative about some Native brothers and sisters who have been critical of one another about who has the "right" to teach the kind of material offered in this text. Briefly reading about these examples will hopefully help the reader gain the needed confidence to go forward with this book's message knowing that if even Indian country is mired in such concerns, we will never bring this wisdom to light in these urgent times if we do not smile, acknowledge the concerns and understand their source, attend to the respectful prerequisites in this book, and go forth.

One of the most prominent critics is one I have quoted in previous pages. Elizabeth Cook-Lynn, an enrolled member of the Crow Creek Sioux, writes,

> In American Indian scholarship and art, the works of writers who call themselves mixed-bloods abound. Their main topic is the discussion of the connection between the present "I" and the past "They" as well as the present pastness of "We." (2008, p. 340)

Then, after offering a list of ten well-known mixed-blood authors, she continues,

> While there is in the writings of these intellectuals much lip service given to the condemnation of America's treatment of the First Nations, there are few useful expressions of resistance and opposition to the colonial history at the core of Indian/White relationships. Instead, there is explicit and implicit accommodation to the colonialism of the "West." (p. 340)

Later, she describes her main concern:

> A great deal of the work done in the mixed-blood literary movement is personal, invented, appropriated, and irrelevant to First Nation status in the United States....Moreover, no important pedagogical movement will be made toward those defensive strategies that are among the vital functions of intellectualism: to change the world, to know it and to make it better by knowing how to seek appropriate solutions to human problems. (p. 341)

Although she mostly likely did not intend this last quotation to apply to non-Indians teaching Indigenous knowledge in mainstream schools, it nonetheless supports such an agenda. What she describes is exactly what the goals are for indigenizing mainstream education. Cook-Lynn's efforts are intended to protect intellectual property of Indians in light of the dire continuation of genocide and the misappropriation of culture. However, in her attacks on mixed-bloods, she falls into the trap she warns against about "accommodating colonialism." She is participating in the "divide and conquer" strategy used against Indigenous Peoples around the world for centuries. Identity and blood quantum issues have especially divided American Indian communities, and definitions of Indian identity are multiple and varied. Even Scott Momaday, whose work Cook-Lynn admires for its ability to "explore traditional values, revealing truth and falsity about those values from a framework of tribal realism" (p. 342), defines an Indian as

> someone who thinks of themselves as an Indian. But that's not so easy to do and one has to earn the entitlement somehow. You have to have a certain experience of the world in order to formulate this idea. I consider myself an Indian; I've had the experience of an Indian. (Quoted in Bordewich, 1996, p. 67)

Cook-Lynn cannot know the life experiences of all the mixed-blood scholars to whom she refers, and if she did, she could not sufficiently judge most of them. For example, I "call myself" a mixed-blood even though I was raised in a suburban setting with little reference to Indigenous ways of knowing. My mother would seldom speak of her Cherokee father, rarely mentioning his life or his suicide except when intoxicated with whiskey. I learned to dismiss and, like most of white society, even degrade my heritage. After my time in the U.S. Marine Corps and my disillusionment with the Vietnam War and my government's deceptions, I wound up questioning Mom's perspective as well, although I did little to act on it until a near-death experience in Mexico, where I was rescued by Tarahumara Indians as mentioned earlier. This event accelerated my desire to reclaim this heritage. For the past several decades I have had many experiences that now cause me to "think of myself as Indian." Such experiences include, but are not limited to, completing four Sun Dances with Rick Two Dog's Medicine Horse group on the Pine Ridge Reservation; living and working with the Oglala, the Seri and the Raramuri; studying deeply numerous Indigenous cultures at the doctoral level; working as an activist for Indigenous causes; and living as best I can according to a Nature-based ethic. I am also "authorized" to "pour the water" in my continuing use of *inipi* ceremonies by virtue of my having met all of the requirements in the Lakota "Declaration of War against Exploiters of Lakota Spirituality," unanimously passed by 500 representatives on June 10, 1993. I have written prolifically in ways that many other Indigenous scholars support, such as Daniel Wildcat, who wrote about my edited text *Unlearning the Language of Conquest* (2006), "Outstanding scholarship…giant first steps towards the goal of providing a truthful and constructive understanding of indigenous worldviews" (Back Cover).[23] I do not know if scholars like Cook-Lynn would think I am by virtue of my lifestyle "accommodating colonialism," but great care must be taken when a scholar says someone else is "not Indian enough" to teach Indigenous spiritual perspectives if we are to realize such perspectives in our world again.

An example of how such allegations divide Indians against one another is the Ward Churchill affair. Cook-Lynn was one of many Native People who testified against him in this now infamous case. In July 2007 a prolific professor and "self-proclaimed mixed-blood" at the University of Colorado was fired for his comments about people who were killed in the Twin Towers on 9/11. In a blog after the event, he essentially said many of the people were "not so innocent," claiming they were functionaries of globalization, as was Adolf Eichmann when he was coordinating trains bringing Jews to concentration camps. Cook-Lynn was one of many who attacked Churchill with comments implying that his claim of Indian ancestry was fraudulent. This issue continues to divide Indian Country almost in half. Russell Means and Dennis Banks, two well-known Indian activists and co-founders of the American Indian Movement, were on different sides of this issue. As it turned out, Churchill's identity claim seems to have had as much to do with his loss of tenure as the substance of his original statement![24] The Churchill situation reveals the absurdity and the danger of well-intended academics going *too* far in protecting Indigenous intellectual property, ultimately risking that vital knowledge will be prevented from helping "all our relations." As I discuss below, I also think such conflicts in Indian Country expose a loss of courage, a virtue that leads to the quality of fearlessness, which has been foundational for Indigenous cultures for thousands of years.

In a book chapter entitled "Spirituality for Sale" (2000), a mixed-blood Indian named Christopher Ronwanien Jocks writes in praise of Churchill, referring to him as "the most energetic opponent" of those who appropriate American Indian identity and wisdom (p. 63). Jocks, at the time a professor of Native American studies at Dartmouth College, is of Mohawk and Irish descent.[25] In the same chapter where he defends Churchill as having authority to speak of things Indian, however, he writes the following about our guest author Eagle Man (a.k.a. Ed McGaa):

> A number of the most sharply attacked "plastic medicine men" are of Native blood, and some of them can recount deep connections to their Indian contexts earlier in their lives. Once they have started on the road of selling their native spirituality to paying customers elsewhere, however, relations back home invariable go bad. Some, like Ed McGaa, also known as "Eagle Man," assert nonetheless that their "mission" to the wider world was the result of visionary experience, a claim that leaves nonparticipant readers as well as many Indian people in something of a quandary. The line between authenticity and quackery is not always easy to draw, and in fact many of the most traditional-minded will simply refrain from doing so as a matter of policy. (p. 67)

It is difficult to tell whether Jocks is himself attacking Eagle Man or is merely reporting that others do this. I take the latter view in light of his saying that the most traditional-minded elders would not draw such lines. However, it is likely he was making a negative example of Eagle Man. Otherwise, in singling him out, he could also have defended his authority to teach Indigenous spirituality. He might have said that Eagle Man's experiences authorize him to write books that share Indigenous knowledge with the world, such as having participated in six Sun Dances back when the courage needed to do so was increased by the fact they were illegal according to the ban on Indian religious activities.[26] Or if this act of courage and generosity was not considered sufficient to meet Scott Momaday's idea of entitlement, quoted above, he might also have written that Eagle Man:

- Flew 110 combat missions over Vietnam as a Marine Corps pilot in an F-4 jet
- Exposed boarding school realities in nine of his books, presenting legal and artistic evidence of the crimes against Indians in places like Canton Federal All Indian Insane Asylum to further verify the inhumanity and unconstitutional persecution to which Indians were subjected, including evidence of 140 graves on the fourth and fifth fairways of the Canton Golf Course, when few others even talked about such things.
- Was asked by Chief Fools Crow to invite representatives of the American Indian Movement (AIM) to come to the Sun Dance and protect it from the dangerous detractors who threatened opposition

to the lone Pine Ridge Sun Dance, which broke the power of the missionaries and the laws they helped sustain.

- Was a negotiator at Wounded Knee.
- Was honored by thousands at the Rosebud Fair and Pow Wow in 2011 and awarded an eagle feather by Leonard Crow Dog, primary medicine leader among the Sichangu, whose members gave two powerful speeches that day acknowledging Eagle Man's fight for the return of Indigenous spiritual ways of being in the world.
- Has written books that have inspired tens of thousands of people to live more balanced lives.

It may not be surprising for an academic to criticize a non-academic like Eagleman, but to show how complex and sensitive issues about teaching Indigenous spirituality is, consider that Eagle Man challenges the authority of Vine Deloria Jr. to write and teach about Indigenous spirituality. For those unfamiliar with Deloria, *Time* magazine named him one of the most important religious thinkers of the world in the early 1970s. A member of the Oglala Lakota tribe, he was a lawyer, professor and author of numerous books, chapters and articles, many about Indigenous spirituality. Vine died during the publication of a book I was editing to which he contributed a chapter entitled "Conquest Masquerading as Law." A friend and colleague of his, I dedicated the book to him, writing, "May his courage, spirit, and wisdom be remembered, and may his belief that we can and must unlearn the language of conquest—for the sake of all our futures—be realized in time" (Four Arrows, 2006).

Eagle Man, also an Oglala, feels strongly that Deloria was guilty of offering "implicit accommodation to the colonialism of the West" as much or more than anyone Cook-Lynn has identified (although Cook-Lynn would likely disagree). Eagle Man, also a respected friend and colleague of mine, feels that Vine's affiliations with Christianity, especially during the 1960s and 1970s, kept him from being a true ally in the struggle against the missionaries and the government during a crucial time when the Civil Rights Movement gave American Indians who wanted to reclaim their traditional spiritual ways a fighting chance to do so. Discussing the control of the missionaries and the struggle to reclaim Lakota spiritual paths, Eagle Man largely dismissing Vine's many published challenges to doctrine and dogma in Western Christian traditions when he states,

> Vine Deloria offers no such exposure or such writing nor involvement with we who were in the Trenches of Change back in the 60s and 70s. His family, leading Missionaries, well

knew of the existence of Canton,[27] yet nary a word from Vine. It was I whom Chief Fools Crow sent to invite AIM to come to the Sun Dance and protect it from the detractors….Vine never danced with us. (Personal e-mail, August 10, 2012)[28]

I think it is clear from Deloria's critiques of Christianity in his books that he and Eagle Man share much common ground. For example, in *God Is Red* (1973), Deloria writes about the polarity that exists between Native spirituality and Christianity because of the latter's relative disregard for the sacredness of place and because of its emphasis on fear, including fear of death. At the same time, there can be no doubt about his Christian affiliations. Deloria's grandfather and father were ministers, and he himself went through the ministry. It is also true that he did not participate in traditional Lakota Sun Dances and other spiritual ceremonies and that his family arranged his memorial service so that it was presided over by an Episcopal priest who was a friend of the family. Deloria makes an interesting statement in the close of his book *Singing for a Spirit* (2000) that deserves analysis as well: "There is no question that Christianity served as a bridge to enable the Sioux people to make the transition from their life of freedom to a new life confined within the small boundaries of a reservation" (p. 216). Obviously, he is not saying that being moved to reservations was good for Indians, but we must consider that the Christian church's enabling of this move was likely the nail in the coffin of Indian internment.

Eagle Man's critique of Deloria can be seen as an attack on his authority to teach about Indigenous spirituality. Even if Deloria did not sufficiently participate in the courageous acts of resistance that others like Eagle Man did, this is not an authority or identity issue but rather a matter of fear and courage. In the case of Eagle Man's historical concerns about Deloria, it is best to try to discover how Christian affiliations may have influenced him and his decisions—for example, his decision not participate in the Sun Dance. We must try to understand his thoughts about whether the transition that he says Christianity "enabled" caused the ongoing problems on reservations and how the continuing movement of Native People into Christian religions plays out for all of us today.

The interrelated views of the three Indigenous writers I have been discussing hopefully help reveal some of the tensions that Indigenous People continue to suffer in their efforts to protect their highly vulnerable cultures (and perhaps in some cases, their vulnerable careers) from even more destruction. Eagle Man's perspective is especially important because it essentially represents the belief of many that Christianity and Indigenous spirituality are incompatible, in spite of the growing numbers of Indians joining Christian faiths throughout North America. This question of compatibility makes for an important dialogue during any effort to teach "about" religion or spirituality, especially in schools where many students and teachers are Christians. It is also important in the context of our ecological crises in light of the connection between Indigenous spirituality and ecological sustainability.

Notes

1. It is likely that the use of "Great Spirit" is a mistranslation of the Lakota "Wakan Tanka." Frances Densmore in *Teton Sioux Music and Culture*, originally published in 1918, clarifies this in an extensive note, pointing out that "the word Wakan Tanka is composed of wa'kan (mysterious) and tan'ka (great)" (1992, p. 85). This sense of the mysterious is a vital part of most Indigenous assumptions about "God." Indigenous spiritual conversations rarely, if ever, speak about an entity such as "God" except indirectly through the numerous spiritual manifestations of some unknowable energy.

2. As told to Richard Epes Brown and published in *The Sacred Pipe: Black Elk's Account of the Seven Rites of the Oglala Sioux* (1989, p.27).

3. Paul S. Boyer, a professor emeritus of history at the University of Wisconsin, writes in "When U.S. Foreign Policy Meets Biblical Prophecy" that cultural historians have long underplayed the importance of religion in the United States, particularly in the modern era. In fact, religion has always had an enormous, if indirect and under-recognized, role in policy formation" (http://www.alternet.org/story/15221?page=2).

4. I support this view and therefore find Christianity not compatible with Indigenous spirituality. However, Lynn White's position may now be revisited to give additional responsibility to free market ideology and capitalism as well as to globalization, agriculture and education. Other thinkers besides Eagle Man, one of this chapter's guest authors, have questioned the possible role of Christianity in bringing us to the brink. Chet Bowers, in *Rethinking Freire: Globalization and the Environmental Crises* (2005), writes that Paulo Freire's Christian orientation may have prevented his important work in social justice from moving us closer to an ecological ethic.

5. Even Western scholars note the vast connections between the two, especially those whose orientations have moved away from strictly pathological applications and toward the more holistic positivist and humanistic psychology movement that pervades most models today (Joseph, Linely & Maltby 2006). In January, 2012, Columbia University actually began a spirituality concentration in its clinical psychology master's program.

6. I make a distinction between courage and fearlessness in that courage is the phenomenon that causes one to engage that which is causing the fear but with right learning once this happens a degree of fearlessness that incorporates a trust in the cosmos can eliminate the need for courage.

7. The irony is that the separation of church and state was completely ignored when missionaries were put in charge of Indian boarding school education to brainwash Indian children and destroy their cultural wisdom.

8. He does not use the words "Indigenous spirituality" but rather "tribal religions." Deloria's inclination related to his choice of words is explored in more depth later.

9. Although generally censored from U.S. history in mainstream education, Thomas Paine's famous text, *Age of Reason*, frankly declares Christianity and other religions to be a major impediment to freedom, democracy and justice. This text appears in its entirety on the

Internet in several places. If a teacher is committed to indigenizing mainstream education, he or she cannot be afraid to expose students to a book that was written by one of the most important founding fathers.

10. An interesting acronym has become popular that has some bearing- FEAR ="false evidence appearing real" (FEAR), especially as we consider connecting fear to the lack of critical thinking about U.S. history.

11. There will be some critics who say that Eagle Man, not being an academic, is not qualified to contribute to an educational text. Of course, I would dismiss these critics. Even Deloria says that the Indigenous academics from mainstream schools are generally not as capable as those without degrees in teaching Indigenous knowledge. I remember citing Joseph Cambell in a paper for one of my doctoral classes at Boise State University. The teacher gave me an "F" grade and required I pull his name from my paper because he was also not considered an academic scholar.

12. The Maya culture, for example, created systems of mathematics and observations that allowed for learning about astronomy in ways that continue to baffle modern science.

13. Wisdom comes from respectful listening and close observation of the natural world, including animals, birds, fish, insects, plants, rocks and bodies of water. Such entities are the creators of all the virtues, which are gifts that help us know peace.

14. The highest expression of courage is deep generosity.

15. This relates to a genuine belief that no one is above another or superior to the rest of Creation.

16. From a postmodern-integral framework, my research (Fisher, 2010) shows there are at least fifteen different meanings and definitions for "fearlessness." One definition states that it is the virtue of all virtues.

17. In the East, unlike the West (not including Indigenous Peoples and their cultures), a *culture of fearlessness* is deeply embedded in religions like Jainism, Hinduism, and Buddhism and in the associated philosophies and psychology of the peoples. This culture is called (in English translations) the "gift of fearlessness" (Hibbets, 1999; Heim, 2004). I highly recommend that Westerners study this culture and its traditions.

18. Although many today talk about a "culture of fear" and critique it, few really define it. I use this definition: *a culture of fear exists when a system attempts to manage fear by fear-based means, thus producing more fear, not less, and fostering forms of chronic mistrust, coercion and injustices.*

19. From the perspective of "integral nondualism" (Esbjörn-Hargens, 2009, p. 139) and/or integral indigeneity, I perceive no metaphysical pre-given dualism between Nature and culture in this expression. but regard this Natural Way as being much like, but not equivalent to, the dialectic of the Tao (i.e., yin and yang, dark and light) in Taoist philosophy/spirituality. The flow of the Tao, uninterrupted, is also called the "the Way," and in Indigenous writing it is not surprising to hear those who are ethical call for "the Old Ways," which, although ethnico-historically inscribed, is arguably an expression that refers to a time when Indigenous life was lived in harmony with "the Way," or as I call it, the Natural Way, in a metaphysical sense.

20. My guess is that with Sparta, a great Western warrior culture, "fear" was sacred to most people in terms of the human psychology and spirituality of war. No doubt, they were very attuned to when their fear could turn "rotten" and decimate them because of the "bad" advice that it gives and the lack of courage to go to battle and to fight well that it causes and because they knew that violence could corrupt their souls if it became out of balance with love. Part of fight-

ing well, in honorary sacred warrior traditions around the world, is maintaining compassion and never fearing/hating your enemy. For this reason, Spartans, as a culture, are interesting historically in the West. The temple dedicated to fear indicates that on the whole they likely really honored the power of fear and created a sacred site of worship where they could know fear.

21. Much of the following discussion of the CAT-FAWN connection, as condensed from my book *Primal Awareness*, was published as "Wolokokiapi: An Antidote to Neo-liberalism's Influence on War and Peace," *Peace Studies Journal* 3.1 (April 2010) and can be found in a number of other presentations I have given.

22. This idea. which I learned from my vision, led to the publication by Prentice-Hall of my text *Patient Communication for First Responders and EMS Personnel* (1997) in which I showed that people in medical emergencies who are frightened respond to the directives of voices of authority for better or for worse depending on what is said. The book was remaindered after six months because lawyers, on behalf of the psychology industry, said such lifesaving information should be in the hands only of licensed physicians and psychiatrists.

23. Note that such an endorsement actually supports the teaching of Indigenous worldviews to the world and that this edited book was written by full-bloods, mixed-bloods and non-Indians. The point is that it supports the recommendation that mainstream teachers should also help others understand this worldview.

24. If the reader is curious, I supported Churchill openly for reasons I stand by today that relate to the substance of his poorly phrased statement, the realities of 9/11, and his right to claim his Indigenous ancestry.

25. As of this writing, his name was not on the Dartmouth faculty list, and I was not able to locate him in my effort to talk with him about his ideas related to Eagle Man, a subject discussed below.

26. I cannot help but note that most scholars I know who are affiliated with tribes that use Sun Dance ceremonies and who write ardently about Indian identity have not participated in the Sun Dance. The significance of this is discussed below.

27. He refers to Canton Asylum for Insane Indians in South Dakota, a prison for Native Peoples, many of whom died from the despair and injustice before the prison was demolished, leaving only a cemetery to mark where so many lives were tormented and destroyed. Eagle Man spoke against it but claims Vine did not.

28. The interested reader can learn more about Eagle Man's views in his online article "Expose" (2010). (Coincidentally, this short piece includes reference to a debate between him and Cook-Lynn about Deloria's being a negotiator at Wounded Knee. Eagle Man, who was one, says Deloria was not.)

References

Preface

Amundsen, R. (1908). The *north west passage*. London: E.P. Dutton & Co.

Bowers, C. A. (2005). "Is transformative learning the Trojan horse of Western globalization?" in *Journal of Transformative Education*, Vol. 3, pp. 116–125.

Giroux, H. A.(2001). *Theory and resistance in education: Towards a pedagogy for the opposition*, Revised and Expanded Edition (Critical Studies in Education and Culture Series). Santa Barbara, CA: Praeger.

Lipton, B. H. & Bhaerman, S. (2009) *Spontaneous evolution*. Carlsbad, CA: Hay House, Inc.

Momaday, N. S. (1991). "Confronting Columbus again," in Nabokov, P. (Ed.), *Native American testimony: A chronicle of Indian-white relations from prophecy to the present*. New York: Penguin.

Neel, J.V. (1970, Nov.). "Lessons from a primitive people," in *Science*, Vol. 170, no. 3960.

Introduction

Barnosky, A., Hadly, E., Bascompte, J., Berlow, E. Bown, J., Fortelius, M., Getz, W., Harte, J., Hastings, A., Marquet, P., Gillespie, R., Kitzes, J., Marshall, C., Matzke, N., Mindell, D., Revilla, E., & Smith, A. (2012). "Approach a state shift in Earth's biosphere." Nature, 486 (7401): 52. DOI: 10.1038/nature11019

Battiste, M. (2005). "Indigenous knowledge: foundations for First Nations." Retrieved from http://www.sin-hec.org/docs/pdfs/Journal/Marie%20Battiste%20copy.pdf

Bowers, C. A. (1993) *Education, cultural myths and the ecological Crisis: Toward deep changes*. Albany: State University of New York Press.

Bullock, A. Bullock & Trombley, S. Eds. (1999). *The new Fontana dictionary of modern thought*, third Edition. New York. Harper Collins.

Brady, M. (June 17, 2012). "The biggest problem with traditional schooling," in *Truthout*. http://truth-out.org/opinion/item/9829-the-biggest-problem-with-traditional-schooling

Cajete, G. (2000). *Native science: Natural laws of independence*. Santa Fe, N.M.: Clear Light Publishers.

Cook-Lynn, E. (2007) *Anti-Indianism in modern America*. Chicago, Ill.: University of Illinois Press.

Deloria,V. & Wildcat, D. (2001). *Power and place: Indian education in America*. Golden, Colo.: Fulcrum Publishers.

Eberle, J. & Childress, M. (2007). "Heutagogy: It isn't your mother's pedagogy any more." http://www.nssa.us/journals/2007-28-1/2007-28-1-04.htm

Four Arrows (200). *Unlearning the language of conquest*. Austin: University of Texas Press.

Four Arrows, Cajete, G. and Lee, J. (2011). *Critical neurophilosophy and indigenous wisdom*. Rotterdam, Netherlands: Sense Publishers.

Grand, S. (2008). "Red pedagogy: The un-methodology," in Denzin, N., Lincoln, Y. and Tuhiwai Smith, L. *Handbook of critical indigenous methodologies*. Los Angeles, Calif.: Sage.

Hopkins, J. C. (1898) in *Canada. An encyclopaedia of the country*, Vol. 1, Toronto: The Linscott Publishing Company.

In National Social Science Association Journal. http://www.nssa.us/journals/2007–28-1/2007–28–1-04.htm

Jacobs, D. T. & Jacobs-Spencer, J. (2001). *Teaching virtues: Building character across the curriculum*. Lanham, Md.: Scarecrow Education.

Kincheloe, J. L. (1991). Willis Morris and the southern curriculum: Emancipating the Southern ghosts, in Joe L. Kincheloe and William F. Pinar (Eds.), *Curriculum as social psychoanalysis: The significance of place*. Albany: State University of New York Press.

Kincheloe, J. L. & Steinberg, S. R. (2008). "Indigenous knowledges in education: complexities, dangers, and profound benefits," in Kenz, Lincoln, Tuhiwai Smith (Eds.) *Handbook of critical and indigenous methodologies*. Los Angeles, Calif.: Sage.

Lawrence, D. H. (*Columbia world of quotations*). Retrieved January 10, 2012, from http://quotes.dictionary.com/Oh_what_a_catastrophe_for_man_when_he

Mitchell, E. (1997). *Backcover of Shapeshifting: Techniques for personal and global transformation*. New York: Destiny Books.

NCSS (National Council for Social Studies) (1994). Heutagogy. www.socialstudies.org/standards/introduction

Reinhardt, M. & Maday, T. (2005), *Interdisciplinary manual for american indian inclusion*. Tempe, Ariz.: Educational Options.

Roberts, D. (2009). Scientists identify "safe operating space for humanity" in seminal Nature study. http://grist.org/article/2009–09–22-scientists-identify-safe-operating-space-for-humanity-nature/

Slattery, P. (1995) *Curriculum development in the postmodern era*. New York: Garland Publishing

Smagorinsky, P. and Taxel, J. (2005) *Discourse of character education: Culture wars in the classroom*. New York: Routledge

Thompson, G. (2003). *Who was Helen Keller*. Boston: Perfection Learning.

Williams, R. (1977) *Marxism and literature*. Oxford: Oxford University Press.

Zurayk, R. (2010). "Fragmentation and pastoralism." http://landandpeople.blogspot.mx/2010_07_01_archive.html

Chapter One, Anti-Indianism or Survival

Abram, D. (2010). *Becoming animal: An earthly cosmology.* New York: Pantheon Books.

Amster, R. (2010, Dec 28). "Arizona bans ethnic studies and. Along with it, reason and justice." *Truthout* http://archive.truthout.org/arizona-bans-ethnic-studies-and-along-with-it-reason-and-justice66340

Axtell, J. (1987). "Colonial American without the Indians: counterfactual reflections." *Journal of American History*, 73 (March), pp. 981–996.

Bonfil B.G. (1996). Mexico Profundo: *Reclaiming a civilization.* Austin: University of Texas Press.

Clifton, J.A. (1990). *The invented indian: cultural fictions and government policies.* New Brunswick, N.J.: Transaction Books.

Cook-Lynn, E. (2001). Anti-Indianism in modern america: A voice from Tatekeya's Earth. Urbana: University of Illinois Press.

Cook-Lynn, E. (2008) "History, myth and identity in the new Indian story," in Denzin, N., Lincoln, Y. & Smith, L. (Eds.). *Critical and indigenous methodologies.* Thousand Oaks, Calif.: Sage.

Crocco, M.S. & Thornton, S.J. (1999). "Review of the social studies curriculum" In E. W. Ross (Ed.), *The social studies curriculum: Purposes, problems, and possibilities* (pp. 3–19). Albany: State: University of New York Press

Deloria, V. (2006). "Conquest masquerading as law" in Four Arrows (Ed.). *Unlearning the Language of conquest.* Austin: University of Texas Press.

Edgerton, R. (1992). *Sick societies: challenging the myth of primitive harmony.* N.Y.: Free Press.

Ex parte Crow Dog, 109 U.S. 556–569 (1883)

Four Arrows, Cajete, G. & Lee, J. (2011) *Critical neurophilosphy and indigenous wisdom.* Rotterdam, Netherlands: Sense Publications.

Garza, M. (n.d.). "Of myths and realities: implications and consequences." Indigenous Cultures Institute. www.indigenouscultures.org/mythsandrealities.pdf

Grant, A. & Gillespie, L. (1993) *Joining the circle: A practitioner's guide to responsive education for native students.* Full text at http://clas.uiuc.edu/fulltext/c100192.html#biblio

Hagedorn, H. (1930). *Roosevelt in the Bad Lands.* Boston: Houghton-Mifflin.

Hedges, C. (2012). "When civilizations die." *Truthout.* http://truth-out.org/news/item/8808-when-civilizations-die

Johansen, B. (2006). "Adventures in denial: ideological resistance to the idea that the Iroquois helped shape American democracy," in Four Arrows (Ed.). *Unlearning the language of conquest: Scholars expose anti-Indianism in America.* Austin, TX: University of Texas Press.

Leavitt, G.C. (1977) "The frequency of warfare: An evolutionary perspective." *Sociological Inquiry*, 47, pp. 49–58.

Mann, B. (2012, June). Personal communication.

Manitoba Indian Brotherhood (n.d.). *The shocking truth about Indians in textbooks: Textbook evaluation.* Winnipeg, MB: Manitoba Indian Brotherhood.

McDiarmid, G. & Pratt, D. (1971). *Teaching prejudice.* Toronto, ON: Institute for Studies in Education.

McKenna, F.R. (1981). "The myth of multiculturalism and the reality of the American Indian in contemporary America." *Journal of American Indian Education* 221.1 (October). http://jaie.asu.edu/v2151myt.html.

Momaday, S. (1992). "Confronting Columbus again" in Nabokov, P. (Ed.). *Native American testimony: A chronicle of Indian-white relations from prophecy to the present.* London: Penguin Books.

Mooney, J. (1991). *The ghost-dance religion and the Sioux outbreak of 1890.* Lincoln: University of Nebraska Press.

Pinker, S. (2011). *The better angels of our nature: why violence has declined.* New York: Viking Adult.

Reese, D. (2011). http://americanindiansinchildrensliterature.blogspot.mx/

Van der Dennen, J.M.G. (1995). *The origin of war: The evolution of a male-coalitional reproductive strategy.* Groningen, Netherlands: Origin Press, 2 vols.

Weatherford, J. *Indian givers: How the Indians of the Americas transformed the world.* New York: Crown Publishers, Inc.

Whelan, R. (1999). *Wild in the woods: The myth of the peaceful eco-savage.* London: The Environment unit of the Institute of Economic Affairs.

Wilson, W.A.C. (2006) "Burning down the house: Laura Ingalls Wilder and American colonialism in Four Arrows (ED) *Unlearning the language of conquest: Scholars expose anti-Indianism in America.* Austin: University of Texas Press.

Chapter Two, Historical Trauma and Its Prevention in the Classroom

Aboriginal Healing Foundation. (2004). *Historic Trauma and Aboriginal Healing.* Ottawa, Ontario: Anishinabe Printing.

Adams, D.W. (1995). *Education for Extinction—American Indians and the Boarding School Experience 1875–1928,* Lawrence: University Press of Kansas.

Allen, R. (1999). *Education in the Cherokee Nation: An historical overview 1798–1908.* Tahlequah: OK.

American Indian Heritage Support Center. (2012). *Indian Education and Boarding Schools.* Bentonville, AR.

Andrews, T.G. (2002). Turning the Tables on Assimilation: Oglala Lakotas and the Pine Ridge Day Schools, 1889–1920s. *The Western Historical Quarterly*, Vol. 33, No. 4 (Winter, 2002), pp. 407–430.

Baum, R. (2000*). Pedagogical Memory and Second-Generation Witness.* In R. Simon, S. Rosenberg & C. Eppert (Eds.), *Between Hope and Despair: Pedagogy and the Remembrance of Historical Trauma.* Boston, MA: Rowman & Littlefield Publishers, Inc.

Bigfoot. D.S. (2007). *American Indian Youth: Current and Historical Trauma.* The National Child Traumatic Stress Network.

Bigfoot, D. Subia, & L. Burris (2007). Trauma Focused Interventions for Native Children: Project Making Medicine. University of Oklahoma Health Science Center, Center on Child Abuse and Neglect.

Boyer, Paul. (1997). *Native American Colleges: Progress and Prospects.* (An Ernest T. Boyer project of The Carnegie Foundation for the Advancement of Teaching). Princeton, N.J. (ERIC Document Reproduction Service No. ED 409037).

Brave Heart, M. (1998). The return to the sacred path: Healing the historical trauma and historical unresolved grief response among the Lakota through a psycho-educational group intervention. *Smith College Studies in Social Work, 68,* 287–305.

Brave Heart, M., & DeBruyn, L. (1998). The American Indian Holocaust: Healing historical unresolved grief. *American Indian and Alaska Native Mental Health Research, 8,* 60–82.

Braveheart-Jordan, M., & DeBruyn, L. (1995). So she may walk in balance; Integrating the impact of historical trauma in the treatment of Native American Indian women. In J. Adleman, & G.

Enquidanos (Eds.), *Racism in the lives of women: Testimony theory and guides to anti-racist practice*. New York: Haworth Press.

Brock-England, M. (1964). *Writings & Poetry of Minerva Brock England*. Barry County: MO.

Brown, D. (2003). Tribal colleges: Playing a key role in the transition from secondary to postsecondary education for American Indian students. *Journal of American Indian Education, 42* (1), 36–44.

Byers, Lisa G. (2005). "Depression, discrimination, trauma, and American Indian ethnic identity." Ph.D. Dissertation, Washington University.

Cherokee Nation History. (2000). *Section 6: Forced Removal*. In Chad "Corntassel" Smith (Ed.), *Cherokee Nation History Course*. Tahlequah, OK.

Clarke, A. (1993). Sisters in the Blood: The Education of Women in Native America. Center for Bilingual/Multicultural Education, Montana State University. Newton, MA: WEEA Publishing Center.

Cross, T. L. (1998). Cultural competence continuum. *"Focal Point." The Research and Training Center on Family Support and Children's Mental Health*, Portland State University.

Debo, A. (1940). *And still the waters run: The betrayal of the Five Civilized Tribes*. Princeton, N.J.: Princeton University Press.

Debo, A. (1983). *A history of the Indians of the United States*. Norman: University of Oklahoma Press.

Deloria, V., Jr. & D. Wildcat. (2001). *Power of Place: Indian Education in America*. CO: Fulcrum Press.

Deloria, Jr. V. & D. E. Wilkins. (1999). "Racial and Ethnic Studies, Political Science, and Midwifery," *Wicazo Sa Review* 14 (Autumn 1999), 70.

Duran, E. (2006). *Healing the soul wound: Counseling with American Indians and other native peoples*. New York: Teachers College Press.

Duran, E. & Duran, B. 1995. *Native American Postcolonial Psychology*. Albany: State University of New York Press.

Foreman. G. (1934). *The Five Civilized Tribes*. The Civilization of American Indian Series 8. Norman: University of Oklahoma Press.

Gay, G. (2000). *Culturally Response Teaching: Theory, Research and Practice*. New York: Teachers' College Press.

Gover, K. (2000). Address to Tribal Leaders on the occasion of the ceremony acknowledging the 175th anniversary of the establishment of the Bureau of Indian Affairs. *Journal of American Indian Education, 39* (2), 4–6.

Gone, J. P. (2009). A community-based treatment for Native American historical trauma: Prospects for evidence-based practice. *Journal of Consulting and Clinical Psychology, 77*, 751–762.

Grande, S. (2004). *Red Pedagogy: Native American Social and Political Thought*. New York: Rowman & Littlefield Publishers, Inc.

Hitchcock, E. A. (1909). *Fifty Years in Camp and Field: Diary of Major-General Ethan Allen Hitchcock*, ed. W.A. Croffut. New York: Knickerbocker Press.

Holm, T. (1996). *Strong hearts, wounded souls: Native American veterans of the Vietnam War*. Austin: University of Texas Press.

Holm, T. (2005). *The Great Confusion in Indian Affairs: Native Americans & Whites in the Progressive Era*. Austin: University of Texas Press.

Holm, T., D. Pearson & B. Chavis. (2003). Peoplehood: A Model for Extension of Sovereignty in American Indian Studies. *Wicazo Sa Review*, Vol. 18, 1 (Spring, 2003) pp. 7–24.

Hopkins, R. (2011). Epigenetics: Scientific Evidence of Intergenerational Trauma. Retrieved from: http://indiancountrytodaymedianetwork.com/ict_sbc/epigenetics-scientific-evidence-of-inter-generational-trauma.

Jacobs, D. Four Arrows, G. Cajete & L. Jongmin (2010). *Critical Neurophilosophy and Indigenous Wisdom*. Rotterdam, Netherlands: Sense Publishers.

W. K. Kellogg Foundation. (2002). Journeying On: Native American Higher Education Initiative, Phase II. Retrieved 02/01/06 from http://www.wkkf.org/Pubs/YouthEd/NAHEI/Pub3544.pdf

Lankford, R. and J. Riley. (1986). Native American reading disability. *Journal of American Indian Education*, 25 (3), 1–11.

Mankiller, W. & M. Wallis. (1993). *Mankiller: A Chief and Her People*. New York: St. Martin's Griffin.

Our Spirits Don't Speak English: Indian Boarding School. Dir. C. Riche. Rich-Heape Films. 2007.

Pavel, D.M., Skinner, R.R., Farris, E., Cahalan, M., Tippeconnic, J., & Stein, W. *American Indians and Alaska Natives in Postsecondary Education* . Educ Stat Q. 1999; 1(1):67–74.

Phillips, J. (2003). A Tribal College land grant perspective: Changing the conversation. *Journal of American Indian Education, 42* (1), 22–35.

Ringel, S., & Brandell, J. R. (2012). *Trauma: Contemporary directions in theory, practice, and research*. Thousand Oaks, Calif.: SAGE Publications.

Ross, L. (1998). *Inventing the Savage: The social construction of Native American criminality*. Austin: University of Texas Press.

Smith, E. (1991). Ethnic identity development: Toward the development of a theory within context of majority/minority status. *Journal of Counseling & Development, 70*, 181–188.

Smithsonian Institute (2007). Native American History. *A Huron Indian to Jesuit missionary Jean de Brébeuf, 1635*. Smithsonian Institution Press, Washington, D.C.

Sotero M. M. (2006). A conceptual model of historical trauma: Implications for public practice and research. *Journal of Health Disparities and Practice*. 2006; 1(1):93–108.

Spicer, E., (1980). The Yaquis: A Cultural History. Tucson: University of Arizona Press, in Holm, et al., (2003). Peoplehood: A Model for Extension of Sovereignty in American Indian Studies. *Wicazo Sa Review*, Vol. 18, 1 (Spring, 2003) pp. 7–24.

Strickland, R. (1980). *The Indians of Oklahoma*. Norman: University of Oklahoma Press.

Sultzman, L. (2002). Native American village. Retrieved 04/10/12 from http://www.imdiversity.com/villages/native/village_native_american.asp.

United States. 108th Congress, 2d Session, S.J. Res. 37.

U.S. Department of the Interior. Bureau of Indian Affairs. (2005). *Strengthening the Circle: Interior Indian Affairs Highlights 2001–2004*. Washington, D.C.: Government Printing Office.

U. S. Senate. (1969). *Indian education: A national tragedy—a national challenge*. 1969 report of the Committee on Labor and Public Welfare Special.

University of Minnesota (2012). College of Education and Human Development. Institute on Community Integration. Expanding the Circle: Brief History of American Indian Education. Retrieved 04/01/12 from http://etc.umn.edu/resources/briefhistory.htm.

Worcester v. Georgia, 31 US 515, 6 Pet. 515, 8 L.Ed. 483 (1832)

Whitbeck, L. B., G. Adams, D. Hoyt, and X. Chen. (2004). Conceptualizing and Measuring Historical Trauma Among American Indian People. *American Journal of Community Psychology*, Vol. 33, Nos. 3/4, 24–31.

Williams, D., Neighbors, H., and Jackson, J. (2003). Racial/Ethnic Discrimination and Health: Findings from Community Studies. *American Journal of Public Health 93*(2):200–208.

Yellow Horse-Brave Heart, M., & DeBruyn, L. M. (1998). The American Indian holocaust: Healing historical unresolved grief. *American Indian and Alaska Native Mental Health Research, 8*, 56–78.

Zinn, H. (2003). *A People's History of the United States, 1492-Present*. New York: Harper Collins.

Chapter Three, The STAR (Service To All Relations) Navajo School Model

None.

Chapter Four, Indigenous Teaching and Learning Pathways

Aluli-Meyer, M. (2003). Ho'oulu: *Our time of becoming: Hawaiian epistemology and early writings.* Honolulul, HI: Ai Pohaku Press.

Battiste, M. (2002). *Indigenous knowledge and pedagogy in First Nations education.* http://www.afn. ca/uploads/files/education/24._2002_oct_marie_battiste_indigenousknowledgeandpedagogy_lit _review_for_min_working_group.pdf

Beckford, C.L. & Nahdee, R. (2011, Sept). "Research into practice: Incorporating indigenous philosophies and practices." Ontario Association of Dean's Education Monograph 36. http://www.edu.gov.on.ca/eng/literacynumeracy/inspire/research/WW_Teaching_Ecological.pdf

Bowers, C. (2012) *The way forward: Educational reforms that focus on the cultural commons and the linguistic roots of the ecological/cultural crises.* Eugene, Or. : Eco-Justice Press.

Brady, M. (2012, Aug 13). "Eight things wrong with the common core state standards." *Washington Post.*

Brendtro, L., Brokenleg, M. & Van Bockern, S. (1990) *Reclaiming youth at risk: Our hope for the future.* Bloomington, IN:National Educational Service.

Cajete, G. (1994). *Look to the mountain: An ecology of indigenous education.* Skyland, NC: Kivaki Press. Declaration of War: http://www.aics.org/war.html

Facione, P.A., Facione, N.C., & Giancarlo, C.A. (2000). The Disposition toward critical thinking: Its character, measurement, and relationship to critical thinking skill." in *Informal Logic,* 20(1), 61–84

Fremantale, F. (2010) *Luminous emptiness: Understanding the Tibetan book of the dead.* Boston: Shambhala.

Garza, M. (n.d.)"Of myths and realities: implications and consequences." Indigenous Cultures Institute. www.indigenouscultures.org/mythsandrealities.pdf

Grand, S. (2008) "Red pedagogy: The un-methodology," in Denzin, N., Lincoln, Y. and Tuhiwai Smith, L. *Handbook of Critical Indigenous Methodologies.* Los Angeles, Calif.: Sage.

Grimes, R. (1995) Teaching about Native Religions discussion forum at http://www.hartford-hwp.com/archives/41/015.html

Hammond, S. C. & Gao, H. (2002). *Pan Gu's paradigm: Chinese education's return to holistic Communication Studies.* Westport, Conn.: Ablex.

Hampton, Eber (1993). "Towards a redefinition of American Indian education." *Canadian Journal of Native Education,* 20(2), 261–309.

Hampton, E. (1995). Towards a redefinition of Indian education. In M. Battiste & J. Barman (Eds.), *First Nations Education in Canada: The Circle Unfolds* (pp. 5–46). Vancouver: UBC Press.

Jacobs, D.T. (1998). *Primal awareness: A true story of survival, awakening and transformation with the Raramuri shamans of Mexico.* Rochester, VT: Inner Traditions International.

Jacobs, D.T. & Jacobs-Spencer, J. (2001) *Teaching virtues: Building character across the curriculum.* Lanham, Md.: Scarecrow Education.

Slattery, Patrick. (1995). *Curriculum development in the postmodern era.* New York: Garland Publishing,

Teich, H. (2012) *Solar light, Lunar light: Perspectives in human consciousness*. San Francisco: Genoa House.

Chapter Five, Health

Amnesty International (2011, May 7). "Deadly delivery: The maternal health care crises in the U.S."

Angel, B. (1991) "The toxic threat to Indian lands," in Greenpeace Report at www.ejnet.org/ej/toxicthreattoindianlands.pdf

Banks, N.T. (2010). *Aids, opium, diamonds and empire: The deadly virus of international greed*. New York: Universe, Inc.

Brink, S. (2010). "Phys ed redux." *U.S. News & World Report* 132.19 (2002): 50. *Academic Search Premier*. Web. 11 Nov. 2010.

Buckley, S. (2010). "Leaving well enough alone." http://childbirthsolutions.com/articles/leaving-well-alone-a-natural-approach-to-the-third-stage-of-labour/

CDC (2011). National Vital Statistics Report. Vol. 59, Num 10 Tables 16 and 17. http://www.cdc.gov/nchs/data/nvsr/nvsr59/nvsr59_10.pdf

Colomeda, L.A. & Wenzel, E.R. (2000 April). "Medicine keepers: Issues in Indigenous health," in *Critical Public Health*, Vol. 10, No. 2, pp 243–256.

Dunn, O. & Kelley, J.E. (1989). *The diario of christopher columbus's first voyage to America, 1492–1493*. Norman and London: University of Oklahoma Press.

Durie, M. H. (2003). 'The health of indigenous peoples: Depends on genetics, politics and socio-economic [sic] factors.' *British Medical Journal*, 326(7388), 510–511.

Eaton, S.B. & Konner, M. (1985, Jan. 31) "Paleolithic nutrition: A consideration of its nature and current implications." *The New England Journal of Medicine*. 312(5): 283–289.

Education Commission of the United States (1981). "Recommendations for School Health education: A Handbook for State Policymakers." Denver: Education Commission of the States.

Fuchs, E. & Havighurst, R. (1983). To *live on this Earth: American Indian education*. Revised edition. Albuquerque: University of New Mexico Printing.

Gaskin, I.M. (2011) *Birth Matters: A Midwife's manifest*. New York: Seven Stories Press.

Gifford, R. (2007). "U.S. on list of UNIFCEF's worse countries for kids. NPR at http://www.npr.org/templates/story/story.php?storyID=7407245

Global Biodiversity Outlook (2010). http://www.cbd.int/gb03/?pub=6667&section=6689

Grant, A. & Gillespie, L. (1993). "Joining the Circle: A practitioner's Guide to Responsive Education for Native Students," http://clas.uiuc.edu/fulltext/cl00192/cl00192.html#preface

Hall, J. (2012). "From a right to a commodity: Curricular materials and learning experiences sponsored by the transnational water utility service industry." *Critical Education*, 3(2). Retrieved [date] from http://ojs.library.ubc.ca/index.php/criticaled/article/view/182345Abstract

Hampton, E. (1995). Towards a redefinition of Indian education. In M. Battiste & J. Barman (Eds.), *First Nations Education in Canada: The Circle Unfolds* (pp. 5–46). Vancouver: UBC Press.

http://news.yahoo.com/half-americans-suffer-mental-health-woes-cdc-says-180407456.html

Kohr, M. (n.d.). A Worldwide fight against biopiracy and patents on life. *Third World Network* http://www.twnside.org.sg/title/pat-ch.htm

Lawlor, R. (1991). *Voices of the first day*. Rochester, VT: Inner Traditions International.

Nowack, K. M., & Hanson, A. L. (1983). "The relationship between stress, job performance, and burnout in college student resident assistants." *Journal of College Student Personnel*, 24, 545–550.

Obomsawin,R. (2007). Historical and Scientific Perspects on the Health of Canada's First Peoples. http://www.soilandhealth.org/02/0203cat/020335.0bomsawin.pdf

Peat, D.F. (1994). *Blackfoot physics: A journey into the native American universe*. London: Fourth Estate.

Reinberg, S. (2011). HealthDay Reporter | HealthDay—Thu, Sep 1, 2011.

Roger, V.L et al. (2012). "Heart disease and stroke statistics-2012 update: a report from the American Heart Association." www.ncbi.nlm.nih.gov/pubmed/21160056

Roys, R.L. *The book of chilam balam of chumayel* (Norman: University of Oklahoma Press, 1967), 81–84; 138.Internet Source: Internet Sacred Text Archive, *The Book of Chilam Balam of Chumayel*, http://www.sacred-texts.com/nam/maya/cbc/cbc10.htm.)

SGI (2011). at http://www.sgi-network.org/

SHPPS (2006). "School Health Policies and Program Factsheet" http://www.cdc.gov/healthyyouth/shpps/2006/factsheets/pdf/FS_PhysicalEducation_SHPPS2006.pdf

Smith, R.J. & Birnbaum, J.H. (2007). "Drug bill demonstrates lobby's pull" in *Washington Post*, Friday, January 12.

Sturgis, S. (2008). "New evidence of corruption at the Centers for Disease Control and Prevention" at http://www.homeetownhazards.com/2008/02/more-evidence-of-corruption-at-centers.html

Taras, H. (2005). "Physical activity and student performance at school." *Journal of School Health*, 75: 214–218.

Telljohann, S., Seabert, D. & Pateman, B. (2011). Health education: Elementary and Middle School Applications. New York: McGraw-Hill.

The National Health Education Standards: Achieving Health Literacy- An Investment in the Future is a 75 page document (American Cancer Society, 1997) http://opi.mt.gov/pdf/health/nhes.pdf

Verano, J. & Ubulaker, D. (1993).*Seeds of change: Readers on cultural exchange after 1492*. Boston: Addison-Wesley.

Wallbank, D. (2010, Sept. 30). "Senators demand national investigation of indian health service mismanagement" *Minneapolis Post*. http://www.minnpost.com/dc-dispatches/2010/09/senators-demand-national-investigation-indian-health-service-mismanagement

World Health Organization (WHO) (1947) WHO http://who.int/about/definition/en/print.html

Yang, Q. et al. (2012). Trends in cardiovascular health metrics and associations with all-cause and CVD mortality among U.S. *Journal of American Medical Association*. DOI: 10.1001/jama.2012.339.

York, G. *(1989). The Dispossessed: Life and death in Native Canada*. Toronto: Lester and Orpen.

Chapter Six, Music

Adorno,T.W. (1941). "On popular music" in *Studies in philosophy and social sciences,* Vol IX, pp. 17–48).

Cajete, G. (2000). *Native science: Natural laws of interdependence*. Sante Fe, N.M.: Clear Light Publishing.

Carr, W. & Hartnett, A. (1997) *Education and the struggle for democracy*. Buckingham, UK: Open University Press.

Eisner, E. (2002). "The arts and the creation of mind," in *What the arts teach and how it shows*. New Haven, Conn.: Yale University Press.

Freer, P.K. (2012). "Parallel frames and policy narratives in music education and physical education." in *Arts education policy review*, pp. 26–34. http://dx.doi.org/10.1080/10632913.2012.626706

Hart, W.E. (1997). "The culture industry, hip hop music and the white perspective: How one-dimensional representation of hip hop music has influenced white racial attitudes." Doctoral dissertation. University of Texas, Arlington.

Jacobs, D.T. *Primal Awareness: A true story of survival, awakening and transformation with the Raramuri shamans of Mexico.* Rochester, VT: Inner Traditions International.

Jorgensen, E.R. (2011) "How can music education be religious?" in *Philosophy of music education review* 19 (2), pp 155–163.

Kohn, A. (2011, Feb). "STEM Sell: Are math and science really more important than other subjects?" *Washington Post*, 2/17/2011. http://voices.washingtonpost.com/answer-sheet/alfie-kohn/stem-sell-are-math-science-rea.html

Lawlor, R. (1991). *Voices of the First Day.* Rochester, VT. Inner Traditions International, Ltd.

Mathur, N. (2008). "Chanted narratives of indigenous people," in *Asian Ethnology* Volume 67, Number 1, pp. 103–121.

Meyers, D. (2002). "Freeing music education from schooling: Toward a lifespan perspective on music learning and teaching." In *The International Journal of Community Music* 1 (1) pp 49-61.

Neal, M.A. (1997). "Sold out on soul: The corporate annexation of black popular music" in *Popular music and society* 21:3, pp. 117–135.

Negus, K. (1998). "Cultural production and the corporation: musical genres and the strategic management of creativity in the U.S. recording industry" *Media, culture and society.* 20, p. 359.

Richerme, L.K. (2012). "Remain or react: The music education profession's responses to Sputnik and "A Nation at Risk" in *Arts education policy review*, pp. 113:1, 35–44.

Robinson, G., Z. Zeng, and R. Leung. (2008). "Current issues and solutions for physical education in a public educational system." *Proceedings of the International Convention on Science, Education and Medicine in Sport* 3:124–25.

Rose, A.M. (ND). "Music education and the formation of social consciousness." http://www.mun.ca/educ/faculty/mwatch/vol2/rose.html

Spruce, G. (2001). "Music assessment and the hegemony of musical heritage." In: Philpott, Chris and Plummeridge, Charles (eds.). *Issues in music teaching.* London, U.K.: Routledge Falmer, pp. 118–130.

Troutman, J.W. (2009). Indian blues: The indigenization of American popular music. *World Literature Today*, 01963570, May/June 2009, Vol. 83, Issue 3.

Van Dorston, A.S. (1990). "Cultural hegemony in music: A "struggle" of the privileged." http://www.fastnbulbous.com/hegemony.htm

Whitehead, A.N. (Fall,2011). "How can music education be religious?" in *Philosophy of music education review.* Vol.19, No. 2, pp. 155–163.

Chapter Seven, English Language Arts

Apple, M. (2001), "Educational and curricular restructuring and the neo-liberal and neo-conservative agendas: Interview with Michael Apple" in *Currículo sem Fronteiras*, v.1, n.1, pp. i-xxvi, Jan/June 2001. http://www.curriculosemfronteiras.org/vol1iss1articles/appleeng.pdf

Benjamin, B., & Irwin-DeVitis, L.(1998). "Censoring girls' choices: Continued gender bias in english language arts classrooms that identified gender bias. *English Journal*, v 87, pp 64–71.

Bighead, M. E. (1997). *Nikâwiy Okiskinohâmâwina. Mother as Teacher: A Cree First Nations Mother Teaching Through Stories.* Unpublished Masters Thesis, Department of Indian and Northern Education, University of Saskatchewan.

Cajete, G. (1994). *Look to the mountain: An ecology of Indigenous education.* Durango, CO: Kivakí Press.

Chadwick, J.A. (2012). "Green pens, marginal notes: Rethinking, writing and student engagement." *English journal* 101, pp 15–16.

Coles, G. (2003). *Reading the naked truth: Literacy, legislation, and lies.* Portsmouth, NH: Heinemann.

Eigenberger, M.E., Sealander, K.A., Jacobs, J.A. & Shellad, S.M. (2001). Dispostion toward thinking critically: A comparison of pre-service teachers and other university students. *North American journal of psychology,* 3(1), 109–122.

Ford, A. (1992) *Dialogues between Indigenous and Western scientists.* Kalamazoo, Mich.: Fetzer Institute.

Lakoff, G. and Johnson, M. (1980). *Metaphors We Live By.* Chicago: University of Chicago Press.

Lawlor, R. (1991) *Voices of the first day.* Rochester, VT: Inner Traditions International.

MacLean, M. & Wason-Ellam, L. (2006). "American Indian storytelling: When aboriginal and Métis teachers use Storytelling as an Instructional Practice," A Grant Report to the Aboriginal Education Research Network, Saskatchewan Learning http://www.education.gov.sk.ca/Story telling

Nabokov, P. (1991). *Native American testimony: A chronicle of Inidan-white relations from prophecy to the present.* Middlesex, England: Penguin Books Ltd.

Mueller, L. (1980). *The need to hold still.* Baton Rouge: Louisiana State University Press.

Nelson, T. (Ed). (2003). "In response to increasing state and national control over the teacher education profession." *Teacher education quarterly,* 3–8.

Nieto, S. (1996). *Affirming diversity: The sociopolitical context of multicultural education* (2nd ed.). White Plains, NY: Longman.

Gilbert, S. H. (1994). "And they lived happily ever after": Cultural storylines and the construction of gender. In A. H. Dyson & C. Genishi (Eds.). *The need for story: Cultural diversity in classroom and community.* (pp.124–142). Urbana, IL: National Council of Teachers of English.

Palmer, P. (1997). *The courage to teach: Exploring the inner landscape of a teacher's life.* San Francisco. Jossey-Bass.

Pinker, S., (2007). *The Stuff of Thought.* NY: Penguin.

Quinn, C. (2012). "Studies on Critical Thinking for Environmental Ethics." Theses, Dissertations, & Student Scholarship:Agricultural Leadership, Education & Communication Department. Paper 89. http://digitalcommons.unl.edu/aglecdiss/89

Rhodes, R. W. (1988). "Holistic teaching/learning for native American students. *Journal of American Indian Education.* Volume 27, No. 2. January.

Smagorinsky, P. (2008). *Teaching English by design: How to create and carry out instructional units.* Portsmith, N.H.: Heinemann.

Trelease, J. 2006. "All in the family: The Bushes and the McGraws." http://www.trelease-on-reading.com/whatsnu_bush-mcgraw.html

Vizenor, G. (2008). "Aesthetics of survivance." In G. Vizenor (Ed.), *Survivance: Narratives of Native presence* (pp. 1–23). Lincoln: University of Nebraska Press.

Chapter Eight, United States History

Aupaumut, Hendrick. (1827). "A Narrative of an Embassy to the Western Indians." *Memoirs of the Historical Society of Pennsylvania* 2.1: 76–131.

Converse, Harriet Maxwell. "Myths and Legends of the New York State Iroquois." *Education Department Bulletin* 437 (December 1908): 5–195.

Corn Tassel (1785) in (Ed.)Nabakov, P. (1991) *Native American testimony: A chronicle of Indian-white relations from prophecy to the present.* New York: Penguin

DeAngelis, F.T. (2001). *Reflections of a Bankruptee on Debt, Amnesty, Revolution and History* https://www.commondreams.org/view/2012/06/26–1

Deloria, Vine, Jr. (1973). "The Concept of History." In *God Is Red: A Native View of Religion.* 1973. Golden, CO: Fulcrum Publishing.

Foner, P.S. (Ed.). (1945). *The complete writings of Thomas Paine.* New York: Citadel Press.

Gunn Allen, Paula. (1992). "Kochinnenako in Academe: Three Approaches to Interpreting a Keres Indian Tale," in The *Sacred Hoop: Recovering the Feminine in American Indian Traditions* Boston: Beacon Press.

Heckewelder, John. *History, Manners, and Customs of the Indian Nations Who Once Inhabited Pennsylvania and the Neighboring States.* The First American Frontier Series. 1820; 1876, reprint. New York: Arno Press and *The New York Times,* 1971.

Johansen, Bruce Elliot, & Barbara Alice Mann (Eds.) (2000). *Encyclopedia of the Haudenosaunee (Iroquois Confederacy).* Westport, CT: Greenwood Press.

Karlberg, M. (2010). "Education for interdependence: The university and the global citizen" Volume 3, Global studies journal, Number 1, 2010, http://www.globalstudiesjournal.com and http://my web.www.edu/karlberg/articles/GC-Interdependence.pdf

McKinley, J.C. (2010, March). "Texas conservatives win curriculum change." in *New York Times.* http://www.nytimes.com/2010/03/13/education/13texas.html

Parker, Arthur C. *Iroquois Uses of Maize and Other Food Plants.* In *Parker on the Iroquois.* Ed. William N. Fenton. 1913, reprint. Syracuse: Syracuse University Press, 1968.

Shagoury, R. (2012, June). "Who stole Helen Keller?" Common Dreams, June 26, 2012.

Speck, Frank G. "The Wapanachki Delawares and the English; Their Past as Viewed by and Ethnologist." *The Pennsylvania Magazine* 67 (1943): 319–44.

Thompson, G. (2003). *Who Was Helen Keller?* New York: Grosset and Dunlap.

Waters, Frank. (1977). *Book of the Hopi.* New York: Penguin Books.

Chapter Nine, Mathematics

Andreescu, T., Gallian, J. Kane, J.M. & Mertz, J.E. (2008). "Cross-cultural analysis of students with exceptional talent in mathematical problem solving." *Notices of the American mathematical society.* 55, 1248–1260.

Anyon, J. (1981). "Social class and school knowledge." *Curriculum Inquiry* 11, pp. 3–42.

Atweh, W. & Cooper, T.J. (1991,July). "Hegemony in the mathematics curricula: The effect of gender and social class on the organization of mathematics teaching for students." Paper presented at the 15th Conference of the International Grouo of Psycholog of mathematics education. Assisi, Italy.

Barad, K. (1995) "A feminist approach to teaching quantum physics." *Teaching the majority: Breaking the gender barrier in science, mathematics, and engineering.* Ed. Sue Rosser. New York: Teachers College Press, pp. 43–75.

Becker J. (1981). "Differential treatment of females and males in mathematics classrooms. " *Journal for research in mathematics education* 12 (1), pp. 40–53.

Bishop, A. (1988). "Mathematics education in its cultural context." *Educational studies in mathematics,* 19: 179–91.

Cassirer, E. (1944). *An essay of man: An introduction to a philosophy of Huan culture.* New Haven, CT: Yale University Press.

D'Ambrosio, U. (1985). "Ethnomathematics and its place in the history and pedagogy of mathematics" in *For the learning of mathematics,* 5(1), pp.44–48.

Fasheh, M. (1989) "Mathematics in a social context: Math within education as praxis versus within education as hegemony. In Mathematics, education and society: Reports and papers presented in the fifth day special programme on "Mathematics, education, and society" at the 6th International Congress on Mathematics Education. Pares: UNESCO.

Fasheh, M. (1990). Community education: To reclaim and transform what has been made invisible. *Harvard Educational Review,* 60(1), 19-35.

Fauvel, J., Flood, R. and Wilson, R. (eds) (2003). *Music and mathematics: From Pythagoras to fractals.* London: Oxford University Press.

Gatto, J.T. (2003)."Against School." *Harper's Magazine* Sep. 2003, pp. 33—38.

Hiebert, J. (1984) 'Children's Mathematical Learning: The Struggle to Link Form and Understanding.' *The Elementary School Journal,* 84, 5, pp. 496–513.

Hiebert, J. & Carpenter, T. (1992). Learning and teaching with understanding, in D.A. Grouws (ed.). *Handbook of research on mathematics teaching and learning,* New York: Macmillan.

Highwater, J. (1982) *The primal mind.* New York: Penguin.

Jacobs, D.T. and Jacobs-Spencer, J. (2001). *Teaching virtues: Building character across the curriculum.* Lanham, MD: Rowman and Littlefield.

Kitchen, Richard (1995). "Mathematics Pedagogy in the 3rd World: The Case of a Guatemalan Teacher." *ISGEm Newsletter* 10.2: n.p. http://web.nmsu.edu/~pscott/isgem102.htm.

Kutner, M., Greenberg, E., Jin, Y., Boyle, B., Hsu, Y., and Dunleavy, E. (2007). *Literacy in Everyday Life: Results From the 2003 National Assessment of Adult Literacy* (NCES 2007–480).U.S. Department of Education. Washington, DC: National Center for Education Statistics.

Malkowski, R. A. & Schwaller de Lubicz, R. A. (2007). *The Spiritual Technology of Ancient Egypt: Sacred Science and the Mystery of Consciousness.* Rochester, VT: Inner Traditions International.

Millman, D. (1995) *The Life you were born to live.* New York: J.H. Kramer.

Mullis, I.V.S., Martin, M.O., & Foy, P. (with Olson, J.F., Preuschoff, C., Erberber, E., Arora, A., & Galia, J. (2008). "The International Math and Science Report." Chestnut Hill, MA: TIMSS & PIRLS International Study Center, Boston College. http://timssandpirls.bc.edu/TIMSS2007/mathreport.html

Nunes, T. (1992) "Ethnomathematics and everyday cognition" in D.A. Grouws (Ed.) *Handbook of research on mathematics teaching and learning* (pp. 557–574) New York: Macmillan.

Peat, D.F. (1994). *Blackfoot physics.* London: Fourth Estate Limited.

Promak, S. "Our delusional language" at flowpsychology.com/?language. posted 9/29/2010.

Roberts, T. (1997). "Aboriginal maths: can we use it in school? http://www.aamt.edu.au/ICSIMAN/resources/papers/roberts.pdf

Schoenfeld, A.H. (1988). When good teaching leads to bad results: the disasters of "well-taught" mathematics courses, *Educational Psychologist,* 23(2), pp. 145–66.

Rudman, Peter Strom. (2007). *How mathematics happened: The first 50,000 years.* Amhurst, NY: Prometheus Books.

Valverde, G.A., Bianchi, L.J., Wolfe, R.G., Scmidt, W.H. & Houng, R.T. (2002). *According to the Book- Using TIMSS to investigate the translation of policy into practice through the world of textbooks.* Dordrecht: Kluwer Academic Publishers.

Walkerdine, V. (1992, July). "Reasoning in a postmodern age." Paper presented at the Fifth International Conference on Thinking, Townsville, Australia.

Chapter Ten, Economics

Abrams, D. (2011). *Becoming animal. An earthly cosmology.* New York: Vintage.

Adamson, R. (1995) "Changing the rules of the game: Indigenous economics." *Winds of Change,* V 10, no.1, pp 18–22.

Adamson, R. (2008) "The histories of social investing and indigenous peoples: Using the tools of diverse cultures to restore balance to a fractured world." *First Peoples Worldwide.* http://www. nafoa.org/pdf/Histories-of-Social-Investing.pdf

Alex, Carey. (1995). *Taking the Risk out of Democracy,* ed. Andrew Lohrey. Sydney: UNSW Press. p. 27.

Barlow, M. (2001). "Water as commodity—The wrong prescription," Backgrounder, Food First Institute for Food and Development Policy, Summer 2001, Vol. 7, No.1.

Beder, S. (2006). *Free market missionaries: The corporate manipulation of community values.* London: Earthscan.

Bowers, C.A. (2005). Is transformative learning the trojan horse of western globalization?*Journal of transformative education* 3 (2), 116–125.

Carey, A. (1995). *Taking the risk out of democracy: Corporate propaganda versus freddome and liberty.* Chicago: University of Illionois Press.

Coleman-Jensen, Alisha, Mark Nord, Margaret Andrews, & Steven Carlson. "Household Food Security in the United States in 2010." ERR-125, U.S. Dept. of Agriculture, Econ. Res. Serv. September 2011. http://www.ers.usda.gov/Publications/err125/

DeNavas, W. (2011). Current Population Reports, P60-239, Income, Poverty, and Health Insurance Coverage in the United States: 2010, U.S. Census Bureau, U.S. Government Printing Office, Washington, DC.

DeNavas-Walt, Carmen, Bernadette D. Proctor, & Jessica C. Smith. (2011). U.S. Census Bureau, Current Population Reports, P60–239. " Income, Poverty, and Health Insurance Coverage in the United States: 2010." U.S. Government Printing Office, Washington, DC, 2011 http://www. census.gov/prod/2011pubs/p60–239.pdf

Dugger, W.M. (1989). *Corporate hegemony. Contributions in economics and economic history.* Westport, Conn: Greenwood Press.

Four Arrows & Block, W. (2010) *Differing worldviews in higher education: Two scholars argue cooperatively about justice education.* Netherlands: Sense.

Gabbard, D. (2008). *Knowledge & power in the global economy: The effects of school reform in a neoliberal/neoconservative age,* 2nd edition. Mahwah, N.J.: Lawrence Erlbaum Associates.

Galbraith, K. (1999, Jan.). "Free market fraud." *Progressive.* http://www.progressive.org/mag_galbraith0199

Gilson, D. & and Perot, C. (2011). "It's the economy stupid." *Mother Jones online http://*www.motherjones.com/politics/2011/02/income-inequality-in-america-chart-graph#disqus_thread

Heath, J. (2010). *Economics without illusions: Debunking the myths of modern capitalism.* N.Y.: Crown Business.

Hedges, C. (2012, April). "The implosion of capitalism." *Truthout.* truth-out.org/ . . . /item/8808-when-civilizations-die

Hedges, C. (2012) "How are demented system drives people insane." *Democratic underground.* http://www.democraticunderground.com/101628326

Hewith, P. (2002).*Conceptual physics. The high school phsics program.* Englewood Cliffs, N.J.: Prentice Hall.

Mann, B. A. (2009). "All my relatives. The binary fractals of the gift economy." *Reality sandwich.* http://www.realitysandwich.com/gift_economy_fractals—_ftn3 http://www.realitysandwich.com/gift_economy_fractals#_ftn3

Maybury-Lewis, D. (1992). *Millenium: Tribal wisdom for the modern world.* New York: Viking.

Nelson, A. (n.d.) http://www.moneyfreezone.info/prices.html

Schug, M. C. (1985). "Introduction," in *Economics in the school curriculum,* K-12. Washington, DC: Joint Council on Economic Education and National Education Association.

Seiter, D. (1988). "Economics in the curriculum. ERIC Clearinghouse for Social Studies/Social Science Education. http://www.ericdigests.org/pre-929/economics.htm

Stern, S.M. & Stern, J.A. (2011). "The state of state history standards, 2011." Thomas Fordham Institute. http://www.edexcellencemedia.net/publications/2011/20110216_SOSHS/SOSS_History_FINAL.pdf

Survey of the States 2011: The State of Economic and Personal Finance Education in our Nation's Schools http://www.councilforeconed.org/news-information/survey-of-the-states/

Chapter Eleven, Science

Abram, D. (2005). "Animism, perception and earthly craft of the magician" http://www.wildethics.org/essays/animism_perception_magicians_craft.html

Battiste, Marie. "Indigenous knowledge: Foundations for First Nations." Copyright 2005.WIN-HEC. http://www.win-hec.org/docs/pdfs/Journal/Marie%20Battiste%20copy.pdf

Bowers, C.A. (1993). *Education, cultural myths, and the ecological crises: Toward deep changes.* Albany: State University of New York.

Broadway, M. D., & Howland, M. (1991, May). "Science books for young people: Who writes them? *School Library Journal.*

Dunlap, Riley E. and McCright, Aaron M. (2011). "Climate Change Denial: Sources, actors, and strategies." In Constance Lever-Tracy. *Routledge Handbook of Climate Change and Society.* London: Taylor & Francis.

Feyerabend, P. (1978). *Science in a free society* London: New Left Books.

Feynman, R. (1999). "The pleasure of finding things out" in American Scientist, Vol 87, p.462.

Four Arrows, Cajete, G. & Lee, J. (2010). *Critical Neurophilosophy and Indigenous Wisdom.* Rotterdam, Netherlands: Sense Publishers.

Kolat, G. (2011, Oct. 28) "Sports Medicine said to Overuse M.R.I.'s." *New York Times* Health Section.

Loye, D. (2011). *Lost theory: Bridge to a better world.* Pacific Grove, CA; Franklin Press.

McKibben, B. (2012, July 19). "Global warming's terrifying new math" in *Rolling Stone* http://www.rollingstone.com/politics/news/global-warmings-terrifying-new-math-20120719

Peat D. F. (2002). *Blackfoot physics and European minds.* http://www.fdavidpeat.com/bibliography/essavs/black.htm

Samuelshown, D. (2012, Feb 22) "Heartland leader details curriculum." *Politico.* http://dyn.politico.com/tag/heartland-institute

Shafersman, S. (2012, Jan 31). "House bills 220 and 2534 will return Texas to its dark ages." Texas citizens for science http://www.texscience.org/releases/2012Jan31_TCS_Responds_Fordham_State_Science_Standards_2012.htm

Shiva, V. (1988). "Reductionist science as epistemological violence" in Nandy, A. (Ed) *Science, hegemony and violence*, Delhi, India: Oxford University Press.

Suzuki, D. (1992). *Wisdom of the elders*. Toronto, ON: Stoddart.

Chapter Twelve, Geography

Australian Academy of Science (2011). "Toward a geography curriculum for Australia." http://www.ngc.org.au/ See also www.ngc.org.au/report/Towards_a-nat_geog-curric-Final.pdf

Beckford, C. L. (2008). "Re-positioning environmental education in teacher education programs in Ontario." *Journal of Teaching and Learning*, 5(1), 55–66.

Beckford, C.L. & Nahdee, R. "Teaching for ecological sustainability incorporating Indigenous philosophies and practices." http://www.edu.gov.on.ca/eng/literacynumeracy/inspire/research/WW_Teaching_Ecological.pdf

Boehm, R., & Bednarz, S. (1994). *Geography for Life: The National Geography Standards*. Washington, D.C.: National Geographic Society Committee on Research and Exploration.

Bonnet, A. (2008) *What is geography?* London: Sage.

Bowers, C.A. (1993). *Education, cultural myths, and the ecological crisis: Toward deep changes*. Albany: State University of New York Press.

Cohen, M.J. (1990). *Connecting with nature: creating moments that let earth teach*. Portland, Oreg.: World Peace University Press.

Deloria, V. (2001) *Power and place: Indian education in America*: Golden,CO: Fulcrum Publishing

DeMers, M.N. (2010). "Coyote Teaching for Geography Instruction." *Journal of Geography* Volume 109, Issue 3, pp 97–104.

Engel, A. (2007, Aug). "Exposing the myths of high stakes testing." *Fair test* http://www.fairtest.org/exposing-myths-high-stakes-testing

Humphrey, S. (2011, May). "Geography literacy in schools is lacking" in Daily PressJoint Committee on Geographic Education (1984) http://articles.dailypress.com/2011–05–31/news/dp-nws-geography-evg-20110527_1_national-geographic-roper-geography-literacy-geographical-perspective

Jacobs, D.T. (1994). *The bum's rush: The selling of environmental backlash*. Boise, ID: Legendary Press.

Karlin, M. (2012, July 15). "Crony capitalism and the exploitation of labor" in *Truthout* http://truthout.org/news/item/10309-the-1-connection-mexico-and-the-united-states-crony-capitalism-and-the-exploitation-of-labor-through-nafta

Meyer, M.A. (2008) "Indigenous and authentic: Hawaiian Epistemology and the triangulation of meaning" in Denzin, N.K., Lincoln, Y.S. & Smith, L.T. (Eds.). *Handbook of Critical and Indigenous Methodologies*. London: Sage.

Miron, L. (2008). "Transnational, national, and indigenous racial subjects: Moving from critical discourse to praxis" in Denzin, N.K., Lincoln, Y.S. & Tuhiwai Smith, L. (Eds.). *Handbook of critical and indigenous methodologies*. Los Angeles: Sage.

Monmonier, M. (1991). *How to lie with maps* Chicago: The University of Chicago Press.

Mullins, S. (1990). Social Studies for the 21st Century: Recommendations of the National

Commission on Social Studies in the Schools. *ERIC Digest* http://www.ericdigests.org/pre-9219/social.htm

Page, K.R. (1994). "Attitudes suck: The practice of geography instruction in American schools, 1784–1974" in ProQuest Dissertations and Theses.

Plato, "Phaedrus" Translated R. Hackforth (1982). In *The collected dialogues of Plato* (Ed) Edith Hamilton and Huntington Cairns. Princeton, NJ: Princeton University Press.

Schulten, K (2011, July 21). "How much time do you spend in nature." *New York Times* http://learning.blogs.nytimes.com/2011/09/12/how-much-time-do-you-spend-in-nature/

Source Watch http://www.sourcewatch.org/index.php?title=John_Roskam

Sparke, M. (2007) "Geopolitical fear, geoeconomic hope and the responsibilities of geography" in *Annals of the association of American geographers* 97 (2) pp.338–349 http://faculty.washington.edu/sparke/FearHope.pdf

Winders, J. & Schein, R. (Eds.). (2012). *From global dispossess to local repossession: Toward a worldly cultural geography of occupy activism*. Oxford and New York: Wiley-Blackwell.

Chapter Thirteen, From Fear to Fearlessness: Psychology, Religion and Spirituality in Education

Bordewich, Fergus M. (1996). *Killing the White Man's Indian: Reinventing Native Americans at the End of the Twentieth Century*. New York: First Anchor Books.

Bowers, C. A. & Apffel-Marglin, F. (Eds.). (2004). *Re-thinking Freire: Globalization and the environmental crises*. London: Routledge.

Brown, R. E. (1989) *The Sacred Pipe: Black Elk's Account of the Seven Rites of the Oglala Sioux*. 1953. Reprint, Norman: University of Oklahoma Press, 1989.

Cajete, G. (2000) *Native science: Natural laws of interdependence*. Sante Fe, NM: Clear Light Publishers.

Chomsky, N. (1992). *What uncle sam really wants*. Tucson, AZ: Odonian Press.

Cook-Lynn, E. (2008). "History, myth and identity in the new Indian story" in Denzin, N.K., Lincoln, Y. S., & Tuhiwai Smith, L. (Eds.). *Handbook of Critical and Indigenous methodologies*. Los Angels: Sage Publications.

Cooper, T. (1998). *A time before deception: Truth in communication, culture and ethics*. Goldon, CO: Clear Light Publishers.

Deloria, Jr., V. (1973) *God is red*. New York: Grosset & Dunlap.

Deloria, Jr., V. & Wildcat, D. R. (2001). *Power and place: Indian education in America*. Golden, CO: Fulcrum Publishers.

Densmore, F. (1992). *Teton Sioux Music and Culture*. 1918. Reprint, Lincoln: University of Nebraska Press.

McGaa, E. (Eagle Man). (2010). "Expose." *Native Digest*. http://nativedigest.com/expose.html.

Four Arrows (Ed.). (2006) *Unlearning the language of conquest: Scholars expose anti-Indianism in America*. Austin: University of Texas Press.

Four Arrows, Cajete, G. & Lee, J. (2010). *Critical neurophilosophy and indigenous wisdom*. Netherlands: Sense Publishers.

Jacobs, D.T. (1998). *Primal awareness: A true story of survival, awakening and transformation with the Raramuri shamans of Mexico*. Rochester, VT: Inner Traditions International.

Jacobs, D. T. & Jacobs-Spencer, J. (2001). *Teaching virtues: Building character across the curriculum.* Lanham, Md.: Rowman and Littlefield.

Jocks, C. R. (2000) "Spirituality for sale: Sacred knowledge in the consumer age." Irwin, L. (Ed) *Native American spirituality.* Lincoln: University of Nebraska Press.

Joseph, S., Linley, A. P. & Maltby, J. (2006). Positive psychology, religion, and spirituality. *Mental Health, Religion & Culture, 9*(3), pp. 209–212.

Lewis, R. (2004) *Gaj: The end of religion.* Montreal: Hay River Books.

Limbaugh, R. (1992) *See I told you so.* New York: Pocket Books.

Momaday, N. S. (1992). " Confronting Columbus again" in Nabokov, P. (Ed.). *Native American Testimony.* New York: Penguin Books.

Smagorinsky, P. & Taxel, J. (2005). *The discourse of character education: Culture wars in the classroom.* Mahwah, N.J.: Lawrence Erlbaum Associates.

Smith, D.L. (2004). *Why we lie: The evolutionary roots of deception and the unconscious mind.* Boston: St. Martin's Press.

Tinker, G. E (1993). *Missionary conquest: The gospel and Native American cultural genocide.* Minneapolis, MN: Augsburg Fortress.

Tinker, G. E. (2008). *American Indian liberation. A theology of sovereignty.* New York: Orbis Books.

White, L. Jr. (1967). "The historical roots of our ecologic crises." *Science,* 155, 1203–1207.

References to R. Michael Fisher's Essay

Esjbörn-Hargens, S., and Zimmerman, M. (2009). *Integral ecology: Uniting multiple perspectives on the natural world.* Boston, MA: Integral Books/Shambhala.

Ferguson, M. (2005). *Aquarius now: Radical common sense and reclaiming our personal soveriegnty.* Boston, MA: Weiser Books.

Fisher, R. M. (2007/11). Culture of fear and education: An annotated bibliography, 1990–2011. Technical Paper 28. Vancouver, BC: In Search of Fearlessness Research Institute. [available in pdf @ http://csiie.org/mod/page/view.php?id=3.]

Fisher, R. M. (2010). *The world's fearlessness teachings: A critical integral approach to fear management/ education for the 21st century.* Lanham, MD: University Press of America.

Heim, M. (2004). *Theories of the gift in South Asia: Hundu, Buddhist, and Jain reflections on dāna.* New York: Routledge.

Hibbets, M. (1999). Saving them from yourself: An inquiry into the South Asian gift of fearlessness. *Journal of Religious Ethics, 27*(3), 437–62.

Jacobs, D. T. (1998). *Primal awareness: A True Story of Survival, Awakening and Transformation with the Raramuri Shamans of Mexico.* Rochester, VT: Inner Traditions.

Tuan, Y. F. (1979). *Landscapes of fear.* New York: Pantheon Books.

About the Author

Four Arrows (Don Trent Jacobs) has a Ph.D. in Health Psychology from Columbia Pacific University and an Ed.D. in Curriculum and Instruction with a Cognate in Indigenous Worldviews from Boise State University. Former Dean of Education at Oglala Lakota College and a tenured professor at Northern Arizona University, Four Arrows is currently on the faculty in the College of Educational Leadership and Change at Fielding Graduate University. Recipient of Canada's Mid Day Star Award for his service to Aboriginal Peoples and the Moral Courage Award from the Martin Springer Institute on Holocaust Studies, Four Arrows is the author of 20 books and numerous chapters and articles on the positive application of Indigenous perspectives generalized from a number of First Nations on mainstream issues. He lives in a small fishing village in Mexico with his artist wife where he plays arena polo, stand-up paddle surfs and plays one-wall handball. In 2012, he placed fourth in the world championships of "old time piano playing contests" and can be seen in the documentary, *The Entertainers*.

CRITICAL PRAXIS AND CURRICULUM GUIDES

Shirley R. Steinberg and Priya Parmar
Series Editors

Critical Praxis and Curriculum Guides is a curriculum-based book series reflective of theory-creating praxis. The series targets not only undergraduate and graduate audiences but also tenured and experienced teachers of all disciplines. Research suggests that teachers need well-designed, thematic-centered curricula and lessons. This is accomplished when the school works as a community to meet its own needs. Community in this sense includes working collaboratively with students, parents, and local community organizations to help build the curriculum. Practically, this means that time is devoted to professional development workshops, not exam reviews or test preparation pointers but real learning. Together with administrators, teachers form professional learning communities (PLCs) to discuss, analyze, and revise curricula and share pedagogical strategies that meet the needs of their particular school demographics. This communal approach was found to be more successful than requiring each individual teacher to create lessons on her/his own. Ideally, we would love it if each teacher could create his/her own authentic lessons because only s/he truly knows her/his students—and we encourage it, because it is possible! However, as educators ourselves, we understand the realities our colleagues in public schools face, especially when teaching in high-needs areas.

The Critical Praxis and Curriculum Guides series provides relief for educators needing assistance in preparing their lessons. In the spirit of communal practices, the series welcomes co-authored books by theorists and practitioners as well as solo-authored books by an expert deeply informed by the field. Because we strongly believe that theory guides our practice, each guide will blend theory and curriculum chapters, creating a praxis—all, of course, in a critical pedagogical framework. The guides will serve as resources for teachers to use, expand upon, revise, and re-create.

For additional information about this series or for the submission of manuscripts, please contact either Shirley R. Steinberg at msgramsci@aol.com or Priya Parmar at priyaparmar_24@hotmail.com. To order other books in this series, please contact our Customer Service Department: (800) 770-LANG (within the U.S.); (212) 647-7706 (outside the U.S.); (212) 647-7707 FAX; or browse online by series at www.peterlang.com.